hamlyn

GARDEN DESIGN BIBLE

TIM NEWBURY

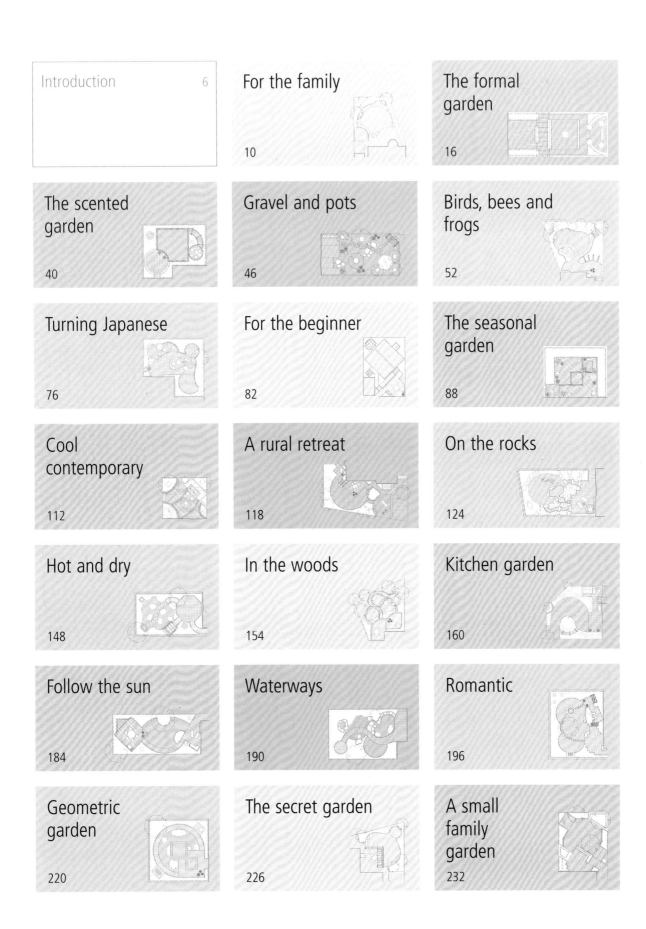

Introduction

Few of us are lucky enough to move into a house that has a garden that is exactly as we would wish it, but imagining how something might be laid out, with different plants and new features, is beyond most of us, especially if we have moved into a house with a garden for the first time. Too often, we introduce features – a shed here, a summerhouse there, a pond in a sunny corner – as we think about them, popping them wherever there happens to be space rather than thinking about their overall impact on the garden as a whole. Most gardeners have the same attitude to plants, which they often acquire one by one, whenever they see something that appeals to them or that appears to be fashionable, but without considering exactly how it will fit in with the other plants and how it will look in five or ten years' time.

If the number of television programmes and books on garden design was a guide, we would all have beautifully laid-out gardens, thoughtfully arranged and planted, with convenient paths, useful patios giving easy access to the kitchen and cosy arbours providing shade on sunny days or shelter in rough weather, not to mention a wonderful selection of plants providing year-round colour and shape.

In fact, of course, the majority of gardens evolve piecemeal, simply because imposing a new design, especially on an established garden, is a rather daunting prospect. The combination of skills required – horticultural, building, architectural and design – can be a deterrent, as can the idea of the disruption that any building work can involve. Deciding what features you want and need, and then choosing the plants that will suit the conditions in your particular garden and that will work well within a particular design, should be enjoyable tasks, but the sheer numbers involved – dozens of styles of sheds and summerhouses and, literally, thousands of plants – makes choosing difficult.

This book will help you make those decisions. It takes 40 types of gardens – from a tiny balcony to a large country garden, from a small urban courtyard garden to a windswept seaside plot – and suggests how these gardens could be laid out and planted. There are gardens for all circumstances and all levels of gardening interest and expertise, including schemes for young families that need to make provision for children and for people whose busy lifestyle leaves little time for gardening, as well as more traditional schemes for people who

Opposite: Some of the most effective designs are also the simplest, using limited colours and clean, crisp lines.

positively enjoy gardening and looking after plants.

Within each garden type, as well as a ground plan to indicate where each feature and plant should go, there is a full-colour illustration to show how the finished garden will look so that you know what you are working towards. Each garden type also includes a special feature – such as an arrangement of plants or something that can be easily constructed – which can be included in the design as illustrated or incorporated into your existing garden or another of the designs included here. Helpful thumbnail sketches indicate how the same features – sheds, pergolas, ponds, paths and patios – can be used in gardens of various shapes and sizes. There are also alternative planting schemes for different colours and different aspects within a garden, so that you will be able to find a scheme for your garden, whether it is

in sun or shade. The suggestions range from the traditional to the modern, so whether you yearn for an old-fashioned cottage garden or long for a minimalist plot you will find something to inspire you.

Throughout, the plants have been chosen for their suitability for each scheme. Many are new or improved forms of old favourites, developed to be robust and reliable, and most are widely available from garden centres and nurseries.

Each garden is described in terms of its suitability for different types of gardener so that you can easily find a plan and a style that will suit your particular needs. Whether you are about to begin work on your very first garden or have enjoyed a lifetime's gardening and are now considering making changes that will enable you to spend less time working in the garden and more time enjoying it, you will find help and advice here.

Above right: Achillea and delphiniums are traditional and reliable perennials, ideal for sunny herbaceous borders.

Opposite: A well-balanced group of urns makes the perfect focal point and finishing detail for this paved area.

For the family

Creating a garden that is safe for young children to play in but that is also a pleasant and attractive place for adults to relax and entertain their friends can be difficult. Meeting the competing claims of everyone in the family can result in a series of unrelated areas, that do not cohere into a pleasing, overall design.

What makes this a good family garden?

✓ A generous patio and lawn for general play and relaxation
✓ A separate play area for use with a swing or slide
✓ An attractive layout that contains something for all the family
✓ A protected area for a kitchen garden
✓ A secure storage area for tools and other gardening materials
✓ A self-contained, no-risk water feature
✓ Year-round interest provided by 'family-friendly' plants
✓ Easy maintenance
✓ Small children can be easily supervised from indoors

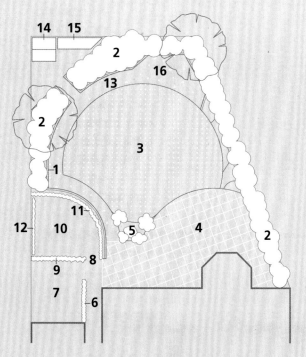

Garden elements key

1 Timber edging
2 Planting
3 Lawn
4 Patio
5 Secure water feature
6 Trellis and climber to screen
7 Utility area or pets corner
8 Gate

9 Trellis and climber for shade

10 Kitchen garden/ herbs

11 'Fedge'

12 Cordon fruit

13 Bark/shingle path

14 Tool shed

15 Compost bins

16 Play area

Mix and match

If you like this garden, but would prefer a different feature, see pages 250–251 for possible variations.

Key features

Children's play area

It's important to site the area where it can be seen from the house so that you can keep your eye on the children, which will usually be from the kitchen window. If the area isn't grassed, make a floor of decking or bark chippings. Use the area for a slide or swing or a climbing frame.

Kitchen garden

Having a source of fresh fruit and vegetables makes even a small area in which a few crops can be grown a welcome addition to the garden. Make sure it is protected from errant balls and bicycles and that there is a gate that can be fitted with a childproof fastener.

Patio for entertaining

There are few things more enjoyable than being able to entertain family and friends on a warm summer day. Position a patio near to the house so that it is easy to transport the food and drinks to it but have fragrant plants growing nearby or in containers so that the scent can be enjoyed close to.

Millstone

In a family garden one of the main reasons for not including a pond is the risk they can pose to small children. Overcome this by building a feature in which most of the water is contained in a way that a child cannot get at it. The simplest way is to have an underground tank or sump that acts as a reservoir, while the chosen feature – a brimming urn, millstone or large stone – rests on a framework of steel rods or mesh laid across the top of the sump. A submersible pump concealed in the sump pumps the water up into, over or through the feature.

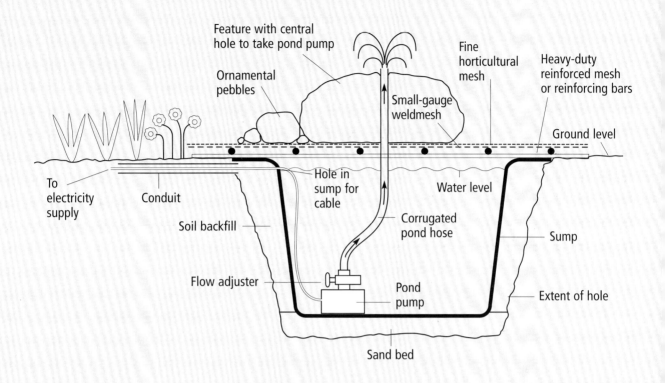

Feature with central hole to take pond pump

Ornamental pebbles

Fine horticultural mesh

Heavy-duty reinforced mesh or reinforcing bars

Small-gauge weldmesh

Ground level

To electricity supply

Conduit

Hole in sump for cable

Water level

Soil backfill

Corrugated pond hose

Sump

Flow adjuster

Pond pump

Extent of hole

Sand bed

You will need

Millstone, ornamental urn or large stone, pre-drilled to accept pond hose

Container or sump

Bag of soft sand – about 27kg (60lb)

Fine soil

Bricks or concrete blocks

Reinforcing bars or heavy-duty reinforced mesh, 60 x 60cm (2 x 2ft)

Small-gauge weldmesh, 60 x 60cm (2 x 2ft)

Fine horticultural mesh, 60 x 60cm (2 x 2ft)

Submersible pump

Hose clip

1m (3ft) corrugated pond hose

Ornamental pebbles, slate or shingle

Step by step

1 Dig a hole for the sump, level the base of the hole using a layer about 2cm (1in) thick of firmed down soft sand, place the sump in the hole, checking it is level and does not stand proud of ground level. Backfill around the sump with fine soil and firm down.

2 Place lengths of reinforcing bars or a square of heavy-duty reinforced mesh across the top of the sump so that it overhangs by at least 15cm (6in) all round. Especially heavy features, such as a large boulder or natural millstone, will require extra support in the form of piers of bricks or concrete blocks. Make sure you leave enough space beneath the feature to feed the pond hose up through it.

3 Connect one end of the pond hose to the feature and put it in position. Connect the other end to the pump. Pass the electric cable from the pump through a small hole drilled just below the top edge of the sump to protect it from chafing against the mesh.

4 Fill the sump with water and turn on the pump. Use the flow adjuster on the pump to achieve the desired outflow from the top of the feature.

5 Place two pieces of small-gauge weldmesh on top of the reinforced mesh so that small pebbles and cobbles do not fall through. If you use small pebbles or gravel lay two pieces of fine horticultural mesh on top of the weldmesh.

6 Place stones, pebbles, slate or shingle to cover the mesh.

Planting

The best plants for this garden

Undemanding, modestly priced shrubs, perennials and grasses are used in this garden. All the plants are child and animal friendly and have been chosen for their durability and resistance to accidental damage. They do not need special growing conditions, apart from reasonable drainage, and the maintenance requirements are straightforward.

Planting key

1 *Clematis montana* var. *rubra* 'Elizabeth'
2 *Jasminum officinale* f. *affine*
3 *Buxus sempervirens*
4 *Hypericum* 'Hidcote'
5 *Geranium sanguineum*
6 *Miscanthus sinensis* 'Silberfeder'
7 *Escallonia* 'Apple Blossom'
8 *Aucuba japonica* 'Crotonifolia'
9 *Pulmonaria saccharata* Argentea Group

7

27

41

47

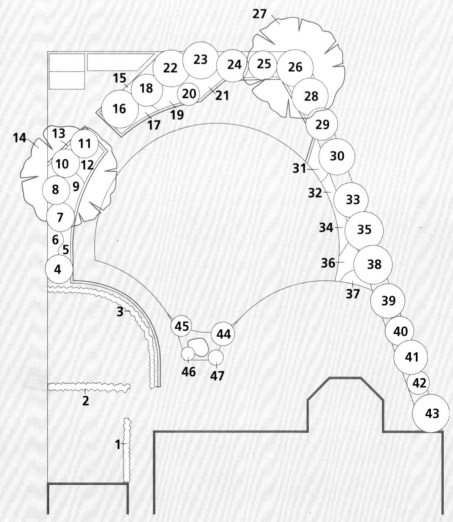

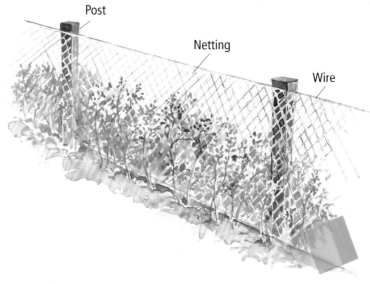

Post
Netting
Wire

A 'fedge'

This combined fence and hedge can be used anywhere you need a sturdy physical barrier – it is ideal for protecting an area from footballs or children – but where something more attractive than a plain fence is needed.

You will need

Posts

Wire

Wire netting

Nails or staple gun

Hedging plants

Step by step

1 Erect a post-and-wire or post-and-rail fence around the area to be protected or screened. The fence should be about 15cm (6in) lower than the final hedge height.

2 Nail or staple wire netting tightly to this fence.

3 Plant the chosen hedging plants at the appropriate distance apart and as close to the fence as possible.

4 Maintain by trimming the sides regularly to keep the 'fedge' narrow and to encourage dense growth. Trim the top once it has reached its final height.

Best plants for a 'fedge'

Evergreens are best, especially those with soft, flexible or small leaves and stems, such as:

- Hedging conifers, including cultivars of *Taxus baccata* (yew) and *Thuja plicata* (western red cedar)

- Shrubs, including *Buxus sempervirens* cultivars (box), *Lonicera nitida* and *Ligustrum* (forms of privet)

- Evergreen climbers, especially forms of *Hedera* (ivy), which is particularly effective for taller, narrow 'fedges' where ground space is limited

The formal garden

In the right situation a simple formal garden, even on a small scale, can be striking. The best formal gardens, regardless of their size, are a blend of symmetry and geometry in which plants are used in an architectural way to create neat, organized shapes that complement the straight edges, angles and precise curves of paving, walls and fountains. A limited colour palette provides gentle relief against this severe background.

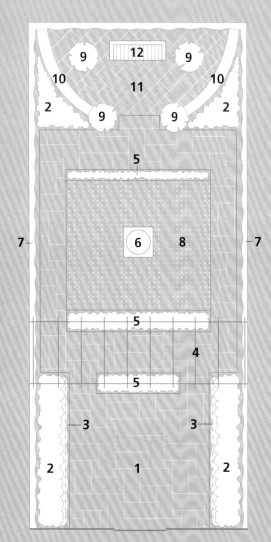

Garden elements key

1 Natural stone flag paving
2 Rose border
3 Dwarf box edging
4 Pergola with wisteria
5 Lavender hedge
6 Urn on stone plinth
7 Climbers on wall
8 Lawn
9 Yew topiary
10 Yew hedge
11 Old brick paving
12 Bench seat

What makes this a good formal garden?

✓ Several distinct yet interlinked spaces

✓ Strong symmetry on either side of the garden, both in the various garden features – paths, walls, pergola – and the planting, particularly the repetition of the climbers

✓ A series of focal points, from the pergola, to the urn, to the bench seat against the tightly trimmed ivy backdrop

✓ Simple, regular shapes, straight lines and curves

✓ Well-trimmed, uniform yew, lavender and box hedges – the yew hedge ends in two tightly controlled topiary shapes

✓ Flower colours in soft, pastel shades that are used either in repeat patterns or in drifts of single colours

Mix and match

If you like this garden, but would prefer a different feature, see pages 250–251 for possible variations.

Key features

Bench seat

Think about how a seat might fit in with the rest of your garden. Traditional designs and materials – such as oak and cast iron – will fit in well with traditionally formal or old-fashioned gardens. More modern materials and styles, including stainless steel and even plastic, will look good as part of a contemporary or architectural design.

Wisteria

Wisteria is a fabulous climber with its long, slightly fragrant racemes of pea-shaped flowers. To get the best out of it, try and restrict the root zone but give the top plenty of room. Growing it over a large pergola displays the flowers to perfection.

Lavender hedge

All forms of lavender make excellent low, fragrant hedges that can be incorporated in both formal and informal designs. Make sure that your hedge is in a sunny, well-drained position and trim it lightly after flowering, and again – slightly harder – in very early spring to keep it neat and shapely, and encourage lots of flower. Don't forget you can cut and dry the flowerheads and bring them indoors.

How to create your own topiary

Ready-topiarized plants can be bought in all sorts of shapes and sizes to give an instant effect in a formal garden. It is satisfying, though, to create your own, even if it takes a bit longer.

Ligustrum ovalifolium 'Aureum' (privet) is an ideal plant to topiarize.

1 Choose your plant. Although it's possible to use some deciduous plants for topiary, evergreens are the best and easiest (see right).

2 Decide whether you want to grow it in a container and plant it in the garden when it is ready; plant it straight in its final position in the ground; or keep it in a container indefinitely.

3 Select a shape. Avoid complicated shapes until you have done one or two. Cones, cylinders, pyramids and spheres are the easiest to begin with.

4 Before planting your chosen shrub or conifer, prepare the ground thoroughly because strong, healthy plants make the best topiary. For container topiary, put potbound plants into a slightly larger pot (don't overpot); if it's not ready to pot on, leave it in its original container for the time being.

5 Prune back the side branches quite hard, by one-third or more, cutting into older wood if required, which will produce far more new shoots than just a light trim. Topiary must be dense and bushy to be really successful. Keep the ultimate shape in mind even at this early stage. For a cone you would cut the topmost side branches back further than the lowest ones so that the basic framework is already partly formed.

6 Feed and water the plant well during the growing season to encourage healthy growth.

7 Trim again in midsummer, reducing new growths by about half. Leave the plant to grow until the following spring and build up a strong root system.

8 In late winter trim quite hard again but do not trim further than the base of the previous season's growth.

9 Continue trimming at regular intervals through the season but only into new, current growths. The last trim should be in late summer to allow a small amount of extra growth to soften the 'just cut' look and so that trimmed stems can heal before winter.

Topiary in various geometric shapes planted alongside a gravel path gives this garden a classical look.

Best plants for topiary

- *Buxus sempervirens* (box) – all sizes according to cv.
- *Chamaecyparis* spp. (cypress) – all sizes according to vigour of cv.
- *Euonymus fortunei* – good for small to medium topiary
- *Ilex aquifolium* (common holly) – better for large topiary
- *Ilex x altaclerensis* (holly) – better for large topiary
- *Lonicera nitida* – all sizes
- *Osmanthus* spp. – good for medium to large topiary
- *Taxus baccata* (yew) – ideal for medium to large topiary

Planting

The best plants for this garden

Unless you want a severely formal planting scheme that relies only on the shape, texture and foliage colour of the plants as a foil for the architectural elements, you will want to have some softening textures and colour, and this design includes the pale flowers of the climbing and bush roses and soft purple-blue of the lavender hedge. The wisteria growing on the pergola is trained tightly to the supports.

Planting key

1 *Taxus baccata* 'Elegantissima'
2 *Hedera hibernica* (on wall)
3 *Taxus baccata* (shaped hedge)
4 *Rosa* 'Buff Beauty'
5 *Lonicera periclymenum* 'Serotina' (on wall)
6 *Lavandula angustifolia* 'Munstead'
7 *Rosa* 'Zéphirine Drouhin' (on wall)
8 *Clematis* 'Rouge Cardinal' (on wall)
9 *Jasminum* x *stephanense* (on wall)
10 *Rosa* 'Madame Alfred Carrière' (on wall)
11 *Rosa* 'Cécile Brünner'
12 *Buxus sempervirens* 'Suffruticosa'
13 *Wisteria floribunda* 'Macrobotrys' (on pergola)

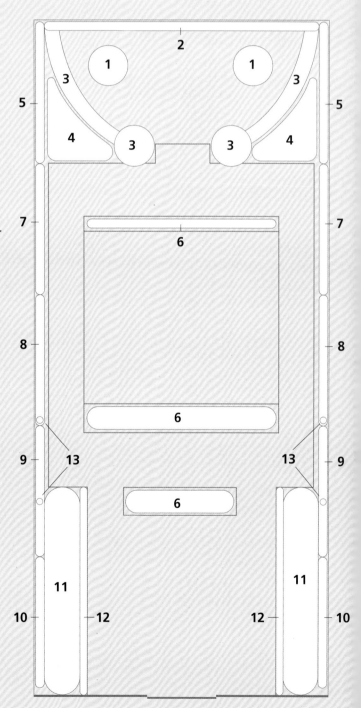

Planting ivies against walls

You should regard ivies as more or less permanent fixtures. They cling by short, aerial roots, which are produced as the plant grows, and walls are difficult to paint and maintain once ivy has been grown on them.

- Make sure that the wall is sound and that the aerial roots produced by the ivy won't damage the face of the brick or the mortar joints

- Some people try to train ivies on wires, but this is rarely successful as they need a flat (but not necessarily rough) surface to grow against

- The existing shoots of newly planted ivies can be held against the wall until new shoots (and roots) form by garden canes pushed into the ground tight against the wall so that the shoots are gently trapped behind them and secured (if necessary) with a piece of natural garden twine

- Ivies purchased from nurseries and tied in to one or more garden canes can already be quite tall, and the shoots will have already produced aerial roots and therefore won't grip on a wall or other flat surface; cut back the stems to 30–45cm (12–18in) and train the vigorous new shoots that will grow and that will cling to the wall

- Small-leaved ivies are sometimes reluctant to climb, often producing low, sprawling mounds, which seem to grow better on the ground than up the wall; placing a long, shallow, vertical board just a few centimetres (inch) in front of the newly planted ivy will reduce the amount of light received at the base of the plant and may encourage it to produce upright growths searching for light, which are more likely to cling to the wall (see right)

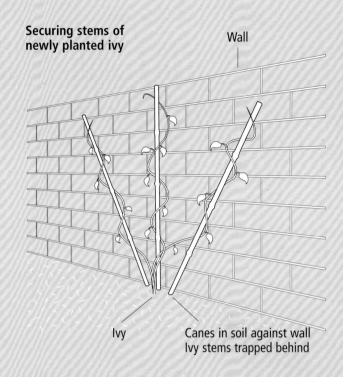

Securing stems of newly planted ivy

Wall

Ivy

Canes in soil against wall
Ivy stems trapped behind

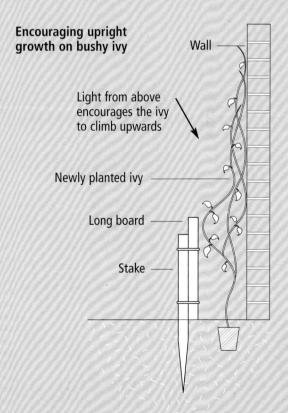

Encouraging upright growth on bushy ivy

Wall

Light from above encourages the ivy to climb upwards

Newly planted ivy

Long board

Stake

On the slope

Most gardens benefit from having one or more level areas that can be used for lawns and patios and for general convenience and comfort in getting around, and gently sloping gardens can usually be easily adapted to provide such areas. If the natural slope is significant, however, you will need to modify it to make the garden more usable on a day-to-day basis.

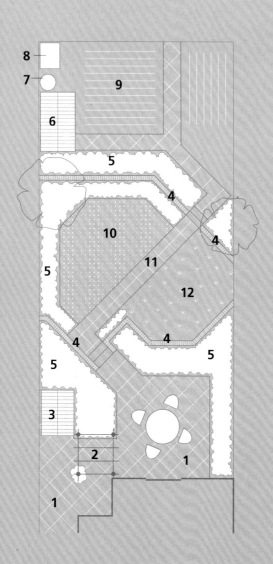

Garden elements key

1 Patio	7 Water butt
2 Pergola	8 Compost bin
3 Garden store	9 Kitchen garden
4 Retaining wall	10 Lawn
5 Border	11 Path
6 Garden shed	12 Play area

What makes this a successful sloping garden?

✓ The division of the garden into three by two low retaining walls enables the areas between to be levelled

✓ Each area is linked by safe, manageable steps and level paving

✓ Planting is designed to make each part of the garden into an almost enclosed space with its own character and purpose

✓ The design not only solves the problem of the slope but is an ideal solution for a long, narrow garden

✓ Each of the three spaces could be made individually secure and safe for small children by the addition of some low fencing or trellis and gates across the steps

Mix and match
If you like this garden, but would prefer a different feature, see pages 250–251 for possible variations.

Key features

Lawn

In some gardens, lawns are treated as a visual aid or foil to set off against colourful planting and assorted garden features. In others, though, lawns are more practical and can double up as play areas, dog runs or patio extensions. Whichever category yours falls into, make sure your ground preparation is very thorough, as if you were going to plant the area with shrubs and perennials rather than grass.

Retaining walls

These are a necessary part of levelling out a sloping garden to make it both attractive and practical. You can make your walls from materials that make them a positive feature or you might want to keep them very low key and disguise them with lots of trailing plants. Combine the walls with matching steps to get you up and down to the various garden areas.

Patio furniture

There's lots of patio furniture available, so take some time and choose a style and colour to fit in with the rest of your garden. Think about whether you'll need to store your furniture out of season and, if so, have you allowed enough storage space. Wooden or painted furniture will probably need to be maintained on a fairly regular basis.

Adapting a design for a smaller plot

If you want to adapt a design you like to suit a smaller plot, you may find that you cannot fit everything in. You'll either need to rationalize the design – for example, combine your lawn and play area – or omit the features that are the least important to you and concentrate on the ones you want most. Here is a square adaptation of the rectangular plan on page 22.

If you can't hide or disguise your garden shed, try to turn it into a positive feature.

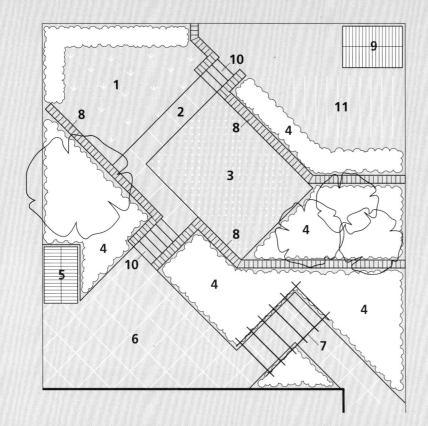

Key

1 Play area
2 Path
3 Lawn
4 Planting
5 Store
6 Patio
7 Pergola
8 Retaining wall
9 Shed
10 Steps
11 Kitchen garden

Garden stores and sheds

Unless you are fortunate enough to have lots of storage space elsewhere, such as an outbuilding or garage, you will need somewhere to put your tools and the multitude of items associated with gardening. Inevitably, whatever size you choose it will not be big enough! More important, however, is the way you incorporate it into the design so that it will be useful and accessible but will not intrude.

If your garden is large enough, you can include an area not only for your garden store but also for other everyday garden items that you may not wish to be visible — compost bin, water butt, greenhouse or cold frames — and separate this from the rest of the garden with a combination of planting and screening. Long, narrow gardens lend themselves particularly well to this solution. In smaller gardens you may find you have to put your store where it is visible to some degree, and you'll therefore want to try and screen or soften it with planting.

• If space is limited plant one or more climbers on the shed walls themselves, but avoid self-clinging plants, such as *Hedera* (ivy), which will make it difficult to maintain the shed; instead, fix wires or trellis to the building and grow climbing species that twine, such as clematis and honeysuckle, and that will tolerate being cut back every few years when you need to carry out essential garden maintenance

• If there is slightly more room mount a trellis or wires on separate posts set a short distance in front of the shed, which will make it easier to maintain later on; making a design feature of the trellis will make the building behind less obvious

• If there is space, create a border in front of the offending structure and plant a mixture of evergreen and deciduous species; link the border with the rest of the planting so that the utility area behind is completely lost

• Treat the store as a positive feature, staining or painting it with different colours to match your garden theme or decorating it with hanging pots or ornaments; include a small paved area around it and treat it as a place for relaxation

Planting

5

14

18

42

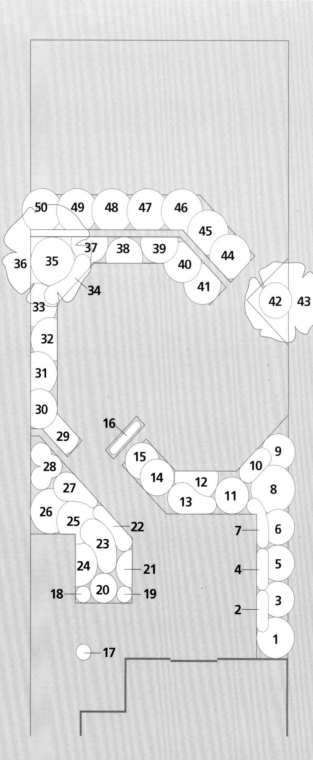

The best plants for this garden

The planting is generally of undemanding, reasonably priced trees, shrubs, perennials and grasses, which have been selected for year-round interest and their suitability for a family garden. The trees and taller shrubs are sited so that they help to emphasize the divisions between the three distinct parts of the garden.

Planting key

1 *Cistus* x *hybridus*
2 *Iris* 'Frost and Flame' (tall bearded)
3 *Cytisus* 'Windlesham Ruby'
4 *Lavandula angustifolia* 'Folgate'
5 *Hibiscus syriacus* 'Oiseau Bleu'
6 *Panicum virgatum* 'Rubrum'
7 *Coreopsis verticillata* 'Zagreb'
8 *Ceanothus* 'Delight'
9 *Miscanthus sinensis* 'Gracillimus'
10 *Geranium wallichianum* 'Buxton's Variety'
11 *Spiraea japonica* 'Anthony Waterer'
12 *Weigela florida* 'Foliis Purpureis'
13 *Hemerocallis* 'Stafford'
14 *Perovskia atriplicifolia* 'Blue Spire'
15 *Juniperus horizontalis* 'Emerald Spreader'
16 *Agapanthus* 'Blue Giant'

17 *Vitis vinifera* 'Ciotat'
18 *Clematis* 'Rouge Cardinal'
19 *Jasminum officinale*
  'Argenteovariegatum'
20 *Astilbe chinense* 'Finale'
21 *Geranium clarkei* 'Kashmir Purple'
22 *Oenothera macrocarpa*
23 *Campanula persicifolia* var. *alba*
24 *Camellia japonica* 'Adolphe
  Audusson'
25 *Lonicera fragrantissima*
26 *Rhododendron* 'Avalanche'
27 *Schizostylis* 'Sunrise'
28 *Potentilla fruticosa* 'Tilford Cream'
29 *Phlox paniculata* 'Sandringham'
30 *Viburnum carlesii* 'Aurora'
31 *Leucanthemum* x *superbum*
  'Aglaia'
32 *Nepeta* 'Six Hills Giant'
33 *Monarda* 'Snow Queen'
34 *Carex oshimensis* 'Evergold'
35 *Skimmia japonica* (1 male, 2
  female)
36 *Robinia pseudoacacia* 'Frisia'
37 *Astrantia major*
38 *Veronica gentianoides* 'Variegata'
39 *Iris sibirica* 'Tropic Night'
40 *Brachyglottis* Dunedin Group
  'Sunshine'
41 *Hemerocallis* 'Pink Damask'
42 *Spiraea nipponica* 'Snowmound'
43 *Malus* x *zumi* 'Golden Hornet'
44 *Euonymus europaeus* 'Red
  Cascade'
45 *Escallonia rubra* 'Crimson Spire'
46 *Viburnum opulus* 'Roseum'
47 *Rhododendron* 'Purple Splendour'
48 *Buddleja* 'Pink Delight'
49 *Viburnum rhytidophyllum*
50 *Ribes sanguineum* 'Tydeman's
  White'

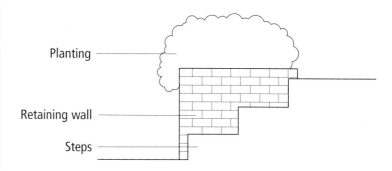

Planting — Retaining wall — Steps

Plants to soften walls

Retaining walls that are higher than 60–70cm (24–28in) tall will usually be built from brick or concrete and sometimes from stone. Regardless of the quality and detail of your chosen material, you may end up with expanses of rather plain vertical surfaces. Fortunately, there are many plants that will not only thrive by being planted immediately behind a retaining wall (where soil conditions may be cool but well-drained) but will cascade or arch down over the top of the wall to give an attractive, softening effect.

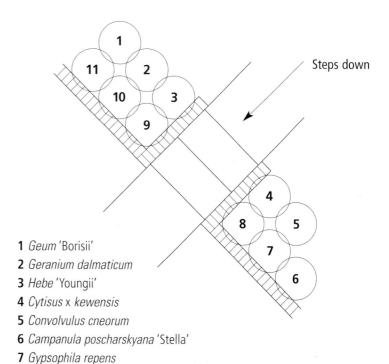

Steps down

1 *Geum* 'Borisii'
2 *Geranium dalmaticum*
3 *Hebe* 'Youngii'
4 *Cytisus* x *kewensis*
5 *Convolvulus cneorum*
6 *Campanula poscharskyana* 'Stella'
7 *Gypsophila repens*
8 *Genista lydia*
9 *Juniperus communis* 'Green
  Carpet'
10 *Helianthemum* 'Wisley Primrose'
11 *Veronica cinerea*

Patio practical

A lawn may not be a practical proposition in a small garden, but if you want an area for play, entertaining and general relaxation, building a patio will provide you with all the space you need. A large, relatively unbroken area of hard landscaping is included in this scheme, and so that it does not look bland and desert-like, the planting has been carefully chosen.

What makes this a good patio garden?

✓ Although it's a large space, the main patio is attractive because it is circular and is broken up with a bold pattern and contrasting edging

✓ The raised terrace adds another dimension and provides a slightly quieter shady area off the main patio

✓ The design includes bold drifts of planting that are in scale with the unbroken areas of paving

✓ Mobile bench seats give flexibility and can either be arranged formally in the corner or brought out into the open space for more informal use

✓ Both the barbecue and water features are accessible but don't encroach on the large usable space

✓ A useful covered storage area is screened off behind the terrace

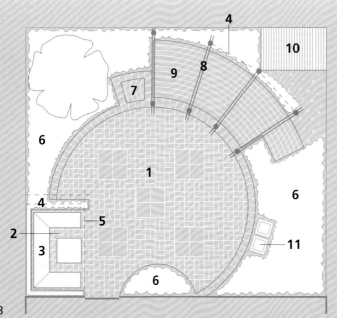

Garden elements key

1 Patio
2 Seating area
3 Mobile box seats
4 Trellis screen and climbers

5 Retractable awning
6 Planting
7 Water feature
8 Pergola and bamboo shading

9 Raised brick terrace
10 Lean-to garden
 store
11 Barbecue

Mix and match

If you like this garden, but would prefer a different feature, see pages 250–251 for possible variations.

Key features

Garden seats

These modular garden seats are very simple boxes on castors. You can put them together to make a formal arrangement around a table or position them in different parts of the garden for informal use. Make them with hinged or removable seats so that they can also act as storage and provide them with cushions for extra comfort.

Water feature

Raised water features make really attractive elements in any garden. Build them about 45cm (18in) high so that you can sit on the edge. Place them where they can be seen from the house and where the sun can catch the moving water.

Barbecue

Built-in barbecues can be designed to match and complement other parts of your garden, such as raised beds or garden walls. Make sure they are not too close to where you will sit and eat and position them in a fairly open area.

Bamboo shading

If you have the time and patience you can make your own bamboo shading to roll out on top of a pergola or gazebo when you need some extra protection from the sun.

Shading made from split or whole bamboo is both attractive and very practical.

1

Drill hole to take cord

3

Stop knot

Cord

Spacer

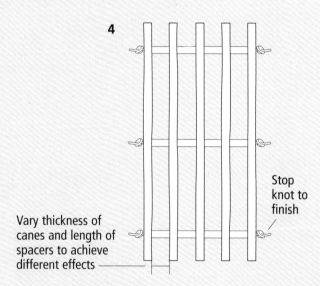

4

Vary thickness of canes and length of spacers to achieve different effects

Stop knot to finish

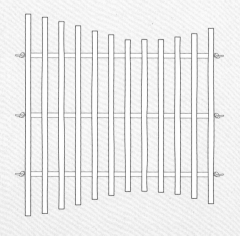

Vary lengths of canes but keep cords parallel

You will need

Bamboo canes; choose a thickness to suit your needs and long enough to match the width of the area you need to cover

Wooden or plastic pre-drilled beads or spacers made from short lengths of cane or thin plastic pipe

Rot-proof cord, preferably in black, brown or dark green

Step by step

1 Cut the canes to the desired length, and drill between three and five evenly spaced holes – depending on the length of cane – just wide enough to thread the cord through.

2 Pass a piece of cord through each hole, to the required length of shading plus some to spare. Fix each cord to the first cane with a large stop knot or tie it around the cane itself.

3 Thread a bead or spacer on to each piece of cord and then pass the cord through the next piece of cane.

4 Repeat the process until the shading is long enough and finish off by tying each length of cord with a stop knot or around the last cane.

Tips

• If you are cutting the canes with a saw, make sure you wear a dust mask

• Vary the thickness of canes and the size or number of beads or spacers between each cane to give different levels of shade

• Make the shading fit different shapes and areas by gradually increasing or decreasing the length of the canes

Planting

The best plants for this garden

The planting is bold and incorporates lots of plants that have been selected for their foliage to balance and contrast with the relatively large areas of hard surfaces. Flowers are of secondary importance, and the emphasis is on shape, colour, size and texture of leaves. The overall effect is unusual and distinctive, but most of the plants are easy to grow and have no special requirements.

Planting key

1 *Rubus henryi* (on trellis)
2 *Aralia elata*
3 *Arundo donax* var. *versicolor*
4 *Elaeagnus pungens* 'Maculata'
5 *Berberis thunbergii* f. atropurpurea 'Red Chief'
6 *Hydrangea aspera* subsp. sargentiana
7 *Catalpa bignonioides* 'Aurea'
8 *Mahonia japonica*
9 *Pleioblastus viridistratus*
10 *Corylopsis sinensis* var. sinensis 'Spring Purple'

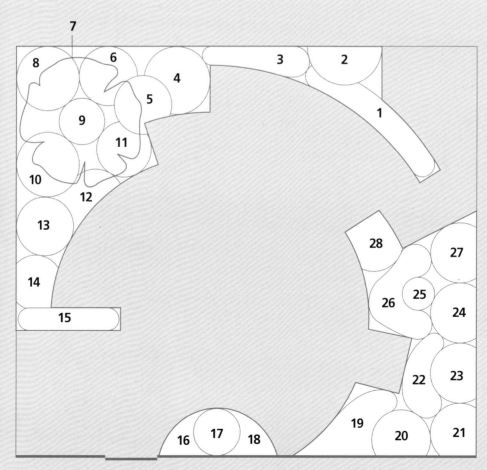

11 *Euonymus fortunei* 'Emerald Gaiety'
12 *Lamium galeobdolon* 'Hermann's Pride'
13 *Atriplex halimus*
14 *Astilboides tabularis*
15 *Vitis vinifera* 'Ciotat' (on trellis)
16 *Geranium macrorrhizum* 'Album'
17 *Salix helvetica*
18 *Ajuga reptans* 'Burgundy Glow'
19 *Hosta* 'Frances Williams'
20 *Cornus alba* 'Sibirica Variegata'
21 *Pseudosasa japonica*
22 *Smilacina racemosa*
23 *Acca sellowiana*
24 *Fatsia japonica*
25 *Eleutherococcus sieboldianus* 'Variegatus'
26 *Euonymus fortunei* 'Emerald 'n' Gold'
27 *Berberis* x *ottawensis* f. *purpurea*
28 *Acer palmatum* var. *dissectum*

Choosing flowers for a corner bed

When you plant a corner bed make sure that the plants you select are not only suitable for the conditions – sun or shade, damp or dry – but are also large enough to hide the walls or fence behind them. This will help to disguise the boundaries and make the garden feel more spacious.

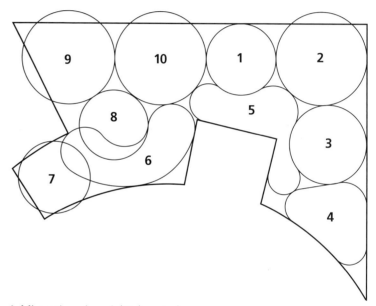

1 *Miscanthus sinensis* 'Malepartus'
2 *Ceanothus* 'Italian Skies'
3 *Viburnum sargentii* 'Onondaga'
4 *Schizostylis coccinea* 'Jennifer'
5 *Oenothera fruticosa* 'Fyrverkeri'
6 *Hemerocallis* 'Sammy Russell'
7 *Spiraea japonica* var. *albiflora*
8 *Potentilla fruticosa* 'Maanelys'
9 *Hibiscus syriacus* 'Oiseau Bleu'
10 *Forsythia* x *intermedia* 'Lynwood'

From the rooftop

Roof gardens are excellent ways of creating green living spaces in towns and cities, especially if you have a flat or apartment that doesn't have any space for a traditional ground-level garden. Of course, you may be fortunate enough to have space for both types of garden, either because the original building already has flat roof space suitable for a garden or you might need to extend the house, perhaps for a garage or extra living room, which will give you an opportunity to create a tailor-made area for a roof garden.

What makes this a good roof garden?

✓ Strong underlying structure to bear weight of plants in containers
✓ Secure perimeter fence or balustrade
✓ Good drainage
✓ Extra space for entertaining and relaxation
✓ Plants and features that screen or enhance existing views
✓ Careful selection of weather-resistant plants

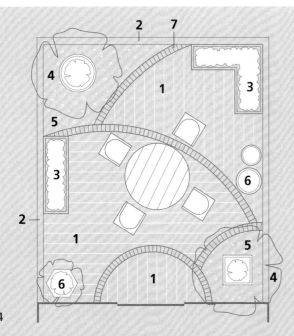

Garden elements key

1 Decking
2 Balustrade
3 Wooden planters to match deck
4 Small tree in container
5 Gravel or stone chippings

6 Container planted shrubs, perennials and grasses
7 Brick pattern set into decking

Mix and match

If you like this garden, but would prefer a different feature, see pages 250–251 for possible variations.

Key features

Trees in containers

Provided that you can look after them properly and that your roof is strong enough, you can plant trees in containers to give valuable height and structure to a roof garden. If possible, fit heavy-duty castors to the bottoms of containers so that you can move them around occasionally. Use them to screen unsightly objects or to frame and enhance a particularly attractive view.

Decking

Decking is an ideal way to cover the 'ground' of your roof garden. It is relatively light and can be laid directly onto the roof structure with minimal preparation. Make different patterns with the decking, mixing it with other materials to create abstract or formal shapes and use coloured stains for extra interest.

The right plants

You may be limited as to how much planting you can include, so make sure that the plants you choose are suitable and provide long periods of interest. Evergreen shrubs will give year-round colour and many grasses look good not only when growing but also in late autumn and winter with their golden-brown foliage and attractive seed heads. Underplant individual large shrubs with small perennials and dwarf bulbs to get maximum interest from your limited space.

Building a planter

Unless you're very fortunate, or able to include your roof garden in an overall building design from scratch, your planting will need to be in containers. You can either buy pots, tubs and other containers or, for a special effect, you can make your own. This planter is fitted with robust castors so that it can be moved to one side when extra space is needed.

Build your containers from boards to match the colour and style of your decking.

You will need

5 x 5cm (2 x 2in) pressure-treated softwood

Spare decking

19mm (¾in) thick marine plywood

Small cabinet brackets

Screws

Stain

Castors (optional); use rubber wheel-type castors, not those sold for indoor furniture

Heavy-duty polythene

Step by step

1 Make a box-shaped frame with the softwood, using the cabinet brackets and screws to make the joins.

2 Cut lengths of decking to the height of the planter and screw to the four sides of the box frame.

3 Cut the plywood to sit inside the planter so that it rests on the bottom of the frame. Drill 1cm (½in) holes about 7.5cm (3in) apart for drainage.

4 Screw a castor to each bottom corner of the planter if you want it to be mobile.

5 Cut lengths of decking to sit along the top edge of the planter, mitred at 45° at each corner to fit together like a picture frame, and screw them down.

6 Stain the planter.

7 Line the inside walls of the planter with the heavy-duty polythene to protect the wood from damp. Fill with your chosen growing medium and plant up.

Roof gardens are most effective when a theme is used, like the silver, pink and white colour scheme in this garden.

Design considerations

Strength

Existing flat roofs were probably not designed to take lots of extra weight. You must check with an expert, such as an architect or civil engineer, that the idea is feasible before you begin. Any new constructions should be designed with this purpose in mind.

Safety

Because they are above ground, roof gardens must have secure perimeters so that no one falls off. If the existing roof edge is not suitable, you must include a proper surrounding wall or balustrade in your design.

Planning consent

Most urban areas, particularly those with historic buildings, are subject to a variety of laws and regulations governing new development and other building works. Check at an early stage to see if your ideas are acceptable to avoid potentially costly and embarrassing problems at a later date if you don't.

Drainage

Rainwater falling on the roof must have somewhere to drain away. You must make a note of how your roof space drains before you build your garden to make sure that your design and any new structures do not interfere with the flow of water.

Planting

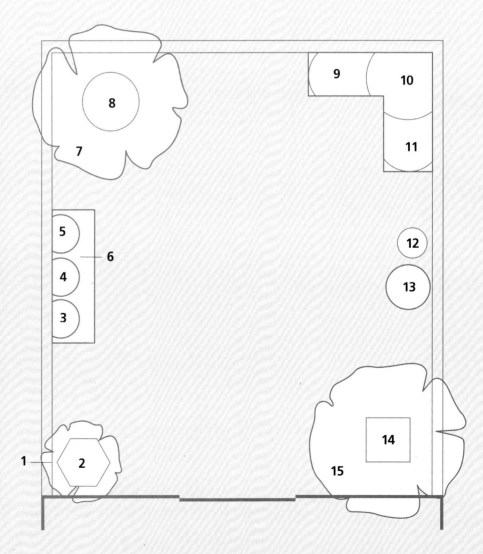

The best plants for this garden

Because most of the planting will need to be in some sort of container or a raised bed, you can choose a growing medium to suit particular plants – an ericaceous or acid soil in which to grow hardy rhododendrons or summer-flowering heathers, for example. This scheme includes a limited number of plants – indeed, in all but the largest of gardens, there will rarely be scope for masses of lavish planting – so those you use must be chosen to give the best results and should have some or all of the following qualities:

- Evergreen, for winter interest
- Wind resistant
- Drought and heat resistant
- A long flowering period
- Interesting foliage or habit of growth
- Suitable for container growing

Planting key

1 *Cornus mas* 'Aurea'
2 *Crocus* purple
3 *Lavandula angustifolia* 'Hidcote'
4 *Yucca filamentosa*
5 *Lavandula angustifolia* 'Hidcote'
6 *Cotoneaster congestus*
7 *Sorbus hupehensis*
8 *Vinca minor* 'Aureovariegata'
9 *Fuchsia magellanica* 'Versicolor'
10 *Elaeagnus pungens* 'Maculata'
11 *Juniperus communis* 'Repanda'
12 *Acanthus mollis* Latifolius Group
13 *Miscanthus sinensis* 'Malepartus'
14 *Hedera hibernica*
15 *Acer negundo* 'Flamingo'

Alternative planting

Here is a plan for a purple and gold colour scheme.

1 *Berberis thunbergii* f. *atropurpurea* 'Red Chief'
2 Dwarf narcissus
3 *Viola riviniana* Purpurea Group
4 *Achillea* 'Moonshine'
5 *Miscanthus* 'Purpurascens'
6 *Rudbeckia fulgida* var. *sullivantii* 'Goldsturm'
7 *Catalpa* x *erubescens* 'Purpurea'
8 *Lysimachia nummularia* 'Aurea'
9 *Potentilla fruticosa* 'Elizabeth'
10 *Pittosporum tenuifolium* 'Purpureum'
11 *Juniperus* x *pfitzeriana* 'Gold Coast'
12 *Artemisia* 'Powis Castle'
13 *Phormium* 'Sundowner'
14 *Ajuga reptans* 'Purpurea'
15 *Acer negundo* 'Kelly's Gold'

Choosing your colour scheme

In a large garden you can successfully introduce an entire bed or border devoted to a single colour – yellow or blue, for example – and this arrangement works particularly well where the design divides the garden into a number of smaller, linked areas. You can't always subdivide small gardens, and a planting scheme of one colour might become overpowering or monotonous. Instead, use two or three complementary colours and link them with the hard landscaping – decks and wooden planters are excellent for this, because it is relatively easy to change the colour if you wish.

No matter what your main colour choice is, include some white and silver plants, which are excellent foils to other colours and lift darker combinations.

The edges of a roof garden are usually strongest, so concentrate your heavier planters and garden features in this zone.

The scented garden

When it comes to designing a bed or border, the visual attractions of plants – flower, foliage texture, shape and colour – are often given priority over another plant attribute – scent. Plants with fragrant flowers or aromatic foliage add an extra dimension to a garden. However, be careful not to plant two (or different) scented plants too closely to one another or their individual fragrances won't be properly appreciated.

What makes this a good scented garden?

✓ An odd shape, with its combination of circular paving and square lawn, encourages visitors to wander around the garden, experiencing a succession of pleasant scents

✓ Something fragrant in the garden at almost any time of the year

✓ Careful planting to avoid potential conflict between fragrances so that each one can be individually appreciated

✓ Enclosing the garden with a wall (or other solid barrier, such as a fence or hedge) helps create shelter and prevents strong breezes from dispersing the fragrances too quickly

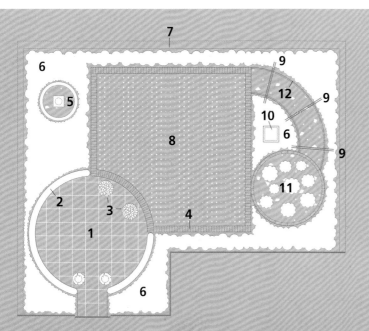

Garden elements key

1 Sun terrace
2 Lavender hedge
3 Annuals in containers
4 Terracotta tile mowing edge
5 Scalloped edge circle with crushed slate and birdbath
6 Planting in border
7 Climbers on wall

8 Lawn

9 Arches planted with climbing roses

10 Statue

11 Thyme 'lawn'

12 Scalloped terracotta edging

Mix and match

If you like this garden, but would prefer a different feature, see pages 250–251 for possible variations.

Key features

Mowing edge

Pristine lawns can make a valuable contribution to a formal or geometric garden design and need crisp edges for the best effect. To keep your lawn looking good, create a mowing strip from tiles, small flagstones or bricks. These will not only emphasize the lawn shape but will also make mowing much easier and stop the lawn edges from crumbling.

Scalloped edge circle and birdbath

Birdbaths and other ornaments make attractive features. To highlight them, put them on a 'base' of crushed slate or shingle surrounded by a circle or square of scalloped edging tiles. Alternatively, you could lay a small area of natural stone paving or bricks and plant around it with low perennials or dwarf shrubs to soften the hard edges.

Rose arches

Arches planted with climbing roses are excellent features for almost any style of garden. Place them in a sunny position where you can walk under them and appreciate the scent. Choose your rose varieties to suit the size and scale of the arches and make sure that the arches are wide enough to pass through without being scratched by thorns.

Lawn shapes

The shape of your lawn will depend initially on the style or theme of your garden. Informal designs will probably look best with an irregularly but gently curved lawn, while more formal styles lend themselves to lawns that have straight edges or that are symmetrical, such as circles.

Circular lawns leave lots of space for planting around the edges and create a secluded garden once plants are established.

Circle or square?

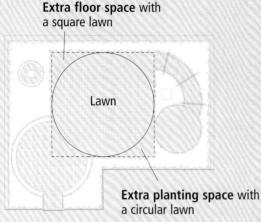

Extra floor space with a square lawn

Lawn

Extra planting space with a circular lawn

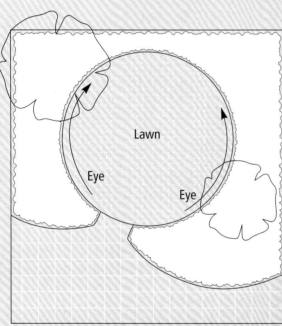

Lawn

Eye

Eye

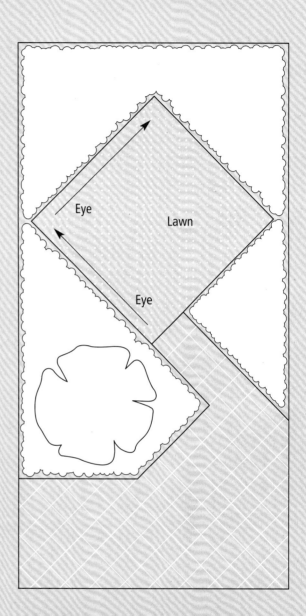

Eye

Lawn

Eye

Disguising a square garden

- A circular lawn will help to disguise an oddly shaped garden by drawing the eye away from corners and straight boundaries

- A circular lawn will take up less space than a square lawn of the same diameter, giving more room for planting and other features

Disguising a long, narrow garden

- A square lawn is useful in a long, narrow garden if it is turned through 45° to create diagonal lines that break up the narrowness

- A square lawn will give you more usable grass area

- A square lawn is easier to cut than a circular one, especially if it is small

Planting

15

20

23

27

The best plants for this garden

The planting has a softness of texture and colour, yet there is enough permanent structure for it to remain interesting through the winter. Within the planting design, the degree of fragrance varies from plant to plant, so that while the fragrance of some strongly scented varieties, such as honeysuckle, will carry some distance, others such as *Phlox* are more localized and invite closer scrutiny.

The plants include some that have no obvious flower scent but instead rely on their aromatic foliage for their attraction. *Salvia* (sage) and *Thymus* (thyme), for example, are best appreciated by rubbing the leaves gently. On the sun terrace this is especially so with the lavender hedge surrounding it and the containers placed strategically near chairs and sunloungers.

Planting key

1 *Mahonia aquifolium* 'Smaragd'
2 *Lavandula angustifolia* 'Hidcote'
3 *Sarcococca ruscifolia*
4 *Wisteria sinensis* 'Blue Sapphire' (on wall)
5 *Lilium martagon*
6 *Phlox carolina* 'Bill Baker'
7 *Salvia officinalis* 'Purpurescens'
8 *Osmanthus delavayi*
9 *Cardiocrinum giganteum*
10 *Mahonia* x *media* 'Charity'
11 *Rhododendron* 'Golden Lights' (azalea)
12 *Filipendula ulmaria* 'Aurea'

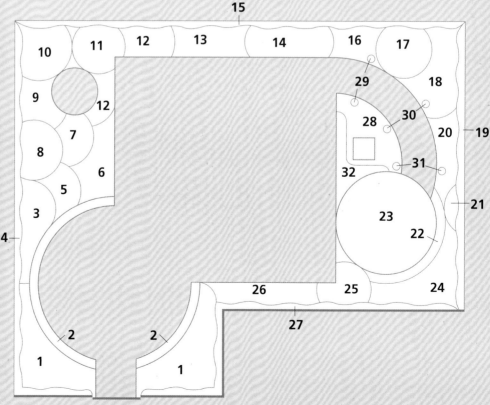

13 *Hosta* 'Honeybells'

14 *Rhododendron* 'Klondyke' (azalea)

15 *Akebia quinata* (on wall)

16 *Geranium macrorrhizum*

17 *Viburnum farreri*

18 *Phlox paniculata* 'Mother of Pearl'

19 *Lonicera periclymenum* 'Serotina' (on wall)

20 *Lilium regale*

21 *Iris graminea*

22 *Lavandula angustifolia* 'Hidcote Pink'

23 *Thymus* cvs. (dotted among gravel bed)

24 *Caryopteris* x *clandonensis* 'Kew Blue'

25 *Philadelphus* 'Silberregen'

26 *Crinum* x *powellii*

27 *Clematis cirrhosa* (on house wall)

28 *Nepeta* x *faassenii* (with *Tulipa* 'Eros')

29 *Rosa* 'New Dawn' (white form)

30 *Rosa* 'Goldfinch'

31 *Rosa* 'Aloha'

32 *Dianthus* 'Devon Dove'

Place a bench next to a scented shrub, such as *Philadelphus coronarius* 'Aureus' (mock orange), for a private seating area with a lovely fragrance.

Choosing plants for scent

You'll come across many plants that provide scent during the summer months, but there isn't so much choice for plants with winter scent. It is worth taking the trouble to find one or two winter-scented plants and positioning them somewhere in your garden that you will use in the winter – perhaps near to front or back doors.

Best hardy climbers for scent

- *Clematis armandii*; *C. cirrhosa* var. *balearica*
- Summer-flowering forms of *Jasminum* (jasmine), including *J. officinale*, *J. polyanthum* and *J.* x *stephanense*
- *Lonicera* (honeysuckle), including *L. periclymenum* and cvs., *L. implexa* and *L. japonica*
- Roses, including *Rosa* 'Albertine' (vigorous), *R.* 'Zéphirine Drouhin', *R.* 'Galway Bay' and *R.* 'Paul's Lemon Pillar'
- *Trachelospermum* spp. and cvs.
- *Wisteria* spp.

Best hardy shrubs for scent

- *Chimonanthus* (wintersweet)
- *Choisya ternata* and cvs. (Mexican orange blossom)
- *Daphne* spp.
- *Lonicera* (winter-flowering honeysuckles), including *L. fragrantissima* and *L.* x *purpusii*
- *Mahonia* spp.
- *Osmanthus* spp.
- *Philadelphus* spp. (mock orange)
- *Sarcococca* spp. (Christmas box)
- *Syringa* spp. (lilac)
- Viburnums, such as *Viburnum* x *bodnantense*, *V.* x *carlcephalum* and *V. carlesii*

Gravel and pots

From time to time you'll come across a garden or backyard where, for a number of reasons, it's not feasible to plant directly into the ground. The ideal solution is to put all your plants in containers and cover the rest of the garden with attractive materials.

What makes this a good container garden?

✓ A good mixture of plants for variations in colour, shape and texture
✓ Larger containers with trees and specimen shrubs to provide scale and structure in the design
✓ A mulch of gravel, stone chippings or other loose materials cover up the rest of the garden area and disguise and level unsightly ground surfaces
✓ An arch, with wooden posts bolted to the concrete (if necessary) with angle brackets, provides extra height

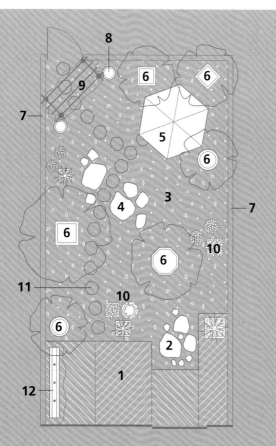

Garden elements key

1 Raised deck modules
2 Rock water feature
3 Gravel, stones, pebbles groundcover
4 Rock feature
5 Parasol and bench seat
6 Small tree or large shrub in container
7 Boundary wall

8 Climbers on arch
9 Arch
10 Shrub / perennial /
grass / bamboo in
container groupings

11 Stepping stone path
12 Planting trough
with climbers

Mix and match
If you like this garden, but would
prefer a different feature, see pages
250–251 for possible variations.

Key features

Parasol

Although you can grow trees quite satisfactorily in large containers, it's unlikely that you'll be able to grow one big enough to cast any serious shade. Therefore, in hot, sunny gardens you might want to use a parasol. Match it to your garden furniture if you can. As the season progresses you can keep rearranging your whole garden – containers, seats and parasol – to follow the sun or not!

Decking

Building your deck in small, portable sections makes it much easier to assemble and also gives you lots of flexibility to change the arrangement from time to time and add extra modules to increase the deck space. With any deck, don't forget to prevent weed growth coming up from below by mulching with heavy black polythene or proprietary fabric before laying the decking.

Groups of containers

Smaller containers will usually look better if grouped together whereas very large ones are often more effective placed in some isolation. Protect terracotta containers from frost damage by storing them somewhere dry in winter. If this is not possible, stand them on pot feet to lift them off the damp ground, and paint the top of the rim with brick waterproofing agent.

Modular decking

An alternative way to construct a simple deck to put on top of an existing hard surface is to build a series of small modules, which you can arrange in whatever pattern you want and add to if and when you need to extend the area of decking.

For a single module make the overall size no bigger than one or two people can easily handle, about 1.8 x 1.2m (6 x 4ft), say.

Make decking in manageable modules for ease of construction and flexibility.

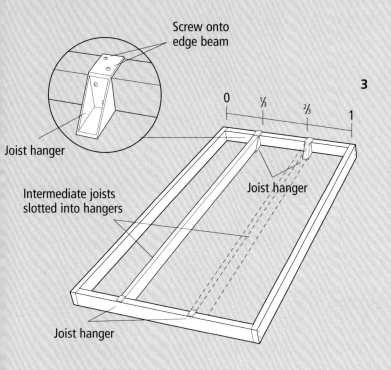

Screw onto edge beam

Joist hanger

Intermediate joists slotted into hangers

Joist hanger

3

0   ⅓   ⅔   1

Joist hanger

You will need

Lengths of 5 x 10cm (2 x 4in) pressure-treated softwood, to form the edges and beams

Lengths of decking of your choice

Joist hangers to take the 5cm (2in) thick softwood beams (available from builders' merchants)

Roofing slate

Screws and nails

Step by step

1 Cut two lengths of beam 1.8m (6ft) long and two lengths 1.2m (4ft) long. Nail or screw them together to make a simple rectangular frame.

2 Divide one narrow end of the frame into three and nail a joist hanger to the inside face at the one-third and two-third marks. Repeat with the other end.

3 Cut two beams long enough to fit snugly in the opposite pairs of joist hangers so that the frame now consists of four long parallel beams and two short ones, one across each end.

4 Cut lengths of decking to match the width of the frame and screw the pieces to the frame, leaving a gap between deck boards of 4–6mm (about ¼in) to allow for drainage and movement.

5 You now have a manageable deck module, which you can place anywhere you wish on your concrete or tarmac yard base. It is simply now a matter of raising each corner, if necessary, with one or more pieces of thin slate to make the whole thing level. Make sure there is at least one piece of slate beneath each corner to keep the beams off the ground and free from damp.

6 If you want to join two modules together remove a couple of deck boards from each module and bolt, screw or nail together the edge beam of each, before replacing the boards.

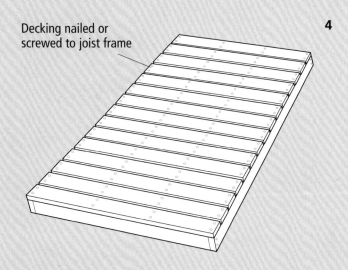

Decking nailed or screwed to joist frame

4

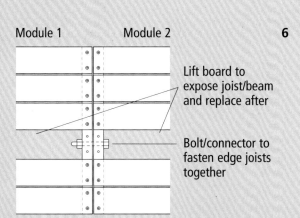

Module 1   Module 2   **6**

Lift board to expose joist/beam and replace after

Bolt/connector to fasten edge joists together

Planting

1

10

17

20

The best plants for this garden

Trees and larger shrubs are needed to provide scale and height and they have been selected so that they are suitable for growing in containers. Perennials and grasses look better in smaller containers, and cultivars have been suggested that will thrive in these particular growing conditions. Arrange them in small groups rather than placing them individually. Because the number of plants is relatively small, each one has been chosen to provide maximum height.

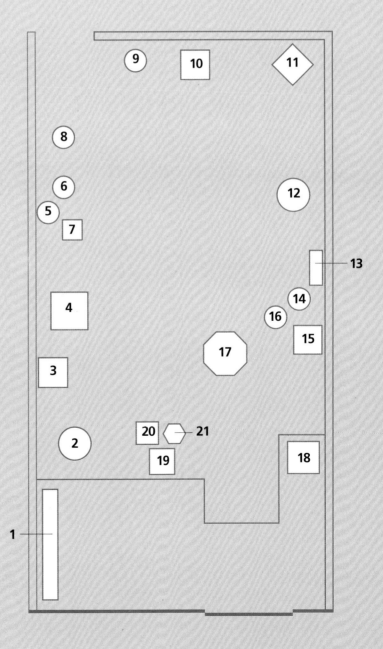

Grouping containers for different effects

When you're putting together a collection of several containerized plants in close proximity for a combined effect, don't put all the containers together in a random fashion but follow the same principles that would apply if you were planting them in the ground – lower soft, mound-forming or trailing plants towards the front with taller, upright forms towards the back. Remember, too, to allow enough room for each plant to fill out naturally without becoming cramped by its neighbours.

Container plants for foliage effect

1 *Cornus florida* 'Rainbow'
2 *Artemisia* 'Powis Castle'
3 *Pleioblastus variegatus*
4 *Heuchera micrantha* var. *diversifolia* 'Palace Purple'
5 *Hosta* 'Wide Brim'
6 *Chamaecyparis pisifera* 'Filfera Aurea'

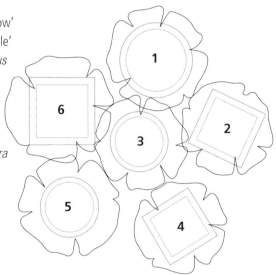

Container plants for a blue and silver theme

1 *Abies koreana* 'Silberlocke'
2 *Ceratostigma willmottianum*
3 *Agapanthus* 'Blue Giant'
4 *Convolvulus cneorum*
5 *Lavandula angustifolia* 'Munstead'
6 *Rhododendron* Blue Tit Group

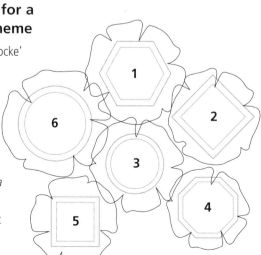

Birds, bees and frogs

As natural habitats decline, many birds, insects, amphibians and small mammals are coming to rely on gardens as sources of food and shelter and places to breed. Many gardens, both urban and rural, contain plants and features that are potentially attractive to wild fauna, but because they are isolated and few and far between they are of limited value, except to occasional visiting creatures.

What makes this a good wildlife garden?

✓ A continuous framework of trees and shrubs provides a permanent corridor around the garden, particularly for birds

✓ The tree species are ideal for nesting and roosting

✓ A range of plants provides lower level cover for smaller birds, mammals and amphibians and provides various food items throughout the year – pollen, berries, seeds

✓ Mini-habitats encourage the widest possible range of wildlife

✓ Overwintering quarters for amphibians, mammals and smaller birds

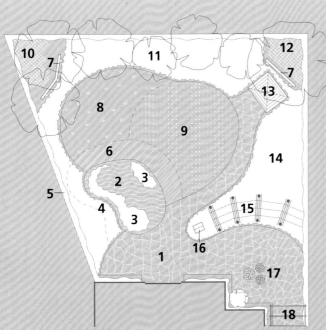

Garden elements key

1 Patio	7 Log screen
2 Pond	8 'Meadow'
3 Marginals in pond	9 Lawn
4 Bog garden	10 Amphibian
5 Fence	hibernation zone
6 Damp 'meadow'	11 'Woodland'

Mix and match

If you like this garden, but would prefer a different feature, see pages 250–251 for possible variations.

Key features

Bird feeding station

This is an easy and comfortable way for birds – and sometimes small mammals – to find food, especially in winter. Make a feature of it and place it where you can observe and enjoy it from indoors in inclement weather. However, make sure it is not too enclosed so that the birds have plenty of escape routes from predators such as cats.

Different habitats

The ultimate aim of this garden is to create and maintain a collection of 'habitats' to attract and hold various forms of wildlife, including a pond, woodland, meadow and hibernation zones. Nevertheless, the garden is also designed to look good and function from the human point of view.

Bog garden

Bog garden planting – such as hosta, astilbe, iris – is often associated with ponds, pools and streams. However, you can create a bog garden without a body of water. Plant up a naturally damp part of the garden or make an area artificially damp by burying a piece of pond liner or heavy polythene so that it will retain moisture.

How to create a wildlife pond

Ponds don't need to be particularly deep (unless you're going to keep fish) but at least one deep zone – about 90cm (3ft) deep – will allow you to grow a wider range of aquatic plants, and the extra volume of water will help avoid wide temperature fluctuations, which can sometimes lead to green, algal growth.

A pond provides a great habitat for all kinds of wild creatures, including frogs, newts and dragonflies.

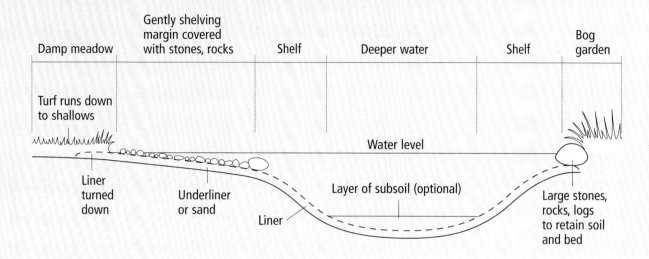

Damp meadow

Gently shelving margin covered with stones, rocks

Shelf

Deeper water

Shelf

Bog garden

Turf runs down to shallows

Water level

Liner turned down

Underliner or sand

Liner

Layer of subsoil (optional)

Large stones, rocks, logs to retain soil and bed

Dig the pond with gently sloping sides along at least part of its edge to make it easy for frogs, toads and other amphibians to get in and out of your pond during the breeding season and for birds and small mammals to bathe or drink.

Cover the shallow area with a mixture of large and small stones and gravel so that if water levels fluctuate you will not have an unsightly strip of pond liner below the highwater mark.

How to maintain a wildlife garden

- Prune shrubs, trees and climbers in late winter, before birds begin to build their nests

- Don't tidy up dead perennials and grasses at the first sign of autumn because the material provides winter cover for many insects and the birds may find seedheads to eat

- Use heavy prunings from trees together with other woody material from shrubs and conifers to top up the hibernation zones

- Pile bricks and other large pieces of material in a low heap to make a good basis for a hibernation zone for amphibians and also for snails

- When you tidy up perennials and grasses in early spring, leave piles of fine, dried material where birds can get at it for nesting material

- Avoid using chemicals in the garden and once the wildlife population has developed it will help to control many garden pests, such as aphids and slugs

- Don't feed meadow areas or you will encourage the growth of coarse grasses, which can take over and suppress the fine-leaved forms and wildflowers that need low nutrient levels

- Stack dried leaves out of sight under the trees as potential bedding for small mammals

The seedheads of grasses provide a good source of food for birds in winter.

- Build a compost heap to encourage worms and other beneficial animals

Planting

The best plants for this garden

The plants have been selected to satisfy the requirements of both appearance and wildlife. The larger shrubs and trees provide a basic framework around which perennials, grasses and climbers are planted to give continuous variations in colour, texture and form. The scale and density of the planting completely masks the boundaries of the garden and helps create a feeling of seclusion and quiet that perfectly suits the needs of the wildlife.

Planting key

1 *Cotoneaster horizontalis* (against wall)
2 *Osmanthus* x *burkwoodii*
3 *Clematis armandii* (against wall)
4 *Pyracantha* 'Mohave'
5 *Lavandula angustifolia* 'Munstead'
6 *Hedera helix* 'Buttercup' (on framed trellis on wall)
7 *Vitis amurensis* (on fence)
8 *Origanum laevigatum* 'Herrenhausen'
9 *Bergenia* 'Wintermärchen'
10 *Filipendula ulmaria*
11 *Viburnum opulus*
12 *Ligularia dentata* 'Desdemona'
13 *Astilboides tabularis*
14 *Stipa calamagrostis*
15 *Euphorbia amygdaloides* var. *robbiae*
16 *Pinus sylvestris*
17 *Humulus lupulus*
18 *Acer campestre*
19 *Prunus laurocerasus* 'Zabeliana'
20 *Symphytum* 'Hidcote Pink'
21 *Hypericum calycinum*
22 *Crataegus monogyna*
23 *Corylus avellana*
24 *Thuja plicata* 'Zebrina'
25 *Lonicera periclymenum*
26 *Betula pendula*
27 *Vinca minor*

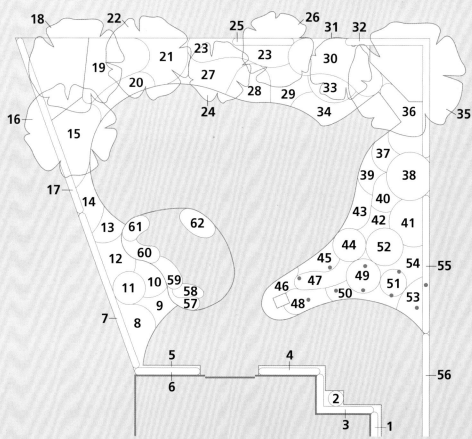

28 *Mahonia aquifolium*
29 *Polygonatum multiflorum*
30 *Ilex aquifolium* (2 female, 1 male)
31 *Betula pendula*
32 *Hedera helix*
33 *Symphoricarpos* x *chenaultii* 'Hancock'
34 *Lamium galeobdolon* 'Hermann's Pride'
35 *Alnus glutinosa*
36 *Fargesia robusta*
37 *Aster amellus* 'Brilliant'
38 *Cotoneaster frigidus* 'Cornubia'
39 *Veronica gentianoides* 'Variegata'
40 *Persicaria bistorta* 'Superba'
41 *Miscanthus sinensis* 'Variegatus'
42 *Rudbeckia* 'Goldquelle'
43 *Salvia* x *sylvestris* 'Mainacht'
44 *Juniperus* x *pfitzeriana* 'Sulphur Spray'
45 *Centranthus ruber*
46 *Erica carnea* 'Springwood White'
47 *Iris sibirica* 'Sparkling Rose'
48 *Aster* x *frickartii* 'Mönch'
49 *Rosa rubiginosa*
50 *Centaurea montana* 'Parham'
51 *Potentilla fruticosa* 'Goldfinger'
52 *Viburnum carlesii* 'Aurora'
53 *Acanthus mollis*
54 *Digitalis purpurea*
55 *Clematis vitalba*
56 *Parthenocissus henryana*
57 *Caltha palustris*
58 *Sagittaria sagittifolia*
59 *Typha minima*
60 *Pontederia cordata*
61 *Butomus umbellatus*
62 *Iris pseudacorus*

Bog gardens

Boggy areas don't always occur next to open bodies of water, such as streams and ponds. Instead, they can often be found in low-lying areas of meadows or on upland moors. If you want to create a bog garden, it isn't essential to have it next to a pond and although it is helpful if there is a permanently damp spot in your garden that will lend itself to development, this is not necessary either.

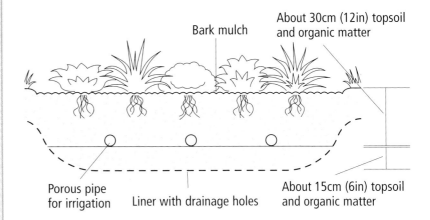

Bark mulch

About 30cm (12in) topsoil and organic matter

Porous pipe for irrigation

Liner with drainage holes

About 15cm (6in) topsoil and organic matter

You will need

Sheet of impermeable material, such as a pond liner or heavy-duty polythene

Clean, weed-free, preferably heavy, soil

Organic matter to condition the soil

Length of porous irrigation pipe and appropriate connections to top up moisture levels in long, dry periods (optional)

Suitable plants

Step by step

1 Select a site for the bog garden, ideally in a low spot in the garden where one might occur naturally, and mark out its shape on the ground.

2 Clear the area of weeds, turf (if lawn) and any other vegetation or debris.

3 Dig out the area to a depth of 45cm (18in), keeping the topsoil and subsoil in separate piles.

4 Make holes in the membrane, about 15cm (6in) apart, to allow some drainage. Although the soil must retain moisture it must not be allowed to become waterlogged and stagnant.

5 Lay the membrane in the hole and backfill with about 15cm (6in) of soil (or subsoil if found). Mix in copious quantities of organic matter.

6 Lay the porous pipe in a serpentine fashion across the top of this layer, remembering to leave one end sticking out just above ground level so that it can be connected to your hosepipe or tap. Seal the other end.

7 Replace the rest of the soil, again mixing in organic matter. If the soil is particularly heavy or sticky, add sharp sand or grit to improve the texture.

8 Position the plants in the garden and plant them.

The sunken garden

Raised beds can be useful and attractive features, introducing changes of level and raising plants, especially low-growing species, to a height where they can be appreciated. As a variation on this theme, this garden has been designed around a sunken lawn so that when you're on the lawn, the rest of the garden is really a raised bed!

What makes this a good sunken garden?

✓ Interesting changes of level are created by sinking the central lawn area, with steps leading down to it and up again at the far end
✓ The level changes emphasize the transition in character between one area of the garden and the next
✓ An enclosed and private patio area
✓ Traditional herbaceous planting, creating strongly contrasting informal space full of lush tree and shrub planting

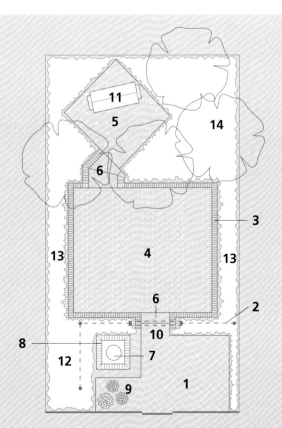

Garden elements key

1 Patio of herringbone red brick

2 Trellis screen

3 Low retaining wall

4 Sunken lawn

5 Open 'glade' in trees and shrubs

6 Steps up from sunken lawn

7 Feature sculpture

Mix and match
If you like this garden, but would prefer a different feature, see pages 250–251 for possible variations.

8 Blue brick square and pebbles

9 Herbs in pots

10 Arch over steps

11 Swing seat

12 Green-and-white planting

13 Perennials

14 Shrubs and trees

Key features

Green-and-white planting

Colour-themed planting is a great way to create atmosphere in a small space. Green and white will make an area seem quite cool. For warmer tones, use pinks, oranges and rich yellows. For a really strong effect, carry your chosen colour theme through into your hard landscaping and garden ornaments as well.

Sculpture

Carefully position sculptures in your garden, making sure they can be seen from your chosen viewpoint. Place them on some sort of base, even it it's only a simple piece of flat stone set among low planting. White or pale pieces will look good if backed by dark evergreens whereas darker sculptures need to be well lit, set against a paler background.

Herbs in pots

Treat herbs in pots as you would any other container-grown plants, with regular feeding, watering, trimming and repotting when necessary. Place them near to your kitchen or patio door so they are easily accessible for cutting and picking. Divide them into sun and shade lovers and position them accordingly so that they are in their ideal growing conditions.

How to create a sunken garden

- Light, sandy or stony soils are usually free-draining and rarely become waterlogged, but heavier, clay soils can retain a lot of water and are often slow-draining. Dig a trial hole in heavy ground during the wettest part of the year to the depth of your intended sunken garden and see if it holds water – if it does you'll need to install some form of drainage to prevent your garden acting as a sump.

- Excavating and carting away lots of topsoil and subsoil can be exhausting and also expensive. Introduce a raised level into your garden as well, where you can incorporate this extra material in new beds.

- When a sunken area is to be planted (or grassed), make sure there is enough depth of topsoil for the purpose when you've finished. Although it's a rather time-consuming process, you'll need to strip off the original topsoil, remove as much subsoil as necessary to create the sunken area and then replace an adequate amount of original topsoil at the new, lower level.

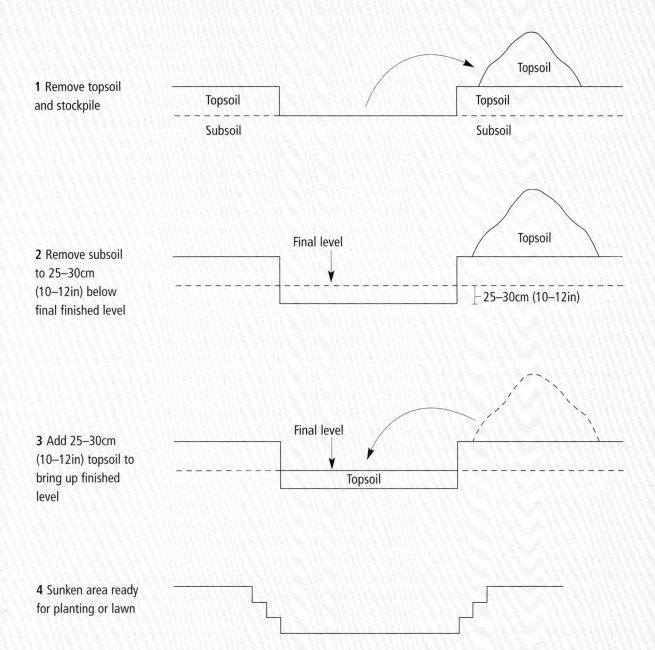

1 Remove topsoil and stockpile

Topsoil

Topsoil

Subsoil

Topsoil

Subsoil

2 Remove subsoil to 25–30cm (10–12in) below final finished level

Final level

Topsoil

25–30cm (10–12in)

3 Add 25–30cm (10–12in) topsoil to bring up finished level

Final level

Topsoil

4 Sunken area ready for planting or lawn

Sunken seating area

If you would like a change of level but a raised bed or similar feature is not possible – for example, against the wall of a house where damp might be a problem – you can sink some paving into the ground and make an attractive little corner for sitting in.

Planting

The best plants for this garden

The planting will create a different effect in each part of the garden. Around the patio a combination of shrubs, climbers and perennials provide a cool, restrained theme of green and white with an emphasis on evergreen foliage. By contrast, the sunken lawn is flanked by borders of traditional, easy-care perennials and climbing roses to give a bright splash of colour in summer. Moving up into the furthest area, the mood changes with masses of informal planting – trees, large shrubs, bamboos and drifts of perennials with lots of emphasis on foliage and shape.

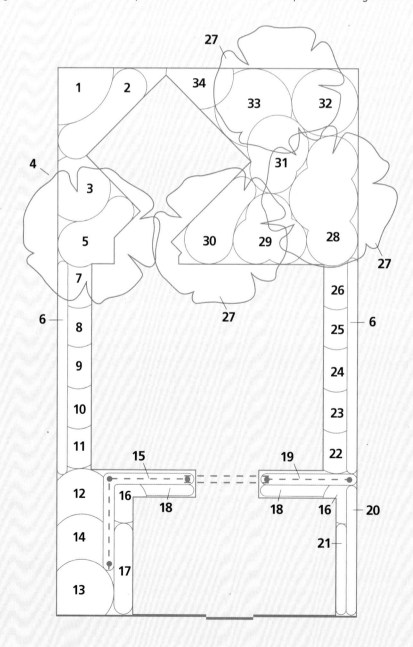

Planting key

1 *Hydrangea aspera*
2 *Pleioblastus variegatus*
3 *Cercis canadensis* 'Forest Pansy'
4 *Malus tschonoskii*
5 *Hypericum forrestii*
6 *Rosa* 'Albertine' (on fence)
7 *Geranium himalayense*
8 *Achillea* 'Anthea'
9 *Iris sibirica* 'White Swirl'
10 *Nepeta* 'Porzellan'
11 *Oenothera fruticosa* 'Fyrverkeri'
12 *Elaeagnus* x *ebbingei*
13 *Osmanthus decorus*
14 *Prunus lusitanica* 'Variegata'
15 *Clematis armandii* (on trellis)
16 *Skimmia japonica* 'Rubella'
17 *Carex ornithopoda* 'Variegata'
18 *Epimedium* x *youngianum* 'Niveum'
19 *Rubus henryi* var. *bambusarum* (on trellis)
20 *Trachelospermum jasminoides* (on fence)
21 *Erica carnea* 'Springwood White'
22 *Phlox carolina* 'Bill Baker'
23 *Leucanthemum* x *superbum* 'T.E. Killin'
24 *Salvia* x *sylvestris* 'Mainacht'
25 *Rudbeckia fulgida* var. *sullivantii* 'Goldsturm'
26 *Sedum spectabile* 'Indian Chief'
27 *Sorbus aucuparia*
28 *Hydrangea serrata* 'Grayswood'
29 *Cornus alba* 'Elegantissima'
30 *Rheum alexandrae*
31 *Prunus laurocerasus* 'Zabeliana'
32 *Rubus cockburnianus* 'Goldenvale'
33 *Euphorbia griffithii* 'Fireglow'
34 *Ligustrum* 'Vicaryi'

Lychnis chalcedonica has a brilliant flame-red flower that is best used sparingly.

Choosing plants for a family garden

Although the appearance of plants individually and in relation to each other is an essential ingredient of a garden, you must also consider how safe they are if there are small children. This garden has many plants that are quite safe, but there are one or two which you might want to change:

- *Elaeagnus* x *ebbingei* can be thorny, although not as extreme as roses, but the leathery, evergreen leaves tend to mask the thorns – if in doubt, use *Ligustrum lucidum* 'Excelsum Superbum' (Chinese privet) instead

- *Euphorbia griffithii* 'Fireglow' produces potentially irritating sap when stems or leaves are damaged – replace with *Lychnis chalcedonica* (Maltese cross)

- *Rheum alexandrae* is a member of the rhubarb family that is probably not good for young stomachs if eaten – try *Astilboides tabularis* as an effective substitute for its dramatic leaves

- *Rosa* 'Albertine' is tucked away against the boundary, above the retaining wall, but it is a thorny rose and potentially painful – replace with *Clematis* 'Fairy Queen'

- *Rubus henryi* var. *bambusarum* is a climber with rather prickly stems, which might cause a rash on tender skin – *Hedera canariensis* 'Gloire de Marengo' would be a good alternative evergreen climber

- *Rubus cockburnianus* 'Goldenvale' is a striking plant but it has wicked hooked thorns on both stems and leaves – *Physocarpus opulifolius* 'Dart's Gold' is much gentler in all respects

- *Trachelospermum jasminoides* (star jasmine) produces a milky, latex-like sap when stems are cut that is potentially irritating – *Jasminum officinale* f. *affine* does not and has an equally attractive scent

Behind walls

Whether the walls around your garden are centuries-old stone or brand-new brick, they add a great deal not only in terms of their appearance but also in terms of the effect they have on the other elements of the garden, especially the planting. In this design the walls form a major element of the structure, defining it as a deliberate and square arrangement, but the contrasting shape of the near-circular lawn and the soft, varied planting around it have the opposite effect, keeping you uncertain about the real shape of the plot.

What makes this a good walled garden?

✓ A well-designed and detailed wall is a positive design element in a garden and requires the minimum of extra adornment or planting

✓ Walls provide instant privacy and seclusion and are more efficient at excluding noise than other forms of boundary

✓ Other garden features, such as pots and containers full of trailing plants or built-in seats set in alcoves, can be attached to walls

✓ Climbers and wall shrubs add an extra dimension to the planting

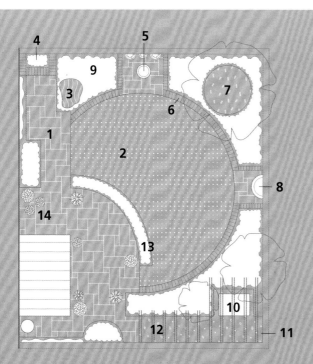

Garden elements key

1 Natural stone patio	5 Statue
2 Lawn	6 Stone mowing strip
3 Informal pond	7 Bark covered circle
4 Raised bed	with log edging

8 Wall-mounted water feature

9 Planting

10 Garden store

11 Gravel path

12 Pergola over path

13 Low hedge

14 Containers

Mix and match

If you like this garden, but would prefer a different feature, see pages 250–251 for possible variations.

Key features

Wall-mounted water feature

These are particularly effective on old stone or brick walls. Try and position your wall-mounted water feature adjacent to a seat or make it into a positive focal point that can be seen from different parts of the garden.

Natural stone patio

Patios are essential areas for sitting outside relaxing and entertaining, and natural stone makes a wonderful material for this type of paving. There are lots of colours available, so choose one to suit your style of garden. Warm colours, such as buff or cream, might suit an informal design edged with soft colourful perennials, whereas cooler coloured stone, in the blue/grey region, would look good in a very formal setting, perhaps, flanked by cool, tightly-trimmed box edging.

Bark covered circle beneath tree

The area immediately beneath some deciduous trees can often be quite bare and difficult to plant. Turn it into a positive design feature by creating a circle or square around the tree with an edging of small logs or old bricks. Cover the bare soil with bark, crushed slate or gravel and place a tiny bench or a couple of chairs for shady summer seating.

Making the best use of walls

Apart from using walls to display a wonderful range of climbers and wall shrubs, you can also use them for other details and treatments to add extra interest to your garden.

Above: Plain walls make an excellent backdrop for plants with delicate flowers and fine leaves.

Top right and right: Use walls and other plain vertical surfaces to hang small planters, ornaments and water features.

Building the garden

Overall, reasonably high levels of skill and knowledge will be required to build this garden, and you may need to employ a professional for some of the work, particularly the walls and piers and possibly also the flag paving. The cost for the hard landscape elements will be above average, due chiefly to the use of natural stone and oak for the pergola. The plant costs will be about average, and you should be able to obtain most of them easily, although a few may be available only from more specialized nurseries.

The main features and skill level required are:

- Walls – high
- Stone piers – high
- Flag paving – high if pointing with mortar but medium high if filling joints with sand
- Oak pergola – medium high
- Mowing strip – medium to medium high
- Wall-mounted fountain – medium to high, depending on whether you have access to the back of the wall
- Log edging – medium
- Planting – medium
- Lawn – medium

- Make the wall a feature in its own right by laying the bricks or stones in different patterns or by using bricks or stones with different colours and textures

- Add colour wash to brighten an unsightly wall, provide a background for plants or create a greater sense of space

- Personalize the wall by painting a mural or *trompe l'oeil*

- Create alcoves in new walls for seats, outdoor shelves for display – perhaps a collection of bonsai trees – or as a frame for a wall-mounted feature, such as a relief sculpture

- If space is limited, use a wall-mounted water feature to create a focal point

- Hang pots and containers at different heights, filling them with seasonal annuals that are replaced every year or with small perennials for long-lasting interest

- Mount lights and display two-dimensional ornaments, such as bronze masks, sculptures, terracotta and glazed plates and dishes

- Build lights into the wall itself, using the special units that take up the space of one brick; alternatively put concealed lighting at the top of an alcove or false arch to cast mood lighting down the wall

- Fix mirrors to create reflections and the illusion of a larger garden

- Build raised beds against walls to give changes of level (but check that you do not compromise any damp proofing)

Planting

The best plants for this garden

A combination of shrubs, perennials and climbers will take advantage of the varying microclimates created within the garden by the walls. Soft colours and textures provide a perfect foil to the natural stone, giving a slightly old-fashioned feel.

Planting key

1 *Primula bulleyana*
2 *Iris sibirica* 'Tropic Night'
3 *Astilbe* 'Sprite'
4 *Filipendula ulmaria* 'Aurea'
5 *Rhododendron* 'Gibraltar' (azalea)
6 *Polygonatum multiflorum*
7 *Hydrangea serrata* 'Bluebird'
8 *Lonicera* x *tellmanniana*
9 *Aruncus dioicus*
10 *Enkianthus campanulatus*
11 *Alchemilla mollis*
12 *Anemone* x *hybrida* 'Honorine Jobert'
13 *Rhododendron* 'Cunningham's Blush'
14 *Prunus* x *subhirtella* 'Autumnalis Rosea'
15 *Geranium phaeum*
16 *Viburnum sargentii* 'Onondaga'
17 *Doronicum* 'Miss Mason'
18 *Potentilla fruticosa* 'Abbotswood'
19 *Clematis macropetala* 'Markham's Pink'
20 *Solanum laxum*

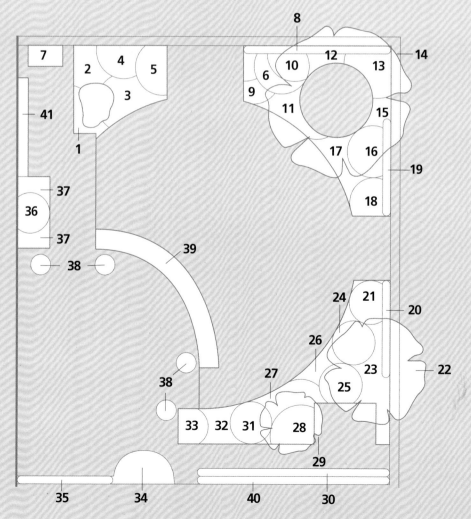

How to train climbers on posts

Many gardeners struggle to keep climbers successfully trained against posts in the first year or two until they are established, using a combination of nails, wire, string and clips. There is a reliable method of keeping them well tied in until they reach the top of your arch or pergola, by which time they should be able to support themselves.

You will need

Galvanized wire, not less than 1.5mm (¹⁄₁₆in) in diameter
Zinc-plated eye-hooks; eye diameter 1–1.5cm (about ½in), overall length at least 3–3.5cm (1¼–1½in)
Soft hessian garden twine (avoid the thinnest)
Pliers

Step by step

1 Screw eye-hooks into each face of the post at top and bottom, about 5cm (2in) from each end. If the posts are round, space each of the four eye-hooks roughly equidistant from each other.

2 Connect a length of wire between each pair of eye-hooks as tightly as possible, using pliers to twist each end around itself several times. Trim off any waste.

3 Plant the climber.

4 Tightly wrap a length of twine, 15–20cm (6–8in) long, twice around the wire and make a simple overhand knot (see right). You should end up with two, roughly equal lengths of twine tied to the wire, with no slippage, and ready to tie around the climber's stem. Tie in the climber exactly where you want until it is self-supporting.

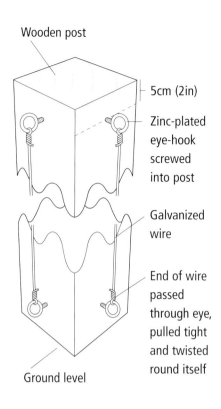

Wooden post
5cm (2in)
Zinc-plated eye-hook screwed into post
Galvanized wire
End of wire passed through eye, pulled tight and twisted round itself
Ground level

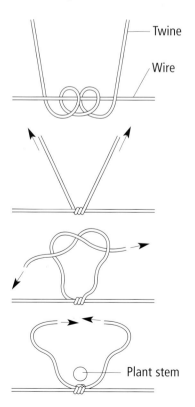

Knot sequence
Twine
Wire
Plant stem

The right-angled garden

Straight lines and right angles are traditionally associated with formal gardens, but it's possible to use these same elements in a completely different way to create a distinctive garden.

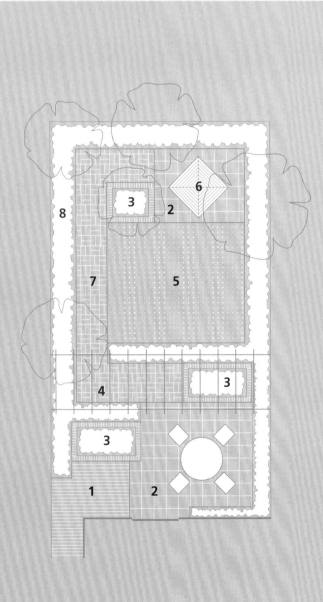

Garden elements key

1 Decking	**5** Lawn
2 Flag paving	**6** Parasol
3 Raised bed	**7** Brick paving
4 Pergola	**8** Narrow border

What makes this a good right-angled garden?

✓ A relatively long, narrow garden is cleverly divided into two parts with a pergola, raised beds and low lavender hedge, yet the two halves still form an obvious whole

✓ Rectangles, squares and straight lines are incorporated into the design to form an almost abstract pattern, with various changes of direction and raised beds for added interest

✓ Paved areas at each end of the garden provide the opportunity to sit out in the sun (or shade) at any time of the day

✓ The rigid lines and corners are contrasted by soft, informal planting

✓ The apparently intricate design gives a manageable and accessible garden

Mix and match
If you like this garden, but would prefer a different feature, see pages 250–251 for possible variations.

Key features

Narrow borders

Sometimes you can only fit very small or narrow beds and borders in a garden. When this is the case, choose your plants carefully. If you need tall planting, select shrubs, grasses and perennials with a pronounced upright growth habit that will reach the desired height without exceeding the width of your garden borders.

Raised beds

Raised beds are usually very well drained, especially if they're filled with good quality soil on top of a gravelly drainage layer. These conditions are ideal for alpines and other dwarf perennials that don't like excessive moisture at their roots. Another advantage of the raised bed is that they are more accessible for weeding and general maintenance – you can even sit on the edge of the bed while you do it.

Dwarf hedge

Dwarf hedges are not intended to be physical barriers or visual screens. Use them to act as dividers between different areas of the garden or to accentuate or soften the crisp edges of paths or terraces, for example. Plant and look after a dwarf hedge in exactly the same way as you would a larger hedge.

Built-in planter

It is sometimes desirable to break up a large area of decking with softening plants. Although you can use container planting on the deck, you can achieve a better effect by planting through the deck into the ground below. If the deck is a long way above ground level, you can plant into a concealed, bottomless container to keep the base of the plant at deck height.

Large areas of decking can be effectively broken up with individual plants or trees.

You will need

Large plastic or galvanized container – dustbin, plant pot, coldwater tank

Good quality compost

Step by step

1 Decide where on your deck you want to build your planter and lift enough boards to accommodate the container. You might find it easier to mark the shape of your container on the deck first and draw a second identical shape 2.5cm (1in) inside that – this will make the board cutting simpler when you lift them off.

2 Saw off the bottom of the container so that when it's placed in the open space on the ground below the deck, it sits just below the finished deck level.

3 Dig and improve the soil in the space and place the open-ended container in it, making sure it's firm and level and at the correct height. Fill the container with good quality compost.

4 Replace the deck boards, cutting them as you go to fit the shape of the container so that they overhang by about 2.5cm (1in) to hide the edge.

5 Plant your chosen plants and water in thoroughly. The open bottom of the container will allow the plant roots to penetrate into the ground as they grow, and they will need less watering and attention than if they were in a normal container.

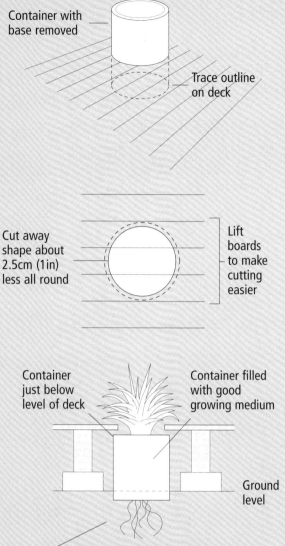

Container with base removed

Trace outline on deck

Cut away shape about 2.5cm (1in) less all round

Lift boards to make cutting easier

Container just below level of deck

Container filled with good growing medium

Ground level

Ground below container prepared by digging and incorporating organic matter

Planting in and around decking

Although it's quite easy to soften flagstone paving or brick with low edging plants or by omitting sections of paving and replacing them with pockets of planting, you need to apply a little more thought with decking that is raised above ground level.

- If the deck is raised slightly – one step of 10–15cm (4–6in), say – you can use rounded or arching plants along the edge that are naturally more than 30–40cm (12–16in) high, so that at least 20cm (8in) will show above the deck and hang over the edge.

- For higher decks use plants that are taller but not so rounded, or much of their distinctive shape will not be visible – irises, grasses, crocosmias, for example.

- Build one or more planters at the edge of the deck so that the soil level will be at the same height as the deck and include a combination of shapes and sizes.

- Create planting pockets within the decking, by using built-in planters, which do not need to be exactly at deck level, but could be slightly higher or have more than one level.

Planting

13

31

35

38

The best plants for this garden

The design includes a mixture of easy-care trees, shrubs, perennials and grasses, selected for their softening qualities and year-round interest and to suit the varying amounts of light and shade that will occur in different parts of the garden. It will, for instance, be sunny against the house wall and shady directly beneath the pergola.

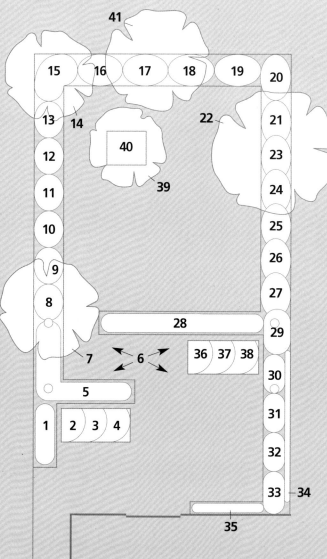

Planting key

1 *Miscanthus sinensis* 'Morning Light'

2 *Helianthemum* 'Rhodanthe Carneum'

3 *Iberis sempervirens* 'Weisser Zwerg'

4 *Campanula carpatica* 'Chewton Joy'

5 *Euonymus fortunei* 'Sheridan Gold' (low hedge)

6 *Wisteria floribunda* 'Domino'

7 *Liquidambar styraciflua* 'Worplesdon'

8 *Chrysogonum virginianum*

9 *Sedum telephium* 'Munstead Red'

10 *Phlox divaricata* 'Blue Dreams'

11 *Knautia macedonica*

12 *Helichrysum* 'Schwefellicht'

13 *Helleborus niger*

14 *Sorbus hupehensis*

15 *Aruncus dioicus*

16 *Hosta* 'Bressingham Blue'

17 *Astilbe* x *arendsii* 'Venus'

18 *Tricyrtis formosana*

19 *Polystichum polyblepharum*

20 *Rodgersia pinnata* 'Elegans'

21 *Iris pseudacorus* 'Variegata'

Soft planting

There are plenty of low, creeping plants to use to disguise hard edges and provide groundcover. These are not always the best solution, however, because they can be flat and, because they will keep growing sideways, they need to be trimmed regularly to keep them off paths – instead of a straight brick or stone edge you end up with a straight 'green' edge. However, there are many perennials to choose that are taller but still provide a soft edge and groundcover without trimming.

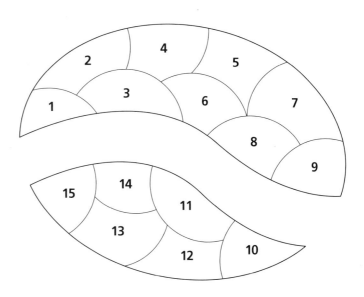

22 *Pyrus calleryana* 'Chanticleer'
23 *Melissa officinalis* 'Aurea'
24 *Euphorbia characias* 'Goldbrook'
25 *Limonium platyphyllum* 'Violetta'
26 *Potentilla* 'William Rollison'
27 *Scabiosa caucasica* 'Miss Willmott'
28 *Lavandula angustifolia* 'Hidcote Pink'
29 *Iris sibirica* 'Papillon'
30 *Geranium* x *oxonianum* 'A.T. Johnson'
31 *Artemisia* 'Powis Castle'
32 *Chrysanthemum* 'Clara Curtis'
33 *Lavandula angustifolia* 'Munstead'
34 *Clematis* 'Vyvyan Pennell'
35 *Abutilon megapotamicum*
36 *Ajuga reptans* 'Burgundy Glow'
37 *Epimedium pinnatum* subsp. *colchicum*
38 *Viola cornuta*
39 *Magnolia* 'Susan'
40 *Omphalodes verna*
41 *Prunus padus* 'Watereri'

'Soft' perennials for a shady spot behind a path or patio

1 *Dicentra* 'Stuart Boothman'
2 *Symphytum* 'Rubrum'
3 *Milium effusum* 'Aureum'
4 *Lamium galeobdolon* 'Hermann's Pride'
5 *Geranium macrorrhizum* 'Czakor'
6 *Saxifraga umbrosa*
7 *Pulmonaria* 'Sissinghurst White'
8 *Viola riviniana* Purpurea Group
9 *Melissa officinalis* 'Aurea'
10 *Geranium* x *cantabrigiense* 'Biokovo'
11 *Liriope muscari*
12 *Aquilegia vulgaris* var. *stellata* Barlow Series 'Nora Barlow'
13 *Luzula pilosa*
14 *Alchemilla alpina*
15 *Geum rivale* 'Album'

'Soft' perennials for a sunny spot behind a path or patio

1 *Geranium robertianum* 'Album'
2 *Campanula* 'Birch Hybrid'
3 *Anthemis tinctoria* 'E.C. Buxton'
4 *Doronicum orientale* 'Magnificum'
5 *Helictotrichon sempervirens*
6 *Aster novi-belgii* 'Heinz Richard'
7 *Geranium himalayense* 'Gravetye'
8 *Diascia barberae* 'Ruby Field'
9 *Artemisia schmidtiana* 'Nana'
10 *Aethionema* 'Warley Rose'
11 *Leucanthemum* x *superbum* 'Snowcap'
12 *Ballota* 'All Hallows Green'
13 *Aster thomsonii* 'Nana'
14 *Hypericum olympicum* f. *minus* 'Sulpuruem'
15 *Anaphalis triplinervis* 'Sommerschnee'

Turning Japanese

Gardens built in the oriental style appeal because of the calm, harmonious way in which plants and materials are brought together and because of the attention that is given to every detail. These gardens do not need to be large, but they should always reflect a respect for the natural elements that are used to create them.

What makes this a good oriental garden?

✓ A balance between paving, plants and other materials

✓ It is not a slavish copy of an original Japanese garden but borrows elements from it and uses them in a way that is in keeping with Western lifestyles and ideals

✓ It uses natural materials obtained (where possible) from local sources so that it is in keeping with and shows respect for its wider environment

✓ The succession of plant groupings and overall effect are in harmony

✓ The colours are generally soft but there are one or two bright hotspots for impact

✓ Ornaments and features are carefully placed in their surroundings and used sparingly to avoid cluttering the space

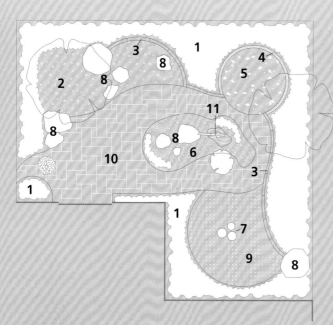

Garden elements key

1 Planting
2 Gravel
3 Log edging
4 Bamboo screen
5 Crushed slate
6 'Pond' of gravel and sand
7 Wood sculpture
8 Boulder
9 Grassless lawn

10 Stone paving
11 Deer scarer

Mix and match
If you like this garden, but would prefer a different feature, see pages 250–251 for possible variations.

Key features

Japanese maple

Japanese maples are available in many forms. Most are best grown in some isolation so that the effect of their colour and shape can be fully appreciated. Use the more vigorous forms as focal points, underplanted with very low groundcover or grow through bark or shingle. Slow-growing, dense forms look good in containers or growing over rock.

Bamboo screen

Natural materials make attractive screens, and bamboo is particularly good as it's readily available and very adaptable. You can build one quickly and simply using ready-made panels or rolls of split or whole bamboo. Alternatively, make your own from scratch and create a unique design. You can do this using whole bamboo canes of different diameters and lengths and fixing them together with thin wire or synthetic twine.

Boulders

Large, individual boulders and rocks are an essential part of oriental garden design. You can, however, use them in all sorts of other situations – especially where the emphasis is on natural appearance. When you place the boulders, sink them slightly into the ground so that they look as if they are natural outcrops. For an even better effect, plant around the boulders with very low groundcover plants, such as ivy (*Hedera*) or periwinkle (*Vinca*).

Deer scarer

Deer scarers are traditional ornaments in Japanese gardens, originally serving the practical purpose of keeping deer and other animals away from crops. They are simple to make once you understand the basic mechanics. You can power one with its own gentle water source as a self-contained feature (see page 150–151) or with some ingenuity you could place it at the side of a stream to catch a little of the water coming over a cascade (see page 193).

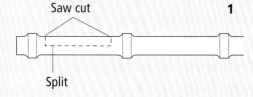

Saw cut

1

Split

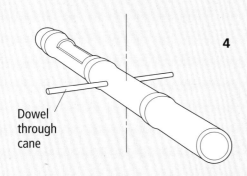

4

Dowel
through
cane

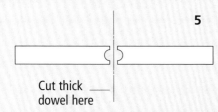

5

Cut thick
dowel here

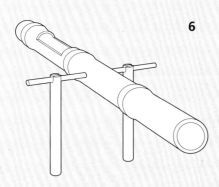

6

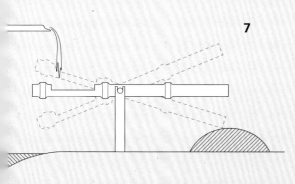

7

You will need

Source of running water
Thick bamboo cane 30–45cm (12–18in) long
Hardwood dowel about 60cm (24in) long and 2.5cm (1in) in diameter
Hardwood dowel about 15cm (6in) long and 1cm (½in) in diameter
Rounded stone or rock
Wood adhesive

Step by step

1 Use a fine saw to make two vertical cuts halfway through the bamboo and towards one end. Carefully split off the top using a sharp knife to create a channel.

2 Roughly balance the bamboo on your finger to find its centre of gravity and mark it.

3 Drill a 1cm (½in) diameter hole through the side of the bamboo about 2.5cm (1in) to the right-hand side of the mark, with the channel on the left-hand side.

4 Push the 1cm (½in) dowel through the hole and glue it in place.

5 Drill a 1cm (½in) diameter hole in the centre of the thicker dowel. Saw it in half exactly through the centre of the hole to leave two short lengths, each with a semicircular notch at one end.

6 Push these into the ground with the notches uppermost so that you can balance the bamboo cane by its dowel to make a see-saw effect. If the ground is soft, concrete the dowel in place. Because of the off-centre position of the dowel it will instantly drop down to one side (the opposite end from the channel). Place your rock or stone exactly under this end so that it is just touching.

7 Provide the water supply, which should slowly and gently run into the channel. As it fills, the centre of gravity will move along the channel until eventually that end becomes heavier, drops and tips the water back into the stream or sump. Immediately, the other end of the bamboo cane will drop back down and strike the rock and the whole cycle begins again! You'll need to experiment to fine-tune your deer scarer. If the 'stone' end of the bamboo cane won't lift up, you'll need to saw bits off the end.

Planting

The best plants for this garden

The texture of foliage and the overall form of plants are as important as flowers, and the plants range from tall, elegant grasses and bamboos through light and feathery perennials to the dark foliage of evergreen shrubs. Ideally, the soil should be of a good quality and slightly on the acid side – that is, with a pH less than 7.0 – to suit rhododendrons and azaleas.

Planting key

1 *Osmanthus heterophyllus*
2 *Rhododendron* 'Praecox'
3 *Polystichum polyblepharum*
4 *Acer palmatum* 'Sango-kaku'
5 *Digitalis purpurea* Excelsior Group
6 *Dryopteris filix-mas*
7 *Skimmia laureola*
8 *Polygonatum biflorum*

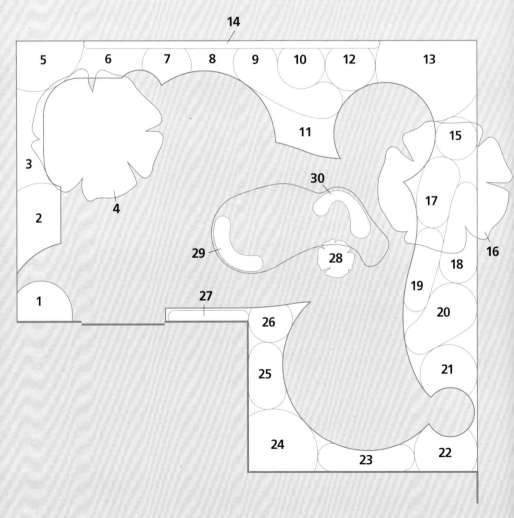

A camomile path will send off a delicious scent when you walk on it.

9 *Rhododendron* 'Blue Danube' (azalea)
10 *Phyllostachys humilis*
11 *Hakonechloa macra* 'Alboaurea'
12 *Enkianthus campanulatus*
13 *Viburnum sargentii* 'Onondaga'
14 *Clematis alpina* (along fence)
15 *Rhododendron* 'Unique'
16 *Acer palmatum* 'Osakazuki'
17 *Sasa veitchii*
18 *Anemone tomentosa*
19 *Hosta* 'Honeybells'
20 *Rhododendron* 'Vuyks Rosyred' (azalea)
21 *Arundo donax* var. *versicolor*
22 *Crinodendron hookerianum*
23 *Iris pallida* subsp. *pallida*
24 *Camellia japonica* 'Doctor Tinsley'
25 *Aruncus dioicus*
26 *Skimmia japonica* 'Rubella'
27 *Festuca glauca* 'Blauglut'
28 *Carex pendula* 'Moonraker'
29 *Ophiopogon planiscapus* 'Nigrescens'
30 *Hakonechloa macra* 'Aureola'

'Grassless' lawns

Several plants other than grass can be used to give the impression of a lawn, and, once established, they require far less maintenance. This type of planting is ideal for areas that are not subject to normal intensive lawn use. Maintaining such a lawn in good condition requires nothing more than a trim once or twice a year across the top and around the 'lawn' edge to keep growth dense and bushy so that the individual plants grow into each other to give a continuous green cover.

Best plants for 'grassless' lawns

- *Ajuga reptans* (bugle) – good in partial shade
- *Chamaemelum nobile* (camomile) – aromatic
- *Cotoneaster congestus* – flowers and berries
- *Erica carnea* (winter heath, alpine heath) – flowers in late winter
- *Hedera* (ivy; green-leaved cvs.) – use small-leaved forms for small lawns or for a neater effect
- *Helianthemum* (rock rose, sun rose), especially prostrate forms, such as *H. nummularium* subsp. *glabrum* – good for dry, sunny positions
- *Juniperus* (juniper), especially horizontal cvs., such as *J. horizontalis* and *J. procumbens* – vigorous and suitable for larger areas
- *Thymus* (thyme; creeping cvs.) – aromatic
- *Vinca minor* (periwinkle) – spring flowers
- *Waldsteinia ternata* – early spring flowers and good in shade

For the beginner

It can be quite daunting for someone who is completely new to gardening to be faced with their own plot for the first time, especially if it's just bare earth! Even though there's plenty of help and information around to explain the basic requirements of growing plants and creating other garden features, it's one thing having ideas and quite another putting them all together in a practical yet exciting way that has a personal touch.

What makes this a good beginner's garden?

✓ It incorporates all the basic features and ideas a beginner might need, with scope to add more as experience and knowledge grow
✓ Each feature is simple and elegant, yet the design as a whole is dramatic and eye-catching
✓ The design incorporates plants that provide year-round interest but at the same time are reliable and tolerant of a wide range of conditions
✓ It is not a difficult or expensive garden to construct as long as there is some help at key stages

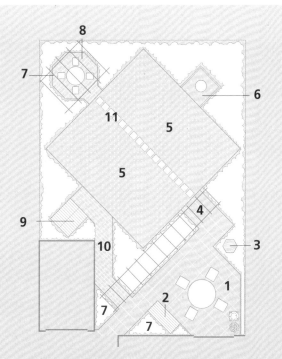

Garden elements key

1 Patio
2 Box seat with lid, or bench
3 Self-contained water feature
4 Pergola
5 Lawn
6 Edged gravel area with statue
7 Shade structure
8 Brick paved sitting area
9 Garden store
10 Brick path
11 Stepping stone path

Mix and match
If you like this garden, but would prefer a different feature, see pages 250–251 for possible variations.

Key features

Year-round interest

Easy-care plants that provide interest throughout the year are an essential part of any garden – especially if you're a gardening novice. You should try to include at least two or three good-sized evergreen shrubs to provide permanent structure and winter colour, and underplant deciduous shrubs with low, shade-tolerant perennials and bulbs to cover the bare ground.

Box seat

A simple wooden box seat (ideally with castors) makes an attractive feature as well as providing extra sitting space. Increase its value by making the lid removable or hinged so that you can store small tools and sundries inside it. When it's not being used as a seat, you can put some containers or small ornaments on top of it for extra decoration.

Patio

If you are a newcomer to gardening and want to build your own natural stone-effect patio, consider using one of the many types of modular paving on the market. These come in a range of sizes and the better-quality brands are very realistic in colour and texture. From a practical viewpoint, they are often non-slip and, because they're actually made from concrete, are frostproof as well.

Long and narrow garden shapes

If you want to adapt a design you like to suit a long, narrow plot, try and use elements such as pergolas, circles, trellis and hedges to break up the view down your garden. It also helps if you can make paths meander or zig-zag. Spread any focal points, such as water features, statues or specimen trees, along the garden so that you don't see them all at once.

Original design

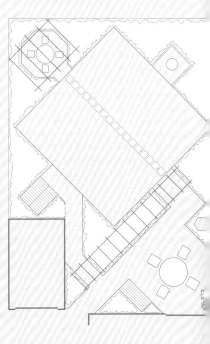

This design for a typical regular plot can be quite easily adapted to suit a different garden shape.

Long and narrow plot

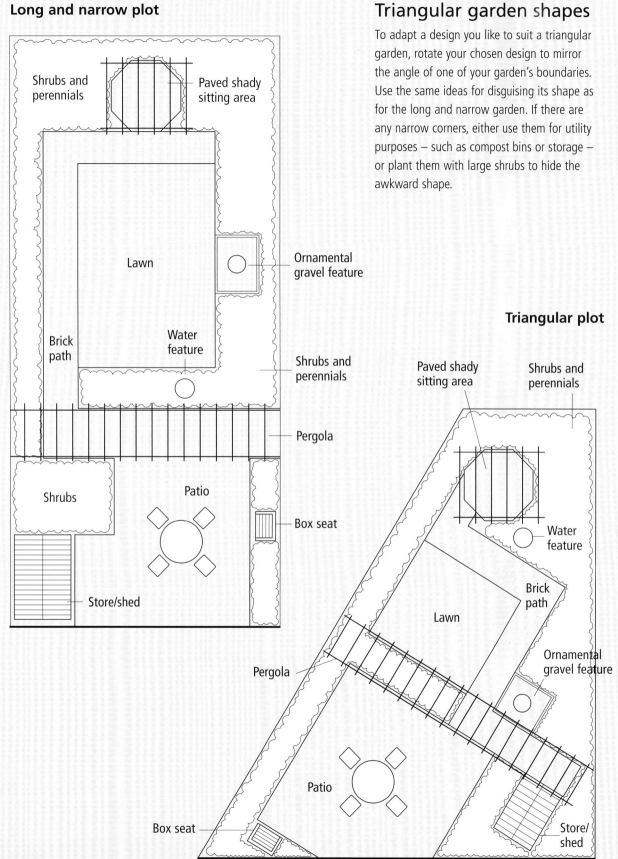

Shrubs and perennials

Paved shady sitting area

Lawn

Ornamental gravel feature

Brick path

Water feature

Shrubs and perennials

Pergola

Shrubs

Patio

Box seat

Store/shed

Triangular garden shapes

To adapt a design you like to suit a triangular garden, rotate your chosen design to mirror the angle of one of your garden's boundaries. Use the same ideas for disguising its shape as for the long and narrow garden. If there are any narrow corners, either use them for utility purposes – such as compost bins or storage – or plant them with large shrubs to hide the awkward shape.

Triangular plot

Paved shady sitting area

Shrubs and perennials

Water feature

Brick path

Lawn

Ornamental gravel feature

Pergola

Patio

Box seat

Store/shed

Planting

13

28

48

51

The best plants for this garden

None of the plants requires any special conditions, and they have been selected because of their general robustness and value for money. All of them are long lived and reliable, whether they are included in the design for their flowers or their foliage. Although it's a fairly small garden and the area devoted to planting is not huge, there is lots of seasonal interest, and the scale of planting balances the summerhouse and masks the fence behind.

Planting key

1 *Kerria japonica* 'Pleniflora'
2 *Prunus lusitanica* 'Variegata'
3 *Vitis coignetiae* (on overheads)
4 *Achillea* 'Moonshine'
5 *Physocarpus opulifolius* 'Diabolo'
6 *Doronicum* 'Miss Mason'
7 *Buddleja davidii* 'Black Knight'
8 *Hemerocallis dumortieri*
9 *Epimedium* x *rubrum*

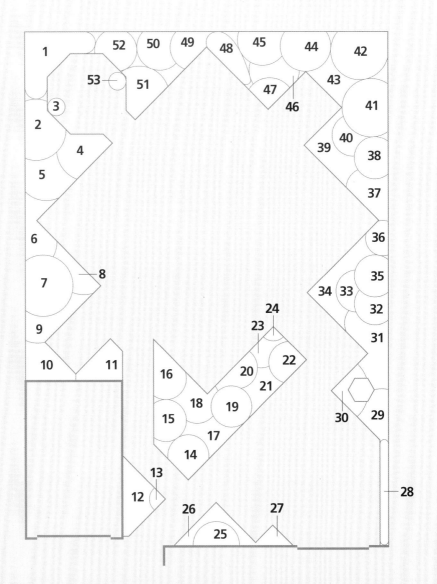

10 *Miscanthus sacchariflorus*

11 *Osmanthus heterophyllus* 'Variegatus'

12 *Garrya elliptica* 'James Roof'

13 *Clematis montana* var. *rubens* 'Tetrarose' (on pergola)

14 *Geum rivale* 'Album'

15 *Spiraea japonica* 'Gold Mound'

16 *Lavandula angustifolia* 'Munstead'

17 *Iris* 'Pearly Dawn' (tall bearded)

18 *Bergenia* 'Bressingham Salmon'

19 *Hebe* 'Autumn Glory'

20 *Viola* 'Clementina'

21 *Aster novi-belgii* 'Schneekissen'

22 *Geranium sanguineum*

23 *Helianthemum* 'Praecox'

24 *Lonicera* x *americana* (on pergola)

25 *Abutilon* 'Kentish Belle'

26 *Geranium renardii*

27 *Hebe vernicosa*

28 *Actinidia kolomikta* (on fence)

29 *Erica* x *darleyensis* 'Ada S. Collings'

30 *Festuca glauca* 'Blauglut'

31 *Campanula persicifolia* 'Bennett's Blue'

32 *Skimmia japonica* 'Rubella'

33 *Phlox paniculata* 'Starfire'

34 *Liriope muscari*

35 *Mahonia aquifolium* 'Apollo'

36 *Skimmia japonica* 'Veitchii'

37 *Aconitum carmichaelii*

38 *Chaenomeles* x *superba* 'Pink Lady'

39 *Coreopsis verticillata* 'Golden Gain'

40 *Rosa* 'Buff Beauty'

41 *Pyracantha* 'Soleil d'Or'

42 *Forsythia* x *intermedia* 'Lynwood'

43 *Lupinus* Gallery Series 'Gallery White'

44 *Cotinus coggygria* Rubrifolius Group

45 *Ilex* x *altaclerensis* 'Golden King'

46 *Iris* 'Kent Pride' (tall bearded)

47 *Incarvillea delavayi*

48 *Echinacea purpurea* cvs.

49 *Aster novi-belgii* 'Audrey'

50 *Taxus baccata* 'Semperaurea'

51 *Geranium himalayense*

52 *Hydrangea macrophylla* 'Lanarth White'

53 *Clematis flammula* (on overheads)

Planting for a sunny, dry corner

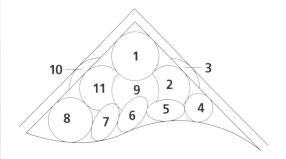

1 *Cytisus* 'Burkwoodii'
2 *Fuchsia magellanica* var. *gracilis* 'Aurea'
3 *Passiflora caerulea* (on fence or wall)
4 *Hebe pimeloides* 'Quicksilver'
5 *Dianthus* 'Devon Cream'
6 *Lavandula angustifolia* 'Nana Alba'
7 *Sedum* 'Ruby Glow'
8 *Salvia* x *sylvestris* 'Mainacht'
9 *Cistus* x *argenteus* 'Peggy Sammons'
10 *Actinidia kolomikta*
11 *Caryopteris* x *clandonensis* 'Kew Blue'

Planting for a shady, damp corner

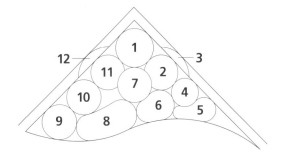

1 *Cornus kousa* var. *chinensis*
2 *Daphne odora*
3 *Lonicera implexa* (on fence or wall)
4 *Helleborus argutifolius*
5 *Athyrium niponicum* var. *pictum*
6 *Astilbe* x *arendsii* 'Fanal'
7 *Viburnum opulus* 'Compactum'
8 *Luzula sylvatica* 'Aurea'
9 *Epimedium* x *youngianum* 'Niveum'
10 *Hosta* 'Krossa Regal'
11 *Hydrangea serrata* 'Diadem'
12 *Clematis* 'Nelly Moser' (on fence or wall)

The seasonal garden

If planting space is at a premium, such as in a small walled backyard, and you're looking for year-round interest, the number of plants you can squeeze in to give winter colour and texture may be limited. However, by using container plantings for your main source of summer colour you will free extra valuable bed or border space for additional winter plants to give you more brightness during the darker months.

What makes this a good seasonal garden?

✓ A generously sized, attractive patio for all-weather use
✓ Lots of winter and spring interest in the borders
✓ Diagonally opposite seating areas to catch the best of the sun or provide shade in hot weather
✓ Gentle, split levels for additional character
✓ Numerous pots and tubs for seasonal planting, especially in summer, leaving more space in the borders for winter and spring plant groups

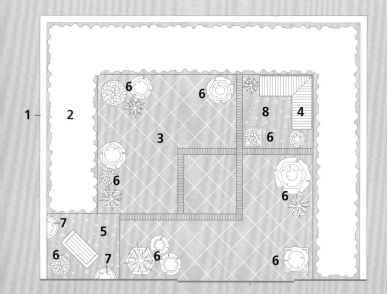

Garden elements key

1 Garden wall with climbers
2 Border
3 Patio
4 Seat
5 Sunken gravel area
6 Containers
7 Wall hanging containers
8 Raised gravel area

Mix and match
If you like this garden, but would
prefer a different feature, see pages
250–251 for possible variations.

Key features

Containers

Put seasonal planting in containers to brighten up potentially dull areas or where space for planting directly in the ground is limited. Use large containers for mixed plantings or group together several smaller containers to create a colourful composition. For a more permanent effect, plant dwarf evergreen shrubs and dwarf conifers surrounded with miniature bulbs such as narcissus, crocus and snowdrops.

Raised gravel area

Add an extra dimension to an otherwise flat garden with a raised area. You can make the upstands with something as simple as old railway sleepers, filling in the space behind with cheap hardcore covered in gravel. Alternatively, make it very formal with, maybe, red or dark blue engineering bricks infilled with old yorkstone paving. Place a statue or urn in the centre as a focal point or, as here, make a simple box seat with removable cushions.

Climbers

In a small, enclosed garden, use climbers to soften and hide walls and fences. Not only do they provide colour and interest but they also disguise the shape and size of the garden. Encourage climbers to spill over the tops of their supports to mask the strong horizontal line of fence or wall tops and try to include one or two evergreen varieties for winter interest.

Choosing containers

Plants in containers should not be regarded as some sort of afterthought or as a means of filling a bare space. They should be used as part of your overall design, and you need to make sure they are used creatively as well as practically. Always choose a container that is appropriate for the plant it holds.

Above: Plant several varieties in larger containers for greater interest.

Above right: Metal containers look great provided they are rust-proof.

- Traditional materials – stone and terracotta – make good containers, but almost any other material – plastic, metal, wood or concrete – can be used provided it won't rot, be damaged by frost or be harmful to plants

- Drainage is essential so make sure there are drainage holes in the bottom of all your containers

- Use good-quality, proprietary compost rather than soil that you have dug out of the garden, which may contain pests, diseases and weed seeds and which has limited nutrient value

- Pick containers to match or complement the theme of the garden – whether it is a colour, a material, such as stone to match the paving, or a style, such as Versailles planters for a formal garden

- Use several small containers to create compositions, which will be more dramatic and effective than having them individually dotted about

- Avoid containers that are much narrower in the neck than in the body for plants that may need regular re-potting – it's difficult, if not impossible, to remove plants from this shape without damaging the root system

- Feed container plants regularly with liquid feed, foliar feed or with fertilizer tablets pushed into the compost – slow-release tablets provide a full growing season's feed

- Water regularly because moisture loss from plants in containers will be greater and more rapid than the same plants in the ground

- Install an automatic drip irrigation system if you've lots of containers and don't have time for watering by hand

- Don't overpot a newly acquired plant but put it into a container that is the next size up from the one you bought it in; gradually increase the size, year by year, until it's in its final chosen container

Containers that are wider at the top than at the bottom are best if you need to re-pot your plants regularly.

Planting

The best plants for this garden

The permanent planting consists of winter- and spring-flowering shrubs, underplanted with spring-flowering bulbs. By the time these have finished flowering, the containers will be planted with annual bedding to provide summer colour.

Planting key

1 *Clematis cirrhosa* var. *balearica*
2 *Rhododendron* 'Praecox'
3 *Magnolia stellata* 'Rosea'
4 *Lonicera standishii*
5 *Viburnum* x *bodnantense* 'Deben'
6 *Enkianthus campanulatus*
7 *Jasminum nudiflorum* 'Aureum'
8 *Camellia japonica* 'Mathotiana Rosea'
9 *Hamamelis* x *intermedia* 'Jelena'
10 *Mahonia* x *media* 'Charity'
11 *Exochorda* x *macrantha* 'The Bride'
12 *Sarcococca hookeriana* var. *digyna*
13 *Clematis armandii*
14 *Prunus incisa* 'Kojo-no-mai'
15 *Chaenomeles* x *superba* 'Rowallane'
16 Spring-flowering bulbs

8

10

11

12

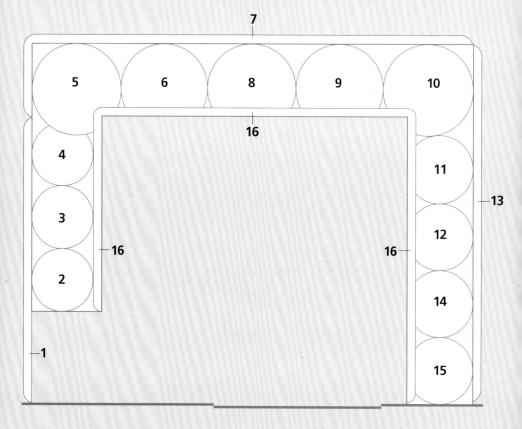

How to plant a mixed container

If you're prepared to accept that your mixed containers are a short-term feature, you can get away with planting them far more densely than you would do if you planted them as permanent displays in a bed or border.

Decide on the arrangement you want in your mixed container rather than buying a selection of plants that you like and then having to struggle to make into a composition.

Remember, large containers are heavy, especially when wet, so put your empty container in its final position before you fill it.

1 Backfill the container to a level where you can stand the largest plant or plants (by pot size) at their finished level; this is much easier than filling it to the top, then digging it out again for each plant.

2 Add more compost and place the next size of plant in the final positions.

3 When all the pot-grown plants are in place, top up the compost level to its finished height – leave it about 2.5cm (1in) below the rim of the pot or container to allow for watering.

4 Plant selected bulbs in the spaces between the other plants; with all but the largest bulbs you'll be able to just push them in and most bulbs need to be planted at a depth about three times the diameter of the bulb itself – that is, a 2.5cm (1in) bulb needs to be covered by about 7.5cm (3in) of compost.

5 Water the container thoroughly and add a little more compost if the level settles.

6 Add a mulch of bark, grit, pebbles or gravel, which will look attractive and also will help to reduce evaporation.

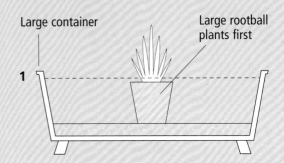

1 Large container / Large rootball plants first

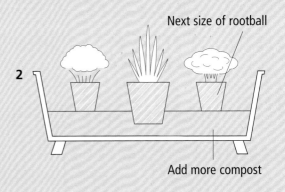

2 Next size of rootball / Add more compost

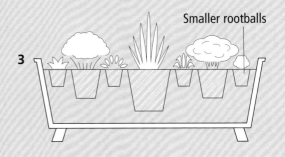

3 Smaller rootballs

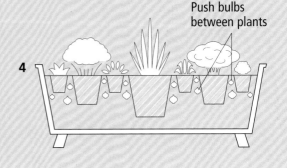

4 Push bulbs between plants

Best bulbs for containers

- *Anemone blanda*
- *Chionodoxa forbesii, C. lucillae* (glory of the snow)
- *Crocus* all spp. and large-flowered cvs.
- *Cyclamen coum, C. hederifolium*
- *Eranthis hyemalis* (winter aconite)
- *Galanthus nivalis* (snowdrop)
- *Iris reticulata, I. danfordiae*
- *Muscari* spp. (grape hyacinth)
- *Narcissus bulbocodium, N. cyclamineus, N. jonquilla*
- *Tulipa*, particularly dwarf cvs and species

Architectural landscape

Using squares, rectangles, circles and straight lines in a garden, emphasized with distinctively shaped plants, can result in an almost formal design that might be termed architectural because of the way it reflects the elements of shape and form of a building.

What makes this a good architectural garden?

✓ A square, angular ground plan with the emphasis on geometric shapes
✓ The repetition of themes in several features, particularly the neat and precise wrought iron screen consisting of regular circles and straight lines
✓ The use of plants that possess architectural qualities, such as distinctive habits of growth and bold, linear leaves
✓ The use of still water in narrow canals that act as mirrors, reflecting both the form of the plants and the man-made elements of the garden

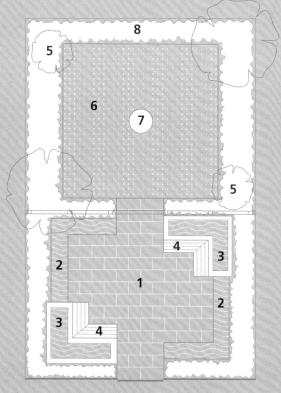

Garden elements key

1 Paving
2 'Canal'
3 Raised 'canal'
4 Built-in seat
5 Trimmed and shaped evergreen
6 Lawn
7 Central sculpture feature
8 Planting

Mix and match
If you like this garden, but would prefer a different feature, see pages 250–251 for possible variations.

Key features

Canals

This distinctive feature is the heart of the design. The edge of the patio forms the top of the canal, and although you could (if you needed a paved area urgently) leave the construction of the raised canals unfinished, you will need to have the base of the wall in place, to just above the finished paving level. This scheme needs careful planning to achieve success.

Circle screen

Making this unusual screen will need special skills, and you will have to provide a template for a local craftsperson.

Built-in seating

Having built-in seating will make a patio even more useful. Ordinary garden furniture often has to be stored in the shed or garage over winter, but this seating will be available all year round.

Top 10 garden design tips

1 Keep the basic design simple and use plants, materials and ornaments to create colour, texture and interest.

2 Decide on a theme, which might be a style – such as formal – a colour or a shape – circles or squares, perhaps.

3 Use plants that will suit your soil and ground conditions rather than trying to change the soil to suit a particular plant.

The stone table and wooden seating and fencing in this garden create a striking combination of materials.

4 Try to plan so that all the 'utilities' – bins, garden store, compost and so on – are in a single area, which will be easier to screen or disguise.

5 Plan for the future; if you've got small children, plan your garden for future changes when they grow up and don't need to use it – making a play area where you'll eventually have a kitchen garden, for example.

6 Before you start work, mark out the garden with canes, string, sand or marker paint and check that all paths and paved areas are big enough for their purpose and that focal points will be visible.

7 Observe where the sun falls during the day and make a note of the sunniest and shadiest spots for locating sitting areas.

8 Make a list of what you want in your garden in order of priority and decide on a budget; then, if you find that your budget does not match your needs, you can trim off the least important items from the bottom of the list.

9 Look at other gardens and try to identify why they are attractive or why you don't like them.

10 Notice which plants grow well in your neighbourhood as a guide in your own choices, then you won't try to grow plants such as camellias or rhododendrons in alkaline soil.

Structure and shape are important in an architectural design – rectangles and squares predominate in this garden.

Planting

The best plants for this garden

The scheme uses plants with distinctive, upright habits or linear foliage, including phormiums, irises, *Carpinus* (hornbeam), *Miscanthus* and *Eremurus*. There are also plants with deliberately contrasting, soft, rounded but neat shapes, such as *Hypericum* (St John's wort), hebes, rhododendrons and berberis. Other plants can be trimmed or controlled to maintain the uniformity and complement the hard landscaping, such as *Prunus*, *Taxus* and *Pinus*.

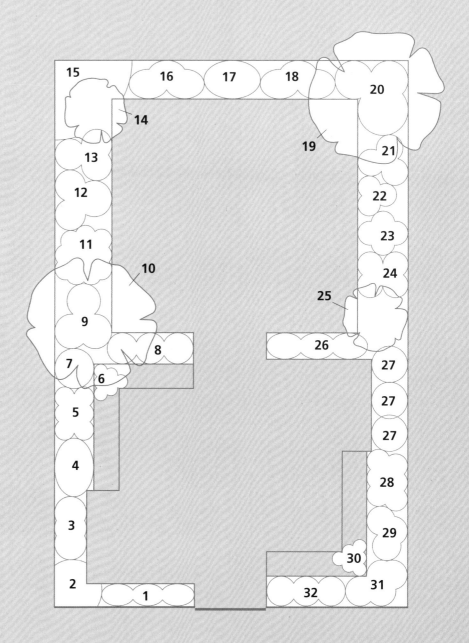

Planting key

1 *Hebe* 'White Gem'
2 *Phormium tenax* Purpureum Group
3 *Kniphofia* 'Percy's Pride'
4 *Pinus heldreichii* 'Satellit'
5 *Carex comans* (bronze form)
6 *Iris ensata* (in canal)
7 *Hypericum prolificum*
8 *Pennisetum alopecuroides*
9 *Prunus laurocerasus* 'Otto Luyken'
10 *Carpinus betulus* 'Fastigiata'
11 *Eremurus robustus*
12 *Rhododendron yakushimanum*
13 *Miscanthus sinensis* 'Sioux'
14 *Taxus baccata* (trimmed)
15 *Aruncus dioicus*
16 *Miscanthus* 'Purpurascens'
17 *Phormium tenax*
18 *Rhododendron yakushimanum*
19 *Carpinus betulus* 'Fastigiata'
20 *Prunus laurocerasus* 'Otto Luyken'
21 *Calamagrostis* x *acutiflora* 'Karl Foerster'
22 *Astilbe* x *arendsii* 'Snowdrift'
23 *Macleaya cordata*
24 *Iris foetidissima* var. *citrina*
25 *Taxus baccata* (trimmed)
26 *Pennisetum alopecuroides*
27 *Pinus mugo* 'Mops'
28 *Iris* 'Jane Phillips' (tall bearded)
29 *Hebe subalpina*
30 *Iris ensata* (in canal)
31 *Spartina pectinata* 'Aureomarginata'
32 *Berberis thunbergii* f. *atropurpurea* 'Atropurpurea Nana'

This border looks hot and fiery – the bright yellow and white planting is enhanced by the orange colour of the retaining wall.

Colour themes

If you're adventurous you can make a garden even more dramatic and eye-catching by restricting your plant colours to certain combinations – blue, pink and purple, or yellow and white, for example. Because the Architectural landscape design (left) is divided into two, you could have a different theme in each half. Here is an alternative planting scheme for the garden.

1 *Hebe* 'Autumn Glory'
2 *Phormium* 'Maori Sunrise'
3 *Iris* 'Jane Phillips' (tall bearded)
4 *Pinus sylvestris* 'Watereri'
5 *Elymus hispidus*
6 *Iris laevigata* 'Variegata' (in canal)
7 *Hydrangea* 'Preziosa'
8 *Pennisetum alopecuroides* 'Little Bunny'
9 *Prunus laurocerasus* 'Zabeliana'
10 *Ulmus* x *hollandica* 'Dampieri Aurea'
11 *Delphinium* Galahad Group
12 *Rhododendron* 'Chikor'
13 *Miscanthus sinensis* 'Strictus'
14 *Taxus baccata* Fastigiata Aurea Group (trimmed)
15 *Astilbe* x *arendsii* 'Weisse Gloria'
16 *Miscanthus sinensis* 'Silberfeder'
17 *Phormium* 'Yellow Wave'
18 *Rhododendron* 'Silver Sixpence'
19 *Ulmus* x *hollandica* 'Dampieri Aurea'
20 *Prunus laurocerasus* 'Zabeliana'
21 *Calamagrostis* x *acutiflora* 'Overdam'
22 *Hosta* 'Royal Standard'
23 *Verbascum* Cotswold Group 'Gainsborough'
24 *Iris pallida* 'Variegata'
25 *Taxus baccata* Fastigiata Aurea Group (trimmed)
26 *Pennisetum alopecuroides* 'Little Bunny'
27 *Pinus sylvestris* 'Beuvronensis'
28 *Iris* 'Sable' (tall bearded)
29 *Hebe* 'Marjorie'
30 *Iris laevigata* 'Variegata' (in canal)
31 *Panicum virgatum* 'Rubrum'
32 *Berberis thunbergii* 'Silver Beauty'

Beautiful balcony

Balconies are about as small as you can get in gardening terms, and when space is limited it can be tempting to cram in an assortment of plants, pots and other garden features. The danger with this approach is that you'll end up with a rather unsatisfactory collection of bits and pieces and probably nowhere to sit and enjoy the view. A better approach is to choose a theme and stick with it, designing your balcony so that not only can the attraction of each element be appreciated individually but the overall effect remains uncluttered but stunning.

What makes this a good balcony garden?

✓ A strong, positive design theme
✓ The use of complementary and sympathetic colours
✓ Maximum use of space for entertaining and relaxation
✓ Movable features to provide lots of flexibility

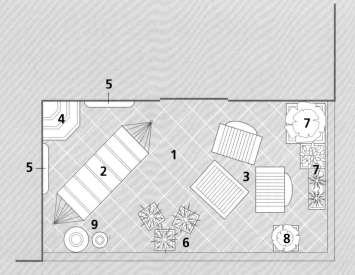

Garden elements key

1 Tile floor
2 Free-standing hammock
3 Safari-type canvas table and chairs
4 Self-contained, corner water feature
5 Wall decorations – dried arrangements or wood carvings

6 Grasses in containers

7 Containers on stands

8 Banana in container

9 Hand-made African
pots or dried gourds

Mix and match

If you like this garden, but would
prefer a different feature, see pages
250–251 for possible variations.

Key features

Garden furniture

In a tiny space garden furniture is unavoidable, both physically and visually, and you should take plenty of time in selecting it, thinking about both the style and material and also the colour. The hammock and canvas chairs and table are redolent of an African safari camp, reflecting the earthy colours associated with the hot, dusty plains. Light and portable, the table and chairs can be moved out of the way when they are not needed and brought indoors to be stored in winter.

Water feature

An essential part of the African landscape, water also adds the qualities of sound, light and movement to a garden. Choose a water feature that is appropriate for your theme. Large water garden suppliers will have a range of small features, and some mail order suppliers also offer a range of small cascades, some of which are solar powered, so you do not have to worry about providing electricity and the associated cabling. In this design the cascades could be of simple terracotta or stone, similar to large, hand-made drinking vessels. Putting it in the corner gives you the opportunity to create some height and it's also an effective way of making the best use of limited space. If your design includes a free-standing water feature, make sure it's self-contained so that you can, if necessary, move it around.

Container planting

Putting plants in containers is an excellent idea when space is limited. Not only does it give you the flexibility of being able to move them around, it also allows you to move them indoors temporarily if, for instance, you need to put out an extra chair or table. If you have a really big, heavy container, consider making a base for it that has castors or small wheels underneath, so that it will be much easier to reposition. Remember that all containers need drainage holes and raising them off the ground prevents the soil mix from becoming waterlogged.

Grasses make excellent container plants, particularly varieties with arching stems that hang down over the container rim. Mulch the top of the compost with shingle or small stones to keep the roots cool and to provide a drier atmosphere at the base of the plant, which many grasses need.

Adapting designs for a different look

A garden is as much a living space as any room in your house, the only differences being that it is outside and subject to the vagaries of climate and season. Approach the task of garden design as you would the decoration of a room, considering what you're going to do in the space and choosing the elements that will achieve the feel and look you want.

Containers are excellent where space is limited and you can move them around to suit your needs.

An alternative design for the same balcony

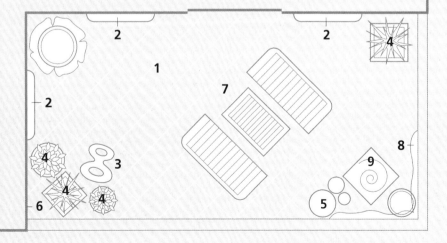

Garden elements key

1 Blue and white tiled floor
2 Reliefs on wall
3 Black abstract sculpture
4 Blue plastic or fibreglass containers in stainless steel or chrome plant pot holders
5 Silver sphere ornaments
6 Pale blue wall
7 Silver-finish furniture
8 Climber on railing
9 Spiral water feature

Planting

The best plants for this garden

Palms, exotic perennials and grasses are suitable for growing in containers and the character of each reflects the theme of the garden.

The slender, spiky habit of grasses captures the feel of the open, dry savannah. Try *Leymus*, *Chionochloa* or *Calamagrostis* (reed grass, smallweed), or, to give the impression of the marshy areas around waterholes, try the moisture-loving but tender *Cyperus* spp.

Palms and bananas – *Chamaerops humilis* (dwarf fan palm), *Musa basjoo* (Japanese banana) – will give a more tropical look, especially when they are combined with exotic flowers, such as *Strelitzia* (crane flower, bird of paradise) and *Osteospermum* cvs. Plants, such as *Musa* spp. (banana), which are not hardy, can be moved inside the house or greenhouse for protection until outside temperatures and conditions are more suitable.

Planting key

1 *Chamaerops humilis*
2 *Strelitzia reginae*
3 *Calamagrostis arundinacea*
4 *Osteospermum*
5 *Musa basjoo*
6 *Leymus arenarius*
7 *Chionochloa rubra*
8 *Carex pseudocyperus*

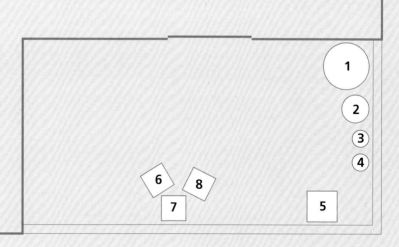

Choosing a different colour scheme

If you like one of the garden designs in this book but would prefer a different range of plants, then why not create your own planting plan – choosing a single colour, a range of colours or even just foliage plants.

This design for the alternative balcony plan on page 103 makes a striking contrast, with a bold, but not brash, colour scheme of blue, white and silver with the tiniest hint of red to create a hotspot. Furniture, containers, water feature and ornaments are contemporary in both style and materials, and the colour theme is continued into the planting.

A silver and white colour scheme will suit almost any situation.

Alternative planting key

1 *Nerium oleander* 'Album Plenum'
2 *Sollya heterophylla*
3 *Astelia chathamica*
4 *Rhododendron* Blue Tit Group
5 *Agapanthus campanulatus*
6 *Crinodendron hookerianum*

By the sea

Coastal gardens are often subject to different climatic conditions from those further inland. The local climate is usually milder, and in many temperate areas frost is rarely a problem. However, these gardens are invariably more exposed to the wind, which often contains minute drops of salt-laden moisture to which many plants are susceptible, resulting in scorched leaves and poor growth.

What makes this a good seaside garden?
✓ Trees and shrubs provide a windbreak against the prevailing winds and create sheltered pockets for less robust plants or areas for sitting
✓ The lawn is sited so that it is sheltered from the main wind direction but allows views out
✓ The patio area takes advantage of the sun and aspect
✓ The trellis and pergola provide shelter on the patio when the wind does not comes from its usual direction

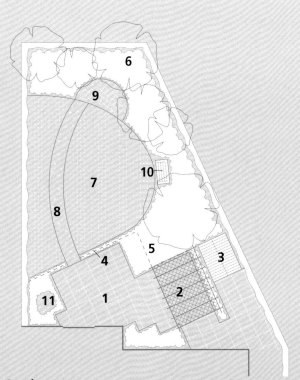

Garden elements key

1 Patio
2 Pergola draped with fishing net
3 Garden store
4 Trellis screen
5 Planting
6 Trees and shrubs for shelter

7 Lawn
8 Path
9 Shady sitting area
10 Bench seat

11 Seaside 'sculpture'
  – driftwood,
  cobbles, shells

Mix and match
If you like this garden, but would prefer a different feature, see pages 250–251 for possible variations.

Key features

Path

Paths are essential to move around your garden, particularly along routes that are frequently used. Make them curved for more interest and use materials that are in keeping with the surroundings — such as beach cobbles and shingle by the sea. Alternatively, link the path with a common theme in your design, for example old bricks in a romantic walled garden.

Trellis screen

When you want a quick, permanent screen or divider, use trellis. For a more solid effect, to give privacy, use tall panels and plant them with climbers. If you only want a suggestion of screening or division, you can use lower panels, perhaps with a very open, lightweight design and put some low plants at the base to soften the trellis.

Hedge

You can use hedges as natural barriers instead of walls or fences. In formal gardens use evergreens trimmed tightly to create geometric and architectural forms. For a less formal and more colourful look, plant flowering hedges such as roses or escallonia that only require an annual trim. Very low hedges — such as lavender — make excellent dividers when you don't want to block views.

Tiled sitting area

This is a very simple seating area that requires a minimum of complex, intricate work.

The key to its success is to make sure that there is a large enough area of tiles (or flags or bricks if you wish) to make a level base for your bench or chairs to sit on. Once you have this core area laid onto a base of hardcore you can add extra tiles and an informal cobble edge to create a soft, random shape around the seat.

Infill the spaces between the tiles and the cobbles with small loose pebbles and shells. You can introduce extra variation by using different sizes of cobbles.

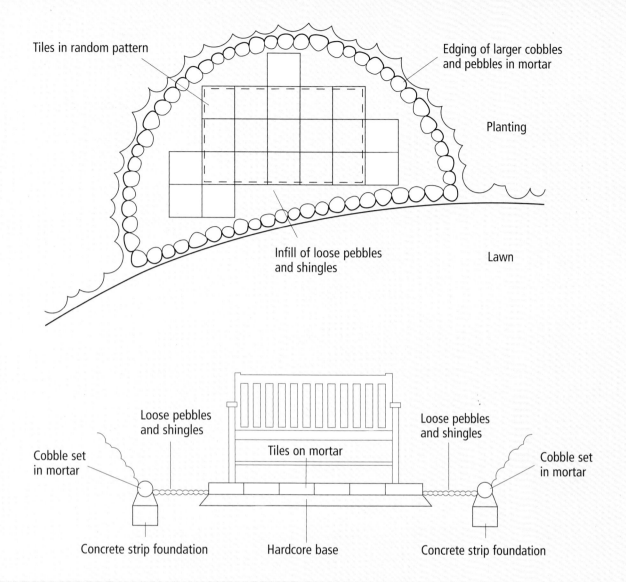

Tiles in random pattern

Edging of larger cobbles and pebbles in mortar

Planting

Infill of loose pebbles and shingles

Lawn

Loose pebbles and shingles

Loose pebbles and shingles

Cobble set in mortar

Tiles on mortar

Cobble set in mortar

Concrete strip foundation

Hardcore base

Concrete strip foundation

Creating a defined garden theme

There is no need for the entire garden to have a single theme. Your design could divide the garden into two or more distinct areas, each of which has a different theme, to add to the element of surprise. Take care, though, that you do not make the garden look bitty and fragmented by having too many discrete areas.

Develop a theme by using a single style throughout the whole garden. Choosing one or two plant colours that run through all the planting will bring unity to a more random mixture of hard landscaping and garden structures. Alternatively, use one or, at most, two colours for all the hard surfaces and introduce a more interesting and varied selection of plant colours. Achieve a stronger effect by using complementary colours or bold contrasts. If you want lots of different colours, use a shape or shapes – a series of circles or squares, for example – to develop a common theme.

You might find inspiration in the landscape beyond your garden. In the countryside a cottage-garden theme is appropriate, while a tiny backyard or roof garden in the heart of the city could be inspired by the architecture around it, not just the shapes and colours, but also the materials, such as glass, polished steel and concrete.

The informal planting and decorative stones, pebbles and shells all add to the coastal theme for this garden.

Planting

The best plants for this garden

Although the plants have been chosen initially for their ability to thrive in the conditions found near the sea and to help establish shelter, the overall design provides stimulating colours and textures throughout the seasons. The larger shrubs, particularly on the side of the prevailing wind, are attractive in their own right and also afford protection for the lower planting of perennials to add to the overall colour palette.

Planting key

1 *Convolvulus cneorum*
2 *Eryngium maritimum*
3 *Agapanthus* 'Bressingham White'
4 *Sedum* 'Herbstfreude'
5 *Armeria maritima*
6 *Elymus hispidus*
7 *Pinus mugo* 'Mops'
8 *Helichrysum* 'Schwefellicht'
9 *Hedera colchica* 'Dentata Variegata' (on trellis)
10 *Lavandula angustifolia* 'Nana Alba'
11 *Cordyline australis* 'Atropurpurea'
12 *Genista lydia*
13 *Lonicera periclymenum* 'Graham Thomas' (on pergola/trellis)
14 *Juniperus* x *pfitzeriana* 'Sulphur Spray'
15 *Anemone* var. *japonica* 'Bressingham Glow'
16 *Alchemilla mollis*

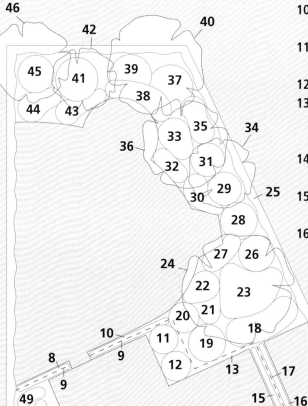

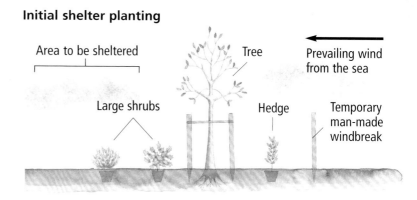

Initial shelter planting

Area to be sheltered

Large shrubs

Tree

Hedge

Temporary man-made windbreak

Prevailing wind from the sea

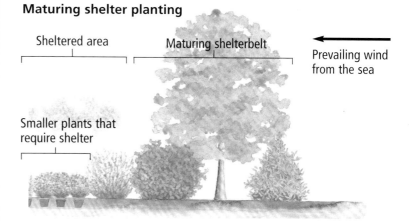

Maturing shelter planting

Sheltered area

Maturing shelterbelt

Smaller plants that require shelter

Prevailing wind from the sea

Establishing shelter plants

Although the trees, boundary hedge and large shrubs will ultimately form the shelter 'backbone' of the garden, it is important to give them as good a start as possible to enable them to grow quickly and begin to do their work.

- Make sure all planting areas are thoroughly dug, are improved by the addition of organic matter and are completely weed free

- Provide regular watering because it is essential that new plants don't suffer from stress caused by inadequate or irregular watering

- Erect a temporary windbreak 'fence' of netting, sacking or twiggy conifer branches to give some instant shelter to the hedge; it should be at least 30cm (12in) higher, more if possible, than the newly planted hedge

- Plant the hedge on the downwind, sheltered side of the windbreak

- Plant the trees, using container-grown ones where possible; avoid potbound trees, which are unlikely to put out strong roots that will anchor the tree firmly in the ground

- Stake the trees to resist the prevailing wind – don't underestimate its force

- Plant the large shrubs, again using container-grown specimens, cutting them back by about one-third so that they are not susceptible to wind-rock but will develop strong, new shoots

- Keep all plants weed free and well watered during the growing season and if possible apply a thick mulch of organic matter, or use a proprietary fabric 'floating mulch', pegged down around the plants

Cool contemporary

Some gardens rely for their effect on a selective and restrained use of contemporary materials, ornaments and plants to give a sleek, sophisticated and uncluttered look. This approach is particularly effective in smaller gardens, especially those in cities and towns where space is always limited, and a carefully thought-out composition can be striking.

What makes this a good contemporary garden?

✓ The quiet elegance of such a design creates a peaceful haven
✓ The scheme is in keeping with the materials used for the house
✓ Although it is small, the design creates the illusion of space

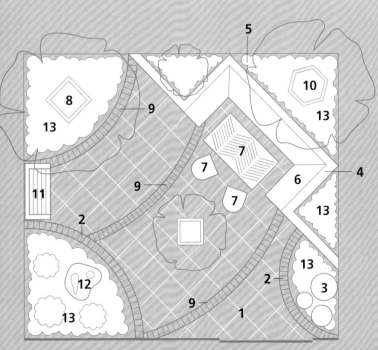

Garden elements key

1 White flagstone paving
2 Red brick edging
3 Illuminated glass spheres

4 Stainless steel coping on wall of raised bed
5 Raised bed
6 Built-in seating

7 Brushed aluminium
table and chairs

8 Tree in container

9 Dark grey brick edging

10 Bamboo in container

11 Wall-mounted bench
seat

12 Chrome-steel sculpture

13 Planting

Mix and match
If you like this garden, but would
prefer a different feature, see pages
250–251 for possible variations.

Key features

Glass spheres

Glass garden ornaments bring an extra dimension to any garden. Put them among planting to provide sparkle and reflections or site them on their own on a bed of pebbles or chippings. Alternatively, combine them with a small water feature so that a fountain or geyser can flow over them and, for a real flourish, put some low-level lighting at the base for night-time attraction.

Built-in seating

Don't just use raised beds for planting – combine them with built-in seating to create an attractive and functional garden feature. Make sure the seating is positioned to suit your needs – for example, in full sun, partial shade or near the kitchen door for good access. Use durable, weatherproof materials and allow time and money for annual maintenance, such as oiling hardwood.

Bamboo in container

Like many plants, some forms of bamboo can be grown in containers. They make excellent specimens used this way and can be planted as focal points, among low planting, on paving to provide vertical contrast or positioned strategically to screen an unsightly view or object. Remember, though, that you should never let them dry out completely. In all other respects, treat them like any other container-grown plant.

Accessorizing with ornaments

Once you have chosen a theme or style for your garden, whether it is Japanese, formal, old-fashioned or cutting-edge modern – you will soon have the paving, lawn, features, pond and plants in place to match it.

Small features often look best when gently tucked into planted areas.

However, if you think of a garden as a room in a house or a new outfit of clothes, it's not quite complete until you've added the finishing touches – the brooch on the jacket, the silver candlesticks on the table! No matter what you choose to accessorize your garden with, it will pay to observe some simple rules:

- Consider the general location of each of your ornaments at the planning stage

- Select items that respect your chosen garden theme or style – perhaps terracotta wall hangings in a Mediterranean garden or a classical stone statue or urn in a Romantic one

- Don't overdo it and fill every nook and cranny with statues, sundials, urns or *objets trouvés*

- Make each ornament a feature and focal point in its own right but make sure that each harmonizes with everything around it

Above right: This simple modern sculpture makes a striking feature.

Right: Use bright colours and crisp shapes to contrast with soft, delicate planting.

Planting

The best plants for this garden

The design uses a limited palette, and the planting is used to emphasize shape and texture while colour plays a background role. All the perennials are excellent for this type of situation. They are long lived and reliable, tolerating a range of conditions, but each has its own individual quality of shape and leaf. The bamboos are excellent features for planting against the walls, where their distinctive habit can be seen to advantage, and together with the tree they give height to the garden without being oppressive. Because flowers are generally low key and pale, the overall greenness of the garden gives it a cool, refreshing feel.

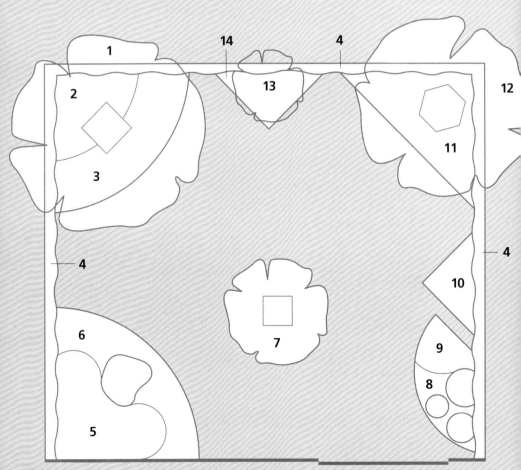

Planting key

1 *Catalpa* x *erubescens* 'Purpurea'
2 *Geranium phaeum* 'Album'
3 *Hosta* 'Halcyon'
4 *Schizophragma hydrangeoides* (on wall)
5 *Phyllostachys nigra* 'Boryana'
6 *Alchemilla mollis*
7 *Acer palmatum* 'Sango-kaku'
8 *Alchemilla mollis*
9 *Iris foetidissima*
10 *Viburnum davidii*
11 *Euphorbia amygdaloides* var. *robbiae*
12 *Phyllostachys aureosulcata* f. *aureocaulis*
13 *Fargesia nitida* 'Anceps'
14 *Alchemilla mollis*

Alternative planting

1 *Jasminum mesnyi* (on wall)
2 *Salix alba* subsp. *vitellina* (as a pollard)
3 *Geum* 'Lady Stratheden'
4 *Humulus lupulus* 'Aureus' (on wall)
5 *Mahonia aquifolium* 'Smaragd'
6 *Iris foetidissima* var. *citrina*
7 *Santolina chamaecyparissus*
8 *Acer negundo* 'Kelly's Gold'
9 *Semiarundinaria yashadake* var. *kimmei*
10 *Waldsteinia ternata*
11 *Clematis* 'Bill MacKenzie' (on wall)
12 *Symphytum* 'Goldsmith'
13 *Filipendula ulmaria* 'Aurea'
14 *Catalpa bignonioides* 'Aurea'

Trees in containers

In a natural environment, the root and crown systems of trees continue to grow and extend as the tree matures. A tree's root system generally spreads as far as the crown to provide stability and to enable the tree to obtain sufficient nutrients and moisture from the ground. However, trees grown permanently in containers do not have this facility, and if they are to do well they need some help.

- The larger the container you provide, the bigger the tree will grow, other things being equal
- Use the best quality potting compost and choose one that is suitable for the purpose – don't use ordinary garden soil
- Support the tree in the early stages to prevent wind rock

Even in winter this combination of polished metal and white tree stems is striking.

- Water regularly and never allow the rootball to become bone dry
- Throughout the growing season apply regular liquid feed or put slow-release fertilizer tablets or pellets into the pot in early spring
- In winter, re-pot the tree into the same container (if it's the final size you want it in) by taking the tree out of the pot, removing about one-third of the old rootball and replanting in fresh growing compost
- If the tree is too large or heavy to repot, scrape away a proportion of growing medium from the top of the rootball and replace it with some fresh compost
- When you are repotting or top-dressing, reduce the crown of the tree by about one-third to keep it in proportion to the roots; also prune off dead, weak or misshapen branches
- Even if the tree is well-rooted in its container, it may blow over in strong winds, so secure it to the ground or nearby walls

Best trees for containers

- *Acer negundo* and cvs. (box elder, ash-leaved maple)
- *Acer palmatum* and cvs. (Japanese maple)
- *Amelanchier* (snowy mespilus)
- *Aralia elata* (Japanese angelica tree)
- *Arbutus unedo* (strawberry tree)
- *Laburnum* spp.
- *Magnolia* x *soulangeana*
- *Malus* spp. (crab apple)
- *Pinus* (pine) – dwarf or slow-growing forms, such as *P. heldreichii* (Bosnian pine); *P. mugo* (dwarf mountain pine)
- *Sorbus cashmiriana*, *S. koehneana*

A rural retreat

When you have plenty of space you may forget to plan your garden properly. It is all too easy to end up with several individual features but with little thought about how they contribute to the overall appearance of your garden.

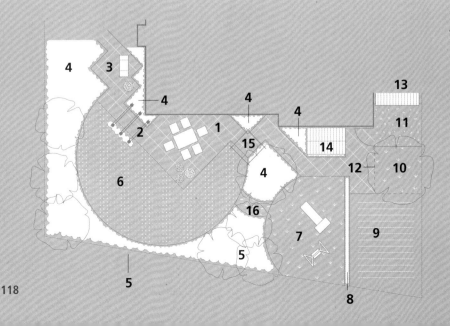

Garden elements key

1 Patio
2 Arches with climbers
3 Patio for late afternoon/early evening
4 Planting
5 Views out over countryside
6 Lawn
7 Play area

What makes this a good rural garden?

✓ Careful zoning separates basic functional areas away from the ornamental and leisure areas

✓ The rough division of the garden into two, combined with perimeter planting and a curved lawn, disguises the rather shallow, wide shape

✓ Views over the surrounding countryside have been maintained and are framed by the trees and shrubs

✓ The style and colour of planting is soft and natural – although the majority of the plants are ornamental varieties – blending in sympathetically with the surrounding landscape

8 Hedge or fence

9 Vegetable garden

10 Rough grass for animal run

11 Paving/gravel for animal run

12 Fence and gate for animal run

13 Animal run

14 Tool shed

15 Pergola

16 Wood chip path

Mix and match
If you like this garden, but would prefer a different feature, see pages 250–251 for possible variations.

Key features

Vegetable garden

In larger rural gardens you can devote more space to growing your own vegetables and could even become self-sufficient. Remember to allocate sufficient space for things like compost bins — you might want two or three for a rotation. Locate your vegetable garden adjacent to your animal runs and other utility areas for convenience and provide a clean paved access to both to make life easier in bad weather.

Arches and pergolas

These features not only provide extra height in a garden but they also allow you to grow a wide range of climbers, including clematis and sweet-scented honeysuckle.

Play area

Providing somewhere safe for children to play will be a priority, but don't forget that the area can be turned into a border or lawn when the children have grown up. Protect features like the vegetable garden with a larger hedge, but use safe plants without sharp thorns or poisonous berries. You'll need to locate your play area where it can be seen from the house, at least until the children are older.

Bringing the countryside into your garden

If your garden backs on to fields or views of open countryside, make it appear to extend into the wider landscape by choosing a boundary that is less obvious. Remember, the more space around, the more likely you are to be exposed to the prevailing weather. Choose your views carefully, preferably in the direction that does not bring strong or cold wind. If you can't do this, narrow your views down and frame them with trees to break up the wind.

Pale, delicate boundary fences allow you to look out over the surrounding landscape so that it appears as an extension of your garden.

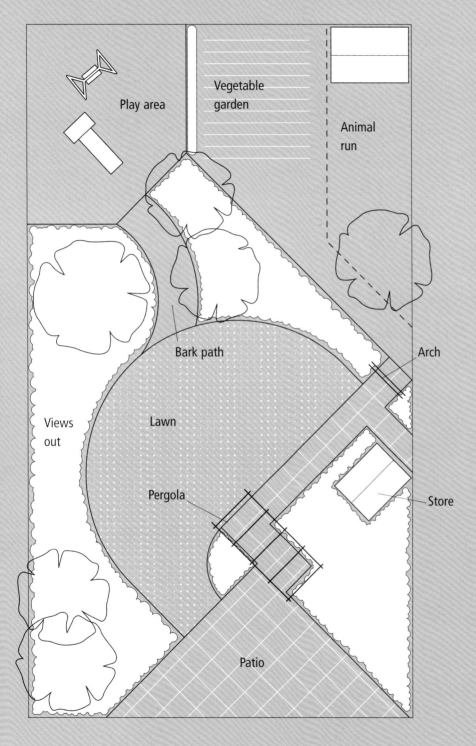

Play area

Vegetable garden

Animal run

Bark path

Arch

Views out

Lawn

Pergola

Store

Patio

Changing the design to suit the shape of your garden

When adapting a design to suit a different garden shape, you might need to change the shapes of individual features such as lawns and patios to fit. Make sure that the new shape is adequate for its purpose – for example, is there enough room on the patio for your garden furniture to fit comfortably?

Try and ensure that the different areas are still roughly in the best position for their intended use – for example, the patio next to the house in a sunny spot, the utility area for compost in a hidden-away corner.

Planting

13

The best plants for this garden

The plants have been selected for their reliability and generally undemanding nature. The planting areas are generous, and species that require minimal maintenance or care have been chosen throughout the scheme. The soft shapes and textures are in harmony with surroundings, and the plan avoids formal, rigid forms. Restrained colours help the garden blend in to the overall landscape.

20

23

28

Planting key

1 *Corylus avellana*
2 *Hypericum calycinum*
3 *Cornus sanguinea*
4 *Prunus avium* 'Plena'
5 *Rhododendron* 'Pink Pearl'
6 *Sarcococca hookeriana* var. *humilis*
7 *Rhododendron* 'Persil' (azalea)
8 *Iris pallida*
9 *Buddleja crispa*
10 *Potentilla fruticosa* 'Elizabeth'
11 *Miscanthus sinensis* 'Graziella'
12 *Lupinus* 'Noble Maiden'
13 *Geranium* x *oxonianum* 'Claridge Druce'
14 *Stipa arundinacea*
15 *Campanula lactiflora*
16 *Spiraea thunbergii*
17 *Rhododendron* 'Christmas Cheer'
18 *Hydrangea arborescens*
19 *Liquidambar styraciflua* 'Worplesdon'
20 *Helleborus argutifolius*
21 *Tilia* 'Petiolaris'
22 *Hydrangea involucrata*
23 *Clematis* x *eriostemon* 'Hendersonii'
24 *Corylus colurna*
25 *Rhododendron* 'Persil' (azalea)

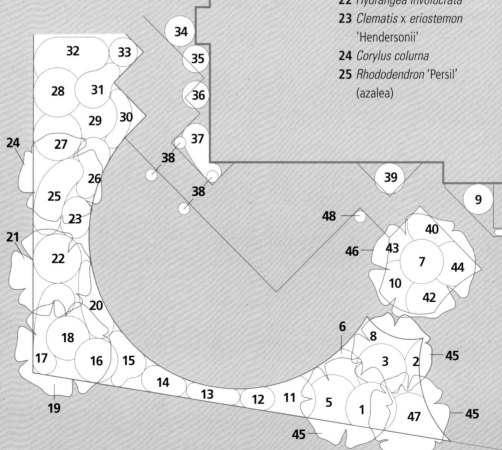

26 *Geranium macrorrhizum* 'Ingwersen's Variety'
27 *Ligustrum japonicum*
28 *Romneya coulteri*
29 *Syringa pubescens* subsp. *microphylla* 'Superba'
30 *Ceratostigma willmotiianum*
31 *Aster divaricatus*
32 *Potentilla fruticosa* 'Primrose Beauty'
33 *Scabiosa caucasica* 'Miss Willmott'
34 *Hebe* 'Midsummer Beauty'
35 *Crocosmia* x *crocosmiiflora* 'Solfatare'
36 *Itea illicifolia*
37 *Geranium himalayense* 'Gravetye'

38 *Lonicera henryi* (on pergola)
39 *Ceanothus griseus* var. *horizontalis* 'Yankee Point' (against wall)
40 *Hypericum prolificum*
41 *Parthenocissus tricuspidata* 'Veitchii' (on shed)
42 *Luzula sylvatica* 'Marginata'
43 *Epimedium* x *rubrum*
44 *Symphoricarpos orbiculatus* 'Foliis Variegatis'
45 *Prunus padus* 'Watereri'
46 *Acer rubrum*
47 *Kerria japonica* 'Picta'
48 *Lonicera implexa* (on pergola)

'Childproof' borders

Many plants will readily recover from occasional interaction with children and their activities, but there are some that will not tolerate regular abuse and will eventually die or look so poor and bedraggled that they won't be worth keeping. On the margins of intensively used play areas include plants that will escape relatively undamaged or that will recover quickly.

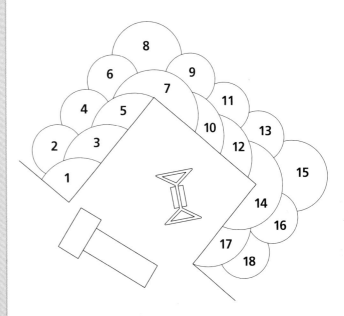

1 *Vinca minor* 'Atropurpurea'
2 *Euonymus fortunei* 'Emerald 'n' Gold'
3 *Geranium clarkei* 'Kashmir Purple'
4 *Buxus sempervirens* 'Elegantissima'
5 *Alchemilla mollis*
6 *Amelanchier lamarckii*
7 *Cotoneaster* x *suecicus* 'Coral Beauty'
8 *Cornus alba* 'Sibirica'
9 *Lonicera nitida* 'Baggesen's Gold'
10 *Hemerocallis* 'Stella de Oro'
11 *Viburnum tinus*
12 *Geum rivale* 'Leonard's Variety'
13 *Aucuba japonica* 'Picturata'
14 *Hedera helix* 'Goldchild'
15 *Corylus maxima* 'Purpurea'
16 *Choisya* 'Aztec Pearl'
17 *Ajuga reptans* 'Pink Surprise'
18 *Viburnum davidii*

41

4

On the rocks

Creating level terraces by building low retaining walls of bricks, concrete or other durable materials can transform an otherwise difficult sloping plot into a series of usable level areas. The same result can be achieved by setting rocks into the slope.

What makes this a good rock garden?

✓ Individual stones positioned to mimic as accurately as possible how they might be found in a natural setting and various sizes incorporated to avoid the feeling of uniformity

✓ A series of informal pools linked by tiny rock cascades adds another natural dimension to the garden

✓ Paths and lower paved areas covered in crushed stone chippings made from the same rock used for the outcrops create a sense of continuity

✓ Ornamental planting including species that are native to upland and alpine regions and that complement the rock and stone

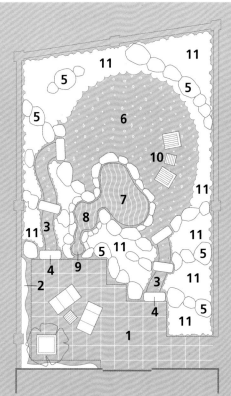

Garden elements key

1 Patio
2 Climbers on patio wall
3 Stone chipping path
4 Stone step
5 Rock formation/outcrop
6 Stone chippings
7 Lower pool
8 Middle pool
9 Upper/top pool
10 Relaxation area
11 Planting bed

Mix and match
If you like this garden, but would prefer a different feature, see pages 250–251 for possible variations.

Key features

Steps

Steps are an essential part of any sloping garden. Choose materials to match or complement other paving. Make sure that they are the right size for safety – between 10cm and 15cm (4in and 6in) is a good height. Very shallow steps are less visible and can trip you up; high steps are uncomfortable and difficult to climb. Think about including a handrail for long flights of steps – perhaps made from ornamental wrought iron or natural oak.

Dwarf conifers

Dwarf conifers are excellent plants for rock and scree gardens. Use them to break up areas of low planting such as alpines and heathers and to give scale and height. Don't plant them too closely together or their individual shapes and characteristics won't be appreciated. They are also excellent when used in containers, particularly where you want to create a more formal effect.

Garden furniture

If you have more than one patio or sitting area, and if you can afford it, invest in extra garden furniture so that you don't have to move your furniture every time you decide to sit somewhere else. Don't forget though that you might need to store it in the winter, so make sure you've enough storage space or select tables and chairs made from durable materials that can be left outside.

A natural pool

The simplest way to build a pond is to line a hole of the desired shape and depth with a flexible pond liner and edge it with natural or artificial flagstones. An edging of random pieces of natural stone (crazy paving) makes a sympathetic finish where a natural look is desired. For an even more natural appearance, you can use solid pieces of stone of the type that are likely to be found around the margins of a real pool. The best way to do this is to build your lined pool first and then add the rocks.

Edging rocks that go into the water give a really natural feel to a pond.

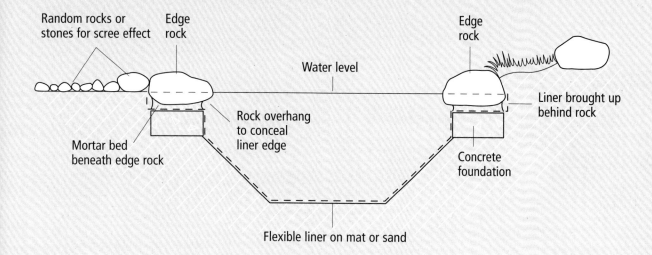

Random rocks or stones for scree effect

Edge rock

Water level

Edge rock

Liner brought up behind rock

Rock overhang to conceal liner edge

Mortar bed beneath edge rock

Concrete foundation

Flexible liner on mat or sand

You will need

A flexible pond liner to suit the overall size of your pool (liner length = maximum length of pool + twice the maximum depth; liner width = maximum width of pool + twice the maximum depth)

Protective mat

Building sand, 20mm (¾in) grade gravel and cement

Selection of large rocks to form the pond edge

Selection of small rocks and stones to finish off

1

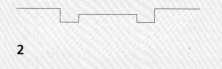

2

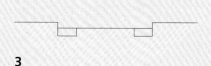

3

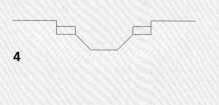

4

5

Step by step

1 Dig your pool to about 25cm (10in) below the proposed finished water level and somewhat wider than the finished water area to accommodate rocks on both sides.

2 Dig out a trench around the perimeter of the excavated area, 10–12.5cm (4–5in) deep and wide enough to accommodate the edging rocks. If the rocks vary greatly in size, decide before you begin which will go where and adjust the width of the trench accordingly.

3 Backfill the trench with concrete (in the proportions 1 part cement, 2 parts sand and 4 parts gravel). Leave the concrete to harden.

4 Dig out the rest of the pool to the required depth and lay a protective mat or about 2.5cm (1in) of soft damp sand over the entire excavated area, including the concrete. Put the pond liner in place.

5 Partly fill the pond with water to tighten the liner.

6 Place a bed of mortar (1 part cement to 6 parts sand) about 5cm (2in) thick on the liner directly above the concrete foundation and lay each rock on it. The mortar needs to be just firm enough not to be squeezed out by the rocks.

7 Bring the edge of the liner up behind the rocks, trim off the excess and secure with soil.

8 Place smaller rocks and crushed stone loosely behind to create a natural finish and top up the pond with water to the maximum finished level.

Planting

10

11

25

30

The best plants for this garden

Low, spreading plants that trail over the rocks contrast
with upright species to provide vertical interest. Most of
the plants in this scheme are small to medium and not too
vigorous, so they will not overpower or dominate the rock
formations and water course.

Planting key

1 *Camellia japonica* 'Lady Vansittart'
2 *Rhododendron* 'Addy Wery'
   (azalea)
3 *Berberis thunbergii* f.
   atropurpurea 'Atropurpurea Nana'

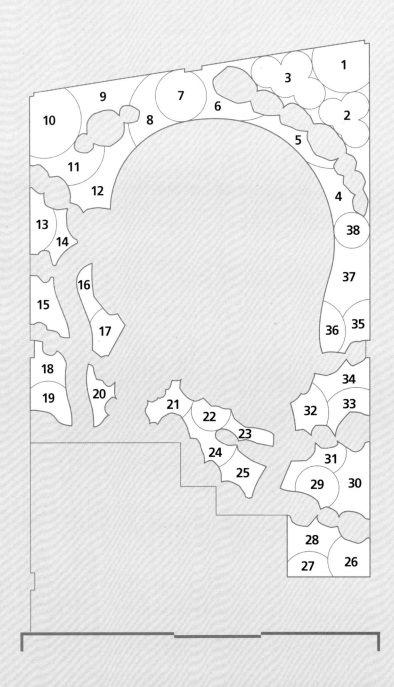

4 *Geranium wallichianum* 'Buxton's
Variety'

5 *Centaurea bella*

6 *Helianthemum* 'Wisley Primrose'

7 *Erica arborea*

8 *Viola* 'Belmont Blue'

9 *Astilbe* 'Sprite'

10 *Rhododendron* 'Praecox'

11 *Pulsatilla vulgaris*

12 *Alchemilla alpina*

13 *Rhododendron* 'Homebush'
(azalea)

14 *Campanula carpatica*

15 *Erica vagans* 'Mrs D.F. Maxwell'

16 *Aurinia saxatilis* 'Citrina'

17 *Berberis* x *stenophylla*
'Corallina Compacta'

18 *Juniperus procumbens* 'Nana'

19 *Erica arborea* 'Albert's Gold'

20 *Geranium* Cinereum Group
'Ballerina'

21 *Erica carnea* 'Myretoun Ruby'

22 *Juniperus communis*
'Compressa'

23 *Armeria maritima* 'Vindictive'

24 *Dianthus deltoides* 'Albus'

25 *Juniperus squamata* 'Blue Star'

26 *Rhododendron* Cowslip Group

27 *Sedum spathulifolium* 'Cape
Blanco'

28 *Artemisia schmidtiana* 'Nana'

29 x *Halimiocistus wintonensis*

30 *Calluna vulgaris* 'H.E. Beale'

31 *Helianthemum* 'Mrs C.W. Earle'

32 *Aster alpinus*

33 *Festuca glauca* 'Blaufuchs'

34 *Persicaria vaccinifolia*

35 *Ceratostigma plumbaginoides*

36 *Achillea* x *lewisii* 'King Edward'

37 *Erica cinerea* 'Velvet Night'

38 *Pinus mugo* 'Humpy'

Miniature rock garden

If your garden is small and flat you can easily create a miniature rock
garden in a sunny corner. Build two low, stepped retaining walls to form
the back and fill the angle between them with topsoil. Rake the soil to a
gentle slope and lay a selection of rocks to form natural-looking outcrops
before planting up.

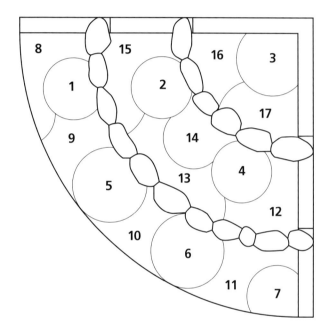

1 *Juniperus squamata* 'Blue Star'

2 *Picea glauca* var. *albertiana*
'Alberta Globe'

3 *Tsuga canadensis* 'Bennett'

4 *Chamaecyparis obtusa* 'Nana
Lutea'

5 *Juniperus horizontalis* 'Grey
Pearl'

6 *Thuja occidentalis* 'Danica'

7 *Pinus mugo* 'Humpy'

8 *Aubrieta* 'Doctor Mules'

9 *Dianthus deltoides* 'Leuchtfunk'

10 *Sempervivum* 'Othello'

11 *Geranium* x *lindavicum* 'Apple
Blossom'

12 *Phlox subulata* 'Oakington Blue
Eyes'

13 *Sedum spurium* 'Erdblut'

14 *Helianthemum* 'Annabel'

15 *Hypericum polyphyllum*
'Grandiflorum'

16 *Arabis alpina* subsp. *caucasica*
'Variegata'

17 *Aster alpinus*

With just a little work

Anything you can do to minimize garden chores – such as staking, tying, weeding and grass cutting – will help you enjoy your garden, even if it is a backyard the size of a postage stamp in the middle of a city or town.

What makes this a good easy-care garden?

✓ There is plenty of interesting paving in a small space
✓ There is an area for outdoor entertaining
✓ Trellis and climbers are used to maximize wall space
✓ The container planting is easy to maintain and includes an automatic watering system
✓ The small water feature is virtually maintenance free
✓ There is a separate barbecue area
✓ A brick plinth for displaying containers and ornaments doubles up as low extra seating and table space, with optional storage cupboards underneath
✓ There is a shaded area for hot, sunny periods

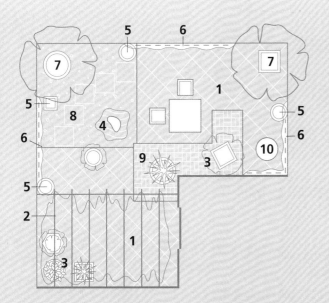

Garden elements key

1 Flag paving
2 Overheads
3 Container planting
4 Small water feature
5 Climber in container
6 Trellis on wall
7 Large shrub or small tree in container

8 Flag stepping stones in
crushed slate

9 Brick plinth

10 Barbecue

Mix and match

If you like this garden, but would
prefer a different feature, see pages
250–251 for possible variations.

Key features

Wall-mounted trellis

This is a simple way to provide support for a range of climbers and disguise unsightly walls. Make sure that your trellis is both strong enough and large enough to match the vigour of your chosen climber. Fix horizontal or vertical battens to the wall and screw your trellis onto these – this will provide more space behind the panel for stems to comfortably twine, and also makes a valuable habitat for small birds and insects.

Brick plinth

This is like a raised bed, but with a hard surface in place of soil and planting. It is ideal for displaying plants and other ornaments or you can use it for seating when you're short of chairs. Provide more interest by varying the types of brick – mix them with other materials like small pieces of flagstone or cover the plinth with wooden boards to create a decking platform.

Flag stepping stones with crushed slate

Crushed slate and other fine, hard materials, such as gravel and chippings, are an attractive and economical way of covering paved areas that are only used occasionally. Spread them onto a smooth, hard base of hardcore or, if you can't do this, put down a sheet of mulching fabric first to prevent it mixing with soil below. Lay stepping stones across any area where you might need to walk on a regular basis.

Using colour to create space and distance

In the natural landscape the general colour of objects, such as fields, forests and mountains, becomes more blue, grey and purple the further off they are, until at the horizon they almost blend into the sky. The brightest and most intense colours are experienced in the foreground, almost under your nose.

This white border is easy to maintain and gives a feeling of space.

How to cut down on garden chores

You may get to a point in your life when for various reasons – too little time, increasing age – you need or want to do less work in the garden. Assuming you don't want to bulldoze your garden and start again from scratch, what can you do to reduce your workload?

- Look at the style of planting, and if it's labour intensive – annual bedding, large rose borders – consider replacing it with dwarf evergreen shrubs or groundcover perennials

- Cut back hard any tall hedges that can only be trimmed with ladders or steps, or consider replacing the hedge with a slower growing species or even a fence or trellis clothed with climbers

- Replace a small lawn with shingle or bark or change an awkward shape to something that is easier to cut and edge

- Remove individual shrubs and small island beds from lawns

- Mulch beds and borders to keep weeds at bay and conserve moisture

- Reduce the number of container plants or else link them to a simple automatic drip irrigation system

- Install an irrigation system to all parts of the garden if your soil is dry and plants need regular watering

- Cover a small pond with heavy-duty mesh and cobbles and shingle and convert it to a safe, low-maintenance water feature

You can exploit this phenomenon even in a small back garden to create an illusion of space and distance. Plants that have flowers or foliage in the blue and purple part of the colour spectrum will appear to be further away than those that are orange, red and yellow, even though the physical distance is the same.

Make your garden – or just one part of it – appear longer by concentrating blue and purple plants at the far end of the area and make sure that any really bright oranges and reds are in the foreground. Mixing a few blue or purple plants among brighter colours will not work – you must group the colours.

Keep bright colours – such as red and orange – in the foreground to make your garden appear longer.

White, silver and other pale colours add an air of spaciousness to a garden, particularly when they're repeated in, say, white boundary walls, white pergolas and arches and cream-coloured paving. The opposite is also true. An abundance of dark earthy colours – dark greens, browns and greys – will close a space in and make it appear small and confined. Consider, for example, the effect achieved in 19th-century, grotto-like plantings of *Aucuba*, laurel, conifers and ferns.

Planting

The best plants for this garden

Shrubs, climbers and perennials will grow happily in containers and require little regular maintenance apart from regular watering and yearly repotting or top-dressing. There is a huge choice of containers available, in a wide range of materials, sizes and prices.

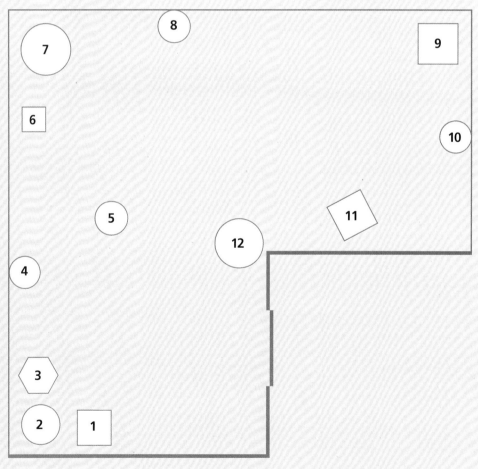

Planting key

1 *Cotoneaster conspicuus* 'Decorus'
2 *Taxus baccata* 'Standishii'
3 *Rhododendron* Elizabeth Group
4 *Actinidia deliciosa*
5 *Stipa gigantea*
6 *Lonicera japonica* 'Aureoreticulata'
7 *Acer negundo* var. *violaceum*
8 *Clematis* 'Jackmanii Superba'
9 *Abutilon* x *suntense* 'Jermyns'
10 *Passiflora caerulea*
11 *Acer palmatum* var. *dissectum* 'Garnet'
12 *Agapanthus* 'Bressingham White'

Climbers and wall shrubs in containers

Climbers and wall shrubs can be successfully grown in containers for training up walls, trellis and other vertical structures. To get the best out of them, remember to feed regularly (liquid feed or foliar feed every 7 to 10 days during the growing season) or use one insertion of controlled release fertilizer pellets, water regularly and re-pot every year. Re-pot or top dress established container-grown climbers and trim them back as necessary.

Jasminum officinale makes a wonderful container plant.

Best climbers and wall shrubs for containers in the sun

- *Abutilon megapotamicum* (trailing abutilon)
- *Actinidia kolomikta*
- *Clematis alpina* cvs.
- *Clianthus puniceus* (glory pea, parrot's claw)
- *Hedera helix* 'Oro di Bogliasco'
- *Jasminum officinale* 'Aureovariegatum'
- *Passiflora caerulea* (passion flower)
- *Trachelospermum asiaticum*
- *Vitis vinifera* 'Purpurea'
- *Wisteria sinensis* cvs.

Best climbers and wall shrubs for containers in the shade

- *Berberidopsis corallina* (coral plant)
- *Clematis* 'Nelly Moser'
- *Euonymus fortunei* cvs.
- *Hedera helix* 'Green Ripple'
- *Hydrangea anomala* subsp. *petiolaris*
- *Jasminum nudiflorum* (winter jasmine)
- *Lonicera periclymenum* 'Graham Thomas'
- *Parthenocissus henryana* (Chinese virginia creeper)
- *Pileostegia viburnoides*
- *Schizophragma hydrangeoides*

In the courtyard

Small gardens enclosed by buildings offer plenty of scope for stimulating designs, not least because of the range of plants you can grow in them. This scheme is for a reasonably sized garden, and within it a succession of small sitting areas has been created in a roughly circular route that provides a natural flow and movement within a square space.

What makes this a good courtyard garden?

✓ A sheltered microclimate, which allows you to include some exotic plants not normally seen in temperate gardens

✓ Lots of vertical surfaces for climbers, wall shrubs and hanging pots

✓ A wide range of growing conditions within a relatively small area – from cool, damp and shady to hot, dry and sunny – giving more opportunities for different plant groupings

✓ The scent from fragrant plants lingers and is more concentrated because of the shelter from the surrounding walls

✓ Painted or coloured walls, which provide contrast with or complement the planting

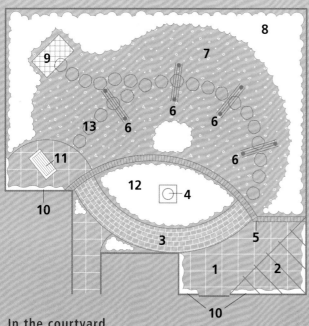

Garden elements key

1 Stone flag paving
2 Pergola for shade
3 Brick path
4 Sundial
5 Brick edging
6 Arch with climber
7 Gravel
8 Perimeter border planting
9 Arbour

10 Wall shrubs and
climbers
11 Bench seat
12 Low planting
13 Stepping stone path

Mix and match
If you like this garden, but would
prefer a different feature, see pages
250–251 for possible variations.

Key features

Stepping stone path

You can use stepping stones purely for appearance or put them where they will serve a real purpose. Use pre-cast flagstones, thin rounds of hardwood (such as oak or alder), natural stone or small squares consisting of paving bricks. Stepping stones look best where they 'sit' in the ground, rather than appearing to be perched on top.

Sundial

Sundials are available in all sorts of shapes and sizes – ranging from traditional forms on small stone plinths to contemporary designs in stainless steel or chrome. You can use them as focal points, perhaps formally in the centre of a lawn on a small brick-edged gravel circle or informally among soft, low perennials. Wherever they go, make sure it is positioned in the sun.

Pergola

Shady areas are very welcome in the heat of summer. Pergolas are a quick and easy way to create shade. You can design the pergola so that it provides shade all year round, with lots of overhead rails and laths or maybe just shade netting. Alternatively, make your pergola simple and more open, and plant it with large-leaved, vigorous climbers that will create shade in summer, but will cast very little shade once the leaves have fallen in the winter.

Arches and pergolas

Overhead structures, such as arches and pergolas, are an excellent way to introduce instant height into your garden and provide support for climbing plants, but you can – and should – also consider using them for other purposes.

Arches can provide a link between two different areas, with or without a gate, or they can frame a distant view or a focal point in the garden.

Pergolas can create a shady area or provide a visual link between your house and an outbuilding, such as a shed.

The materials for these structures should reflect the style of your garden – perhaps wrought iron for an old-fashioned romantic garden; rustic poles in a traditional cottage garden; and maybe brick or stone piers topped with oak for a formal approach.

If your garden has a theme, try and repeat it in your structures – round-topped arches for curving or circular themes or concrete and steel in a very modern garden. Alternatively, you can tie the arch or pergola in with your other garden features, such as furniture and ornaments, by using a strong colour to link them together.

The white flowers of this wisteria look wonderful cascading through the white pergola.

Climbers to provide shade under a pergola

- *Actinidia deliciosa* (summer)
- *Clematis armandii* (year-round)
- *Clematis flammula* (summer)
- *Clematis orientalis* (summer)
- *Hedera colchica* 'Sulphur Heart' (year-round)
- *Lonicera henryi* (year-round)
- *Vitis coignetiae* (summer)
- *Vitis vinifera* 'Purpurea' (summer)

Roses for arches and pillars

- 'Aloha' (rose pink)
- 'Amadis' (reddish-purple)
- 'Casino' (yellow)
- 'Danse du Feu' (scarlet)
- 'Golden Showers' (yellow)
- 'Paul's Scarlet Climber' (scarlet)
- 'Phyllis Bide' (yellow flushed pink)
- 'Pink Perpétué' (pink)
- 'Swan Lake' (white flushed pink)
- 'Zéphirine Drouhin' (deep pink)

Roses are a popular choice for growing over archways and many roses will produce flowers all summer long.

Planting

3

8

25

37

The best plants for this garden

The soft planting has been chosen to create a quiet, contemplative atmosphere. There is an emphasis on pastel flower colours and interesting foliage colours and shapes. The plant associations also reflect the gradual change in growing conditions around the garden, moving from sun to shade and back again.

Planting key

1 *Wisteria sinensis* 'Alba' (on overhead structure)
2 *Lavandula angustifolia* 'Munstead' (around edge of patio)
3 *Chaenomeles* x *superba* 'Crimson and Gold'
4 *Helianthemum* 'Sudbury Gem'
5 *Agapanthus* 'Bressingham White'

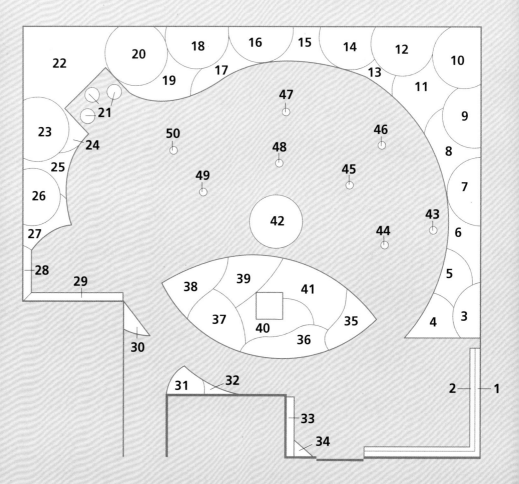

6 *Fuchsia magellanica* var. *gracilis* 'Aurea'

7 *Choisya* 'Aztec Pearl'

8 *Caryopteris* x *clandonensis* 'Heavenly Blue'

9 *Viburnum* x *bodnantense* 'Dawn'

10 *Phyllostachys nigra*

11 *Hemerocallis* 'Hyperion'

12 *Hydrangea macrophylla* 'Forever Pink'

13 *Astilbe* x *arendsii* 'Snowdrift'

14 *Mahonia aquifolium* 'Apollo'

15 *Digitalis purpurea* Excelsior Group

16 *Prunus laurocerasus* 'Otto Luyken'

17 *Ligularia dentata* 'Desdemona'

18 *Fatsia japonica* 'Variegata'

19 *Hosta sieboldiana* var. *elegans*

20 *Acer palmatum* 'Atropurpureum'

21 *Lonicera implexa* (over arbour)

22 *Fargesia nitida*

23 *Camellia* x *williamsii* 'Anticipation'

24 *Astilbe* x *arendsii* 'Bressingham Beauty'

25 *Geranium phaeum* 'Album'

26 *Hydrangea serrata* 'Grayswood'

27 *Luzula sylvatica* 'Aurea'

28 *Clematis* 'Nelly Moser'

29 *Campsis radicans* f. *flava*

30 *Jasminum nudiflorum*

31 *Piptanthus nepalensis*

32 *Sedum telephium* 'Matrona'

33 *Dryopteris erythrosora*

34 *Trachelospermum jasminoides*

35 *Aster amellus* 'King George'

36 *Artemisia* 'Powis Castle'

37 *Achillea* 'Moonshine'

38 *Iris* 'Jane Phillips' (tall bearded)

39 *Nerine bowdenii*

40 *Platycodon grandiflorus* 'Mariesii'

41 *Eryngium variifolium*

42 *Viburnum plicatum* f. *tomentosum* 'Pink Beauty'

43 *Rosa* 'Golden Showers' (on arches)

44 *Clematis alpina* 'Frances Rivis' (on arches)

45 *Rosa* 'Aloha' (on arches)

46 *Jasminum polyanthum* (on arches)

47 *Clematis* 'Ville de Lyon' (on arches)

48 *Ampelopsis glandulosa* var. *brevipedunculata* 'Elegans' (on arches)

49 *Rosa* 'New Dawn' (on arches)

50 *Lapageria rosea* (on arches)

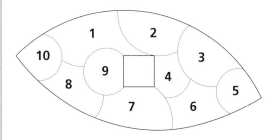

Choose plants that will like the conditions in your garden, such as hostas and ferns for a moist site.

Planting for damp shade

The lens-shaped sundial bed, bounded by the brick edging and the path, is planted with drifts of perennials that thrive in hot, well-drained conditions. However, you can achieve equally attractive plant combinations in shadier, damper conditions.

1 *Dicentra* 'Luxuriant'

2 *Hosta* 'Hadspen Blue'

3 *Saxifraga* 'Rubrifolia'

4 *Tricyrtis formosana*

5 *Filipendula ulmaria* 'Aurea'

6 *Helleborus orientalis* cvs

7 *Matteuccia struthiopteris*

8 *Astilbe* x *arendsii* 'Irrlicht'

9 *Ligularia przewalskii*

10 *Primula florindae*

Simply minimalist

There are so many plants and garden features on offer that it is tempting to fill the garden to overflowing, but adopting a more restrained attitude can be rewarding. It requires a certain amount of discipline and conviction to take just a few simple elements and put them together to form a satisfying composition. The beauty of this approach is that the line, shape, form and colour of each element can be fully appreciated.

What makes this a good minimalist garden?

✓ Space to appreciate the form and habit of growth of a range of interesting plants

✓ The combination of features and architectural planting creates a strong visual statement

✓ The garden appears spacious and has much to commend it from a practical point of view

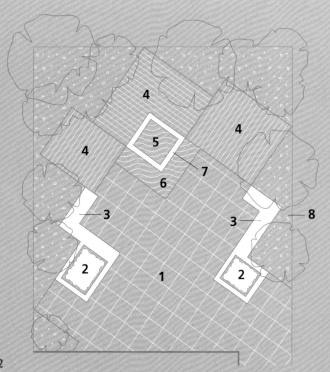

Garden elements key

1 Patio
2 Raised bed
3 Seat built into raised bed

4 Split level deck
5 Raised pool
6 Lower pool at patio level

7 Cascade

8 Gravel/stone/cobble
mulch

Mix and match

If you like this garden, but would
prefer a different feature, see pages
250–251 for possible variations.

Key features

Cascade

Create a glass-like sheet of water cascading from a raised pool into a slightly lower one. The key is to make the lip over which the water flows from a very thin material, such as sheet stainless steel. If your cascade breaks up before it hits the lower pool, try using a slightly bigger capacity pump. For a particularly spectacular effect, put submerged lighting below the cascade.

Split level deck

Make decks more interesting by creating small changes of level to act as steps. Introduce these at obvious points where there is a change of shape or at a corner. Don't introduce too many though or you'll find the individual deck areas may be too small to be practical. You can highlight the step by staining the upright part (the riser) in a contrasting colour to the level areas.

Raised bed

In very flat gardens, use raised beds to create some variations in level. Make the walls a convenient height and width (ideally about 45cm/18in high x 20–30cm/8–12in wide) so that they can double up as seating. For more permanent seating, use planks of smooth wood to cap the wall and have some cushions handy. Ensure that the soil in the bed comes right to the top so that low planting can easily spill over the edge and provide a soft contrast.

Simple deck

The beauty of building a deck is that, in most cases, you don't need to get involved in major excavation and other heavy work which paving with stone or concrete usually requires.

Decks are great if you want a free-draining raised area or if you need to build a large step close against your house wall, but you can't use solid paving because of possible damp ingress into the wall.

Planting around decking can help to disguise the hard lines of its edges.

You will need

Lengths of pressure-treated heavy
   timber, such as old railway sleepers,
   to provide a basic foundation
Sand and cement to make mortar for
   laying the concrete blocks
Lengths of pressure-treated
   softwood, 5 x 10cm (2 x 4in), to
   form the beams or rafters
Lengths of your chosen decking
   board; alternatively, use 2 x 10cm
   (¾ x 4in) sawn softwood boards,
   lightly sanded to remove major
   roughness but not too smooth
Gravel
Mulching fabric
Screws or galvanized nails
Stain

Small changes of level can be incorporated in most gardens to add an extra dimension.

Step by step

1 Clear and level out the area for
your deck.

2 Place the sleepers on the ground
and make sure they are level. If not,
place a thin bed of mortar (sand
and cement) under the appropriate
end until it is level. If the ground is
soft, dig it out until you reach
firm, undisturbed ground. If this
depth is greater than the depth of
the sleepers, then put a layer of
concrete in the bottom and bed your
sleeper on this so that the top of the
sleeper is at least 2mm (⅛in) above
ground level.

3 Cover the ground between the
sleeper foundations with mulching
fabric held down by a layer of gravel
to prevent weed growth.

4 Place the beams or rafters on
edge on top of the sleeper
foundation. Nail or screw them at an
angle through the vertical face into
the sleeper to hold them in place.
(This is not for strength but to keep
them in place when you are fitting
the decking boards.)

5 Place a decking board on top of
the beams and at right angles to

them. Screw or nail it into place,
leaving an overhang of 3.5–4cm
(about 1½in).

6 Continue fixing boards, leaving
gaps of 4–6mm (about ¼in) between
boards for drainage and movement.

7 Take another decking board and
nail or screw it to the ends of the
beams as a soffit to hide the space
under the deck.

8 Complete the deck by staining in
your selected colour.

Planting

The best plants for this garden

The careful choice of plants for such a limited scheme is vital if they are to be successfully integrated into the design. Although only a handful of species has been used, they have been selected for their architectural qualities and cover a range of stem and foliage textures and shapes – tall, slender stems, bold and spiky leaves and dense evergreen foliage. Some forms are almost geometric, others are irregular, like abstract sculptures. The careful siting of each plant will ensure that it can be appreciated, yet the overall planting is balanced and harmonious at all times of year.

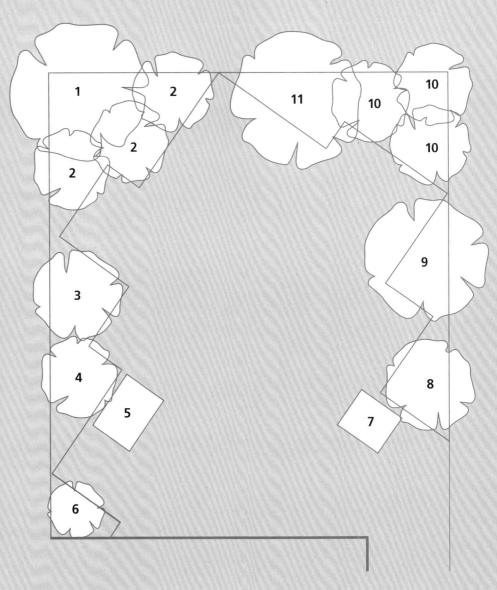

Architectural plants

There would appear to be no precise definition of what constitutes an 'architectural' plant nor any way of measuring one! However, it is a term that is often used in gardening, especially in contemporary or modern designs, and it deserves at least some sort of explanation.

Probably the main feature of an architectural plant is a particular aspect of its foliage or habit of growth – it might be because it has huge, distinctive leaves – for example *Aralia* spp. – or a characteristic shape or habit, such as a yucca. Plants grown primarily for their flowers are rarely classed as architectural – for example potentillas, spiraeas and *Philadelphus* (mock orange). This may be because these plants have small leaves and flowers. Although

Strong, upright-growing grasses like this beautiful *Miscanthus* make good architectural plants.

Buxus (box) and *Taxus* (yew) have small leaves, they could be referred to as architectural when they are trimmed into uniform geometric shapes such as spheres, columns, pyramids – the sort of shapes you might expect to see in the elements of a building. Equally, small plants – alpines, heathers, dwarf perennials and dwarf conifers – don't qualify as architectural.

Best architectural plants

- *Aralia elata* (Japanese angelica tree); *A. spinosa* (American angelica tree)
- Bamboos, such as *Pleioblastus variegatus*; *Pseudosasa japonica*; *Sasa palmata*; *Semiarundinaria yashadake*
- *Catalpa bignonioides* (Indian bean tree); *C.* x *erubsecens*
- *Cordyline* spp. (cabbage tree, cabbage palm)
- Fastigiate trees and shrubs, such as *Cupressus sempervirens* Stricta Group (Italian cypress); *Fagus sylvatica* 'Dawyck' (beech); *Taxus baccata* 'Fastigiata' (yew)
- Grasses – strongly growing forms, such as *Arundo donax* (giant reed); *Calamagrostis* spp. (reed grass, smallweed); *Miscanthus* spp.; *Stipa* spp. (feather grass, needlegrass)
- *Juniperus* (juniper) – strongly growing spp. and cvs.
- *Mahonia* – large forms, such as *M. japonica*, *M.* x *media* 'Winter Sun' and *M. lomariifolia*
- Perennials with big leaves, such as hostas; *Ligularia* spp.; *Phormium* cvs.; *Rheum palmatum* (Chinese rhubarb)
- *Pinus* spp. (pine)
- *Yucca* cvs.

Hot and dry

If your garden is hot and dry you'll need to look at the design from two viewpoints – that of the people using the garden and that of the plants you want to include. Depending on where you live, you may have to choose between providing shelter that will moderate the heat and introducing features that will maximize the available sun and warmth.

What makes this a good hot and dry garden?

✓ There are different places to sit out at different times of day according to whether you want to be in sun or shade

✓ Once they are established the plants will thrive in the hot, dry conditions with the minimum of attention

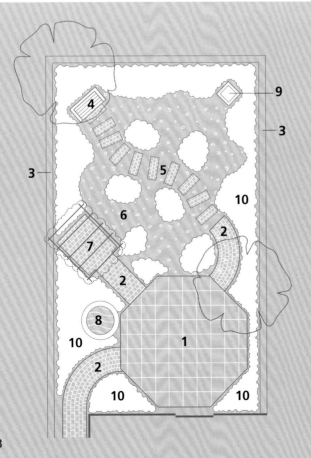

Garden elements key

1 Patio
2 Sett paving
3 Boundary wall
4 Seat in shade of tree
5 Sett 'stepping stones'
6 Gravel bed
7 Shade structure with climber over
8 Self-contained water feature
9 Stone urn
10 Planting

Mix and match
If you like this garden, but would
prefer a different feature, see pages
250–251 for possible variations.

Key features

Shade structure

If there aren't any naturally shady areas in your garden, make a simple shade structure to sit under in the heat of the day. Plant it with vigorous large-leaved climbers like vines (*Vitis*) or strong-growing varieties with scented flowers for added attraction, such as honeysuckle (*Lonicera*) and jasmine (*Jasminum*). For extra shade and coolness, fix trellis panels between the upright supports.

Stone urn

You can use urns as garden features in several ways. Treat them as pure sculpture and leave them unplanted, tuck them into borders to provide hidden surprises or bring them into the open for a more striking focal point. Or plant them with either masses of bright annuals for a real splash of colour or a dwarf conifer for year-round formality.

Planting in gravel

Sun-loving plants such as *Lavandula*, *Anthemis* and *Verbascum* will really benefit from being mulched with crushed stone or gravel because it reflects the heat and also suppresses competition from weeds. Introduce some different-sized rocks or beach cobbles into your gravel area for greater contrast.

Design feature

Building a water feature

Water features are excellent focal points in any garden. Remember the following and make your feature successful and safe.

Electricity

A safe electric supply with RCD (residual current device, circuit breaker) is essential – get advice from a professional electrician if you are at all uncertain. All outdoor electrical connections must be weatherproof and sold for the purpose. Use armoured cable where possible, and protect plastic or rubber-coated cable within a conduit.

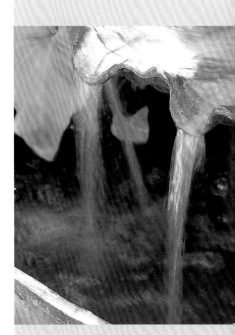

Moving water adds an extra dimension of sound and light.

Reservoirs

Using a large sump for features such as bubble fountains reduces the risk of the water level falling because of evaporation. Nevertheless, remember to check the level every week in hot, dry weather and keep the sump topped up, using soft water if possible.

Make sure that the mesh and reinforcement of 'safe' water features are adequate for the weight of the feature – an urn or millstone, for example – and for any incidental objects, such as boulders or gravel, that will rest on them.

Submersible pumps

Choose a pond pump with slightly more capacity than you actually need. If the flow is too strong, some of it can be diverted back into the sump using a flow adjuster (most pumps are supplied with one). Make sure that the pump is positioned within the sump at a point where you can get easy access for maintenance. Test the pump in a large bucket of water before you install it.

To protect the pump, thoroughly rinse all materials – rocks, stones, gravel and so on – before you place them on the mesh so that sediment isn't washed into the sump. Stand the pump on a piece of flat stone or

Even a small water feature creates a refreshing feel in a hot garden.

a brick so that any coarse silt that falls into the sump isn't sucked into the mechanism.

Use a flexible, corrugated pond hose to pipe the water from its source. Hoses with solid walls are too rigid for such a confined space.

Water safety

Water features can be potentially dangerous to children and you need to decide how you will overcome the dangers before you decide to include water in your garden.

- In a garden divided into two or three separate zones, isolate one area with a fence and gate and put the water feature inside the secure area

- Erect an ornamental rail – wrought iron would look good – around the edge of your pond, making sure that small children can't squeeze through the gaps in the uprights

- Install a 'safe' water feature where the reservoir supplying the fountain or stream is concealed safely below ground

- Cover the pond with black-painted steel mesh that is strong enough to take a child's weight; this is not especially attractive but is a useful solution if you take over a garden and don't want to lose the existing pond

- Build strong mesh into the structure of a new pond so that it sits just below the water level and is barely visible; the depth of water covering the mesh needs to be no more than 2.5cm (1in)

- If you have small children, lay a finer mesh on top of the weight-bearing layer so that their feet can't go through the wire mesh, although this is not a satisfactory arrangement for fish that come to the surface to feed or for floating aquatic plants, such as waterlilies

Planting

The best plants for this garden

There is plenty of soft planting in this garden and a particular emphasis on paler, relaxing colours — white, blues, pinks and yellows. For a really lively, different effect you should introduce some hotter reds, oranges and purples.

Planting key

1 *Campsis radicans* 'Flava'
2 *Iris unguicularis*
3 *Achillea* 'Anthea'
4 *Phlomis fruticosa*
5 *Cistus ladanifer*
6 *Santolina chamaecyparissus*
7 *Lavandula angustifolia* 'Folgate'
8 *Stipa gigantea*
9 *Pittosporum tobira*

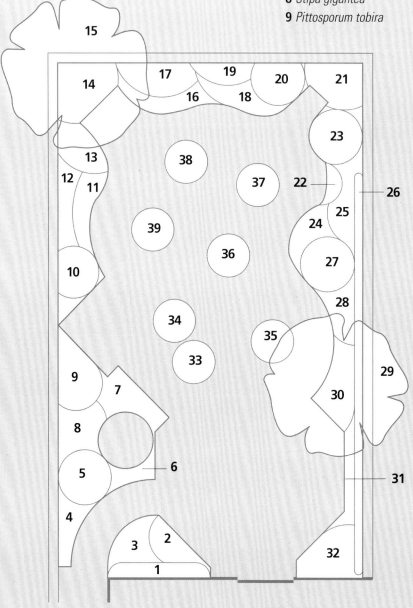

Choosing plants for a hot, dry garden

A reliable way of judging if a plant is suitable for a hot, dry spot is to look at its leaves and stems. One or more of the following characteristics usually means it will suit these particular conditions:

- Very hairy or woolly leaves as on *Stachys byzantina* (lambs' ears) or *Phlomis fruticosa* (Jerusalem sage)
- Grey or silver leaves as on *Lavandula* (lavender) and *Salvia* (sage)
- Thin, wiry stems and small leaves as on *Cytisus* (broom), *Spartium junceum* (Spanish broom) and *Thymus* (thyme)
- Hard or leathery leaves as on *Laurus nobilis* (bay) and *Cistus* (rock rose, sun rose)
- Aromatic foliage as on *Anthemis* and *Rosmarinus* (rosemary)
- Narrow, hard, needle-like foliage as on *Pinus* and *Juniperus*

Looking after the plants

Even sun-loving, drought-tolerant plants need some moisture at their roots, but many species, especially those with silver-grey or woolly foliage, don't appreciate prolonged damp on or immediately beneath their leaves. Low-growing or mat-forming plants seem to be particularly badly affected, and the leaves and sometimes stems are susceptible to rot. Mulching the plants with gravel or stone chippings will allow moisture to drain away quickly and keep the atmosphere around the plants dry. Organic mulches, such as bark and compost, create more humid conditions around the plants. An added benefit of using stone or gravel is that it will reflect heat and light back under the plants.

Planting for a hot, dry bed

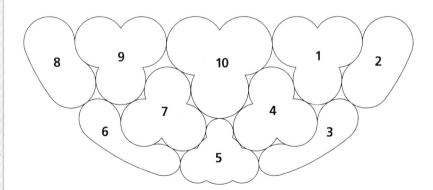

1 *Argyranthemum* 'Jamaica Primrose'
2 *Salvia splendens*
3 *Eschscholzia californica*
4 *Canna* 'Di Bartolo'
5 *Rudbeckia* 'Goldquelle'

6 *Osteospermum juncundum*
7 *Canna* 'Bonfire'
8 *Gaillardia* 'Kobold'
9 *Argyranthemum* 'Peach Cheeks'
10 *Ricinus communis* 'Impala'

In the woods

When broad-leaved trees grow in groups of more than three or four, with their canopies close together or even touching, the combination of reduced light levels, shallow soil and the effects of the tree roots on moisture and nutrient levels in the ground, results in a distinctive type of understorey planting, including shade-tolerant shrubs, bulbs and perennials. These plants have usually grown, flowered and even died away again before the trees are in leaf and compete with them for light and moisture.

What makes this a good woodland garden?

✓ Deciduous trees, including *Betula* (birch) and *Alnus* (alder)
✓ As the trees mature there will be some intermingling of crowns but at the same time there will also be some gaps in the canopy for small amounts of sunlight to penetrate when the trees are in full leaf
✓ The planting beneath the canopy consists of perennials, ferns and bulbs, which will tolerate the cool, shady conditions found there
✓ The planting along the woodland edge contains ornamental shrubs and perennials that are happier in some sun or partial shade

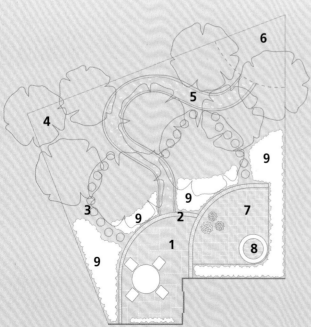

Garden elements key

1 Random rectangular stone patio

2 Brick edging

3 Stepping stone path

4 Deciduous trees

5 Bark-covered, timber-edged path

6 Utility/compost area

7 Brickweave patio
8 Raised pond
9 Planting

Mix and match
If you like this garden, but would prefer a different feature, see pages 250–251 for possible variations.

Woodland planting

You can establish woodland planting beneath almost any deciduous trees or large shrubs, provided you use plants that will either tolerate some shade or complete their life cycle before the trees and shrubs are fully in leaf – such as spring-flowering bulbs. This type of underplanting is an excellent way to make the best use of limited planting space, for example in a tiny town garden.

Timber-edged path

For a quick, relatively inexpensive and easy path, use timber edgings secured in the ground with wooden stakes. They're ideal for natural situations like woodland gardens, especially if they're covered in chipped bark to walk on. They can also be used to make very formal paths with straight edges and corners, and infilled with loose stone chippings or binding gravel. Don't forget to ensure that any wood you use is treated against rot and decay.

Palisade fence

The palisade-style fence – with gaps between individual boards or palisades – is a sympathetic design that allows light through and is not visually 'solid'. In an informal or natural setting, it's best to leave the palisades unstained so that they weather naturally and are more in keeping with their surroundings. Alternatively, stain them in strong colours to match pergolas or arches elsewhere in the garden.

Bark path

A timber-edged bark path is an ideal complement to the natural effect of the woodland. Although it is relatively straightforward to build, the tight curves may require some extra skill and knowledge.

Perennials that thrive in partial shade are ideal for underplanting woodland areas.

You will need

Lengths of pressure-treated softwood edging boards, about
   1.5cm (¾in) by not less than 10cm (4in) deep
Pressure-treated softwood stakes – 3.8–5cm (1½–2in)
   square by at least 30cm (12in) long (longer if the
   ground is soft)
6.5cm (2½in) flat-headed, galvanized nails
Proprietary mulching fabric and pegs to secure it
Ornamental bark chippings

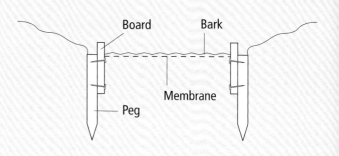

Step by step

1 Dig a shallow trench along both sides of the selected
route, making the trenches deep enough to accommodate
the edging board.

2 Long boards are easier to bend than short ones, and
those between 4.6 and 5.4m (15 and 17ft) are both easy
to bend and manoeuvrable. If you are using short boards,
join two together by nailing a short section, about 35cm
(14in) long, to act as a splint between them.

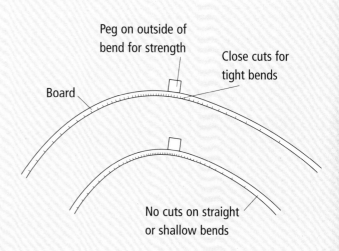

3 Partially drive in stakes along both sides of the path
1–2m (3–6ft) apart. They need to be far enough apart to
keep the boards secure.

4 Lay a board in the trench, using the stakes to help keep
it in position. If you are using thicker boards you may not
be able to achieve a tight enough bend, so relieve the
compression on the inside of the bend by sawing parallel
grooves, to a depth no more than one-third the thickness
of the board. For really tight bends, the grooves may need
to be as close as 1cm (½in) apart. You can vary the amount
of curve along a board by gradually increasing or
decreasing the spaces between the grooves.

5 Once the board is prepared, brush one or two coats of
preservative on the new saw cuts to protect the wood and
maintain its durability.

6 Lay the board back in the trench, moving stakes as
necessary to push it in or out to suit the line.

7 Drive in the stakes to just below the top edge of the
board and secure with at least two of the 6.5cm (2½in) nails.

8 Continue along the path, using the splint method (see
step 2) to connect successive boards where necessary.

9 On really sharp bends place extra stakes on the outer
edge to provide additional resistance against any outward
movement.

10 Remove soil from the path to produce a level base. Cut
the fabric to shape and peg it down.

11 Spread bark over the fabric to a depth of at least 3cm
(1¼in), leaving a gap of about 2.5cm (1in) between the
top of the board and the surface of the bark.

Planting

14

24

26

28

The best plants for this garden

The planting scheme is based on a gradual transition that begins with ornamental plants near the house, progresses through less ornamental plants (though still cultivated varieties) at the woodland edge and ends with a 'natural' effect woodland floor. The plant colours and textures are subtly muted, with just a few deliberate hotspots to lift the garden. The transitional zone at the woodland edge acts as a link between the patio and the woodland area proper, giving views into the woodland when it is at its peak in spring. As the early flowering peak passes, the planting around the patio becomes dominant for the remainder of the season.

1 *Miscanthus sinensis* 'Variegatus'
2 *Geranium wallichianum* 'Buxton's Variety'
3 *Phlox paniculata* 'Prince of Orange'
4 *Hypericum* 'Hidcote'
5 *Lupinus* 'Noble Maiden'
6 *Astilbe* 'Sprite'
7 *Cornus alba* 'Elegantissima'
8 *Tellima grandiflora* Rubra Group
9 *Rhododendron* 'Berryrose' (azalea)
10 *Pulmonaria longifolia*
11 *Aconitum* 'Bressingham Spire'

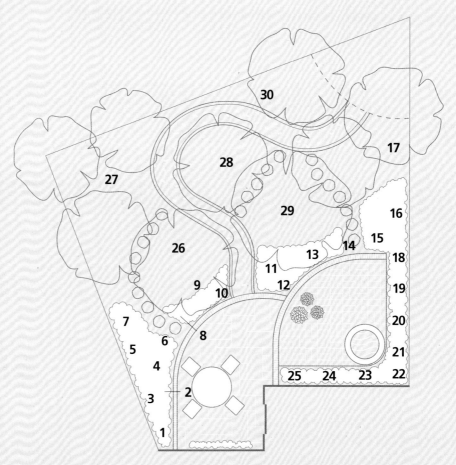

12 *Persicaria affinis* 'Superba'
13 *Taxus baccata* 'Semperaurea'
14 *Geranium sylvaticum* 'Album'
15 *Pieris formosa* var. *forrestii*
16 *Digitalis purpurea* Excelsior Group
17 *Rhododendron ponticum* 'Variegatum'
18 *Astilboides tabularis*
19 *Campanula persicifolia*
20 *Aruncus dioicus*
21 *Hosta* 'Halcyon'
22 *Osmanthus delavayi*
23 *Iris foetidissima* 'Variegata'
24 *Rudbeckia fulgida* var. *sullivantii* 'Goldsturm'
25 *Nerine bowdenii*
26 Mixed understorey of *Cornus canadensis, Narcissus* 'February Gold' and 'Waldsteinia ternata'
27 Mixed understorey of *Dryopteris erythrosora, Hyacinthoides non-scripta* and *Lamium galeobdolon* subsp. *montanum* 'Florentinum'
28 Mixed understorey of *Anemone nemorosa, Hyacinthoides non-scripta* and *Narcissus* 'February Gold'
29 Mixed understorey of *Galanthus nivalis, Polygonatum multiflorum* and *Primula vulgaris*
30 Mixed understorey of *Ajuga reptans* 'Purpurea', *Hyacinthoides non-scripta* and *Matteuccia struthiopteris*

Creating a mini-woodland border

If you have only a tiny garden, you can still create a woodland effect as long as you have an area in your garden that is not in the sun all day or, at least, not when it is at its hottest. The canopy is represented by an open-branched deciduous shrub with an understorey of compact, low perennials and ornamental ferns combined with dwarf winter- and spring-flowering bulbs.

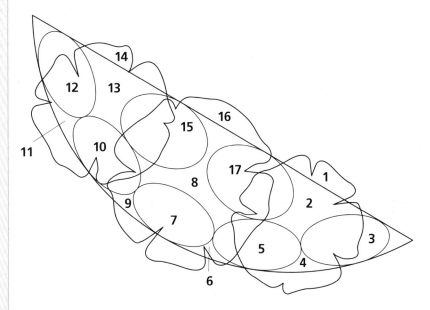

1 *Cornus alba* 'Kesselringii'
2 *Eranthis hyemalis*
3 *Athyrium nipponicum* var. *pictum*
4 *Galanthus nivalis*
5 *Pulmonaria longifolia*
6 *Narcissus jonquilla*
7 *Tiarella cordifolia*
8 *Crocus* large-flowered blue cvs.
9 *Narcissus jonquilla*
10 *Epimedium* x *rubrum*
11 *Galathus nivalis*
12 *Brunnera macrophylla*
13 *Eranthis hyemalis*
14 *Hydrangea paniculata* 'Tardiva'
15 *Blechnum spicant*
16 *Hibiscus syriacus* 'Oiseau Bleu'
17 *Geranium phaeum* 'Album'

Kitchen garden

There is nothing to compare with freshly picked, home-grown vegetables, fruits and salad crops. With careful planning and a little imagination, even a small garden can have space for a productive plot without sacrificing or radically affecting the other aspects of garden design that you would expect to find.

What makes this a good kitchen garden?

✓ An attractive layout with plenty of interesting features
✓ Lots of lawn and patio space as well as a play area
✓ An easy-to-build and relatively economical scheme
✓ Generous areas for growing crops
✓ The efficient use of all available space
✓ A greenhouse to maximize crop production
✓ Year-round structure in the form of trees, shrubby herbs and other garden features
✓ Appeal to a wide range of gardeners

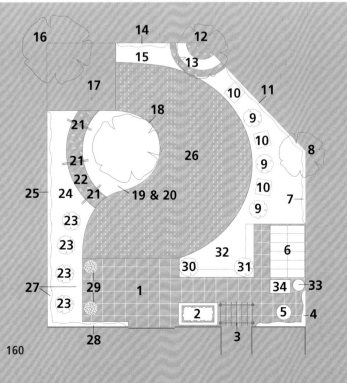

Garden elements key

1 Patio
2 Raised bed for small herbs
3 Pergola with grape vine
4 Trellis for melons
5 Barbecue area
6 Greenhouse
7 Climbing berries on fence
8 *Laurus nobilis* (bay laurel)
9 Columnar apples, e.g. 'Minarette'

10 Obelisks for sweet peas or climbing beans
11 Climbing beans on fence
12 Fig in restricted planting pocket
13 Bench seat on gravel
14 Fan-trained fruit trees on fence, e.g. morello cherry
15 Raspberries in contained bed

16 'Family' pear tree
17 Play area
18 Plum tree
19 Courgettes, marrows
20 Shady herb area –
   mint, lemon balm,
   parsley
21 Beans, nasturtiums
   on arches
22 Bark path
23 Standard currants
   (red, white),
   gooseberries
24 Potatoes
25 Quince and thornless
   blackberries on fence

26 Lawn
27 Tomatoes, capsicums
   and aubergines in
   hot corner
28 Fan-trained
   nectarine, apricot or
   peach
29 Containers for
   seasonal interest
30 Golden bay laurel
   (*Laurus nobilis*
   'Aurea')
31 Rosemary
32 Larger herbs
33 Water butt
34 Coldframe

Mix and match

If you like this garden, but would prefer a different feature, see pages 250–251 for possible variations.

Key features

'Family' pear tree

'Family' fruit trees are an ideal way to grow a selection of top fruit in a relatively small space. Each tree consists of two or three varieties of apple or pear grafted onto a single stem. These varieties are carefully selected by the nursery to give the cross-pollination essential for the best crop, and in many cases they will ripen at different times to give a long season of availability.

Golden bay laurel

The golden bay laurel is one of those plants that can be used for many different purposes. Although its role in a kitchen garden is primarily as a culinary herb it is an excellent evergreen shrub for a sunny, sheltered spot. It makes an excellent subject for topiary – simple shapes such as cones, spheres or mopheads are most effective – or can be grown as a formal hedge.

Grape vine on pergola

In hotter climates and situations, grape vines can be grown not only to provide welcome shade but also as a source of delicious fruit for eating or – if you're ambitious – a bottle or two of home-made wine. Cooler conditions will mean you need to grow your vine in an unheated greenhouse if you want usable fruit or you could just use the young, tender leaves for making your own delicious dolmades.

Raised herb bed

A raised herb bed is a convenient way of growing herbs, especially smaller types, such as thyme. You can easily build one in a sunny spot where you might not be able to, or want to, plant directly into the soil. Raised beds are easy to maintain and you fill them with a top-quality growing medium, which overcomes the problem of impoverished soil in other areas of the garden. In addition, a raised bed is an attractive feature in its own right, and at the right height can double up as a seat. You could convert it to a raised water feature or different style of planting, perhaps a scree garden, if you get tired of growing herbs.

A low willow hurdle makes an attractive alternative to a brick or wooden raised bed.

You will need

Clean, good quality railway sleepers or other heavy timbers that have been treated with preservative
Galvanized, drilled angle brackets and long screws (optional)
Heavy-duty polythene
Gravel or stone chippings
Proprietary woven or spun mulching fabric
Growing medium
Herbs

Step by step

1 Cut the timbers to size and lay them wide-face down in the required location, adding one or two more layers until you reach the desired height for your bed.

2 Secure the timbers with an angle bracket screwed to the inside of each corner.

3 Cut the polythene to size and fit it around the inside face of the sleeper wall. This will both prevent soil from washing through the gaps and extend the life of the timbers by protecting them from contact with the soil.

4 Put a layer of gravel or stone chippings, 2.5–5cm (1–2in) deep, in the bottom and cover with a piece of mulching fabric cut to fit.

5 Add the growing medium or soil mix, firming it down gently as you go.

6 Allow time for the soil level to settle, top up with more as necessary and plant the herbs.

7 Finish off the herb bed with a layer of pebbles, shingle or gravel as an ornamental mulch.

Planting the raised herb bed

1 *Thymus doefleri* 'Bressingham'
2 *Rosmarinus officinalis* 'Severn Sea'
3 *Origanum vulgare* 'Thumble's Variety'
4 *Thymus vulgaris* 'Silver Posie'
5 *Allium senescens* subsp. *montanum* var. *glaucum*
6 *Salvia officinalis* 'Tricolor'
7 *Salvia officinalis* 'Icterina'
8 *Salvia officinalis* 'Purpurascens'
9 *Allium schoenoprasum* 'Forescate'
10 *Thymus* 'Porlock'
11 *Origanum laevigatum* 'Herrenhausen'
12 *Rosmarinus officinalis* 'Severn Sea'
13 *Thymus pulegiodes* 'Aureus'

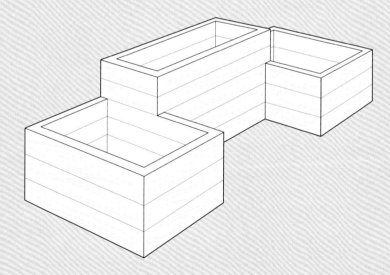

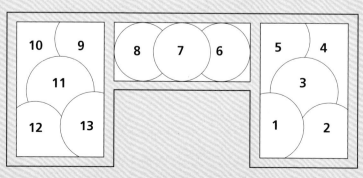

Planting

1

8

10

15

The best plants for this garden

The aim is to produce the maximum amount of edible produce – vegetables, salads, fruits or herbs – from the available space, but the overall effect and appearance should not be overlooked. Woody plants provide a framework, while the annuals – salad crops and vegetables – are planted between in random, informal drifts in much the same way as a herbaceous border, to provide movement and rhythm by avoiding straight lines and rows.

In this type of kitchen garden it is especially important to take sun and shade into account when you position plants. Capsicums and aubergines, for example, are planted in the hottest, sunniest corner, but climbing beans and lettuce will do better against a slightly cooler fence, away from the heat of the day.

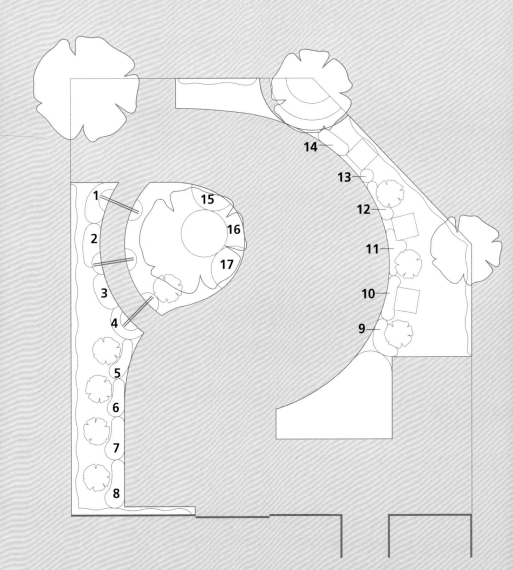

Add interest to your winter vegetable garden by choosing colourful varieties, such as these wonderful purplish-red Brussels sprouts (*Brassica oleracea*).

Planting key (perennials)

1 *Astilbe* 'Deutschland'
2 *Campanula persicifolia*
3 *Iris sibirica* 'Dreaming Yellow'
4 *Geranium renardii*
5 *Dianthus* 'Marshmallow'
6 *Potentilla* x *tonguei*
7 *Dicentra* 'Adrian Bloom'
8 *Lavandula angustifolia* 'Hidcote'
9 *Solidago* 'Cloth of Gold'
10 *Veronica gentianoides*
11 *Tradescantia* Andersoniana Group 'Karminglut'
12 *Nepeta* x *faassenii*
13 *Iris* 'Tinkerbell' (dwarf bearded)
14 *Coreopsis rosea* 'American Dream'
15 *Brunnera macrophylla* 'Dawson's White'
16 *Astilbe* 'Sprite'
17 *Bergenia* 'Abendglut'

Winter interest

The emphasis in a kitchen garden is on providing fresh fruit, vegetables, salads and herbs, and it's inevitable that the area will look its best from mid-spring to autumn. Here's how to make sure you have something of interest in the dormant winter months.

- Plant ornamental quinces, such as *Chaenomeles* x *superba* 'Crimson and Gold' or *C.* x *superba* 'Pink Lady', which will produce fruits, albeit not so large or abundantly as a cultivated form of *Cydonia*, and will also bear masses of pink or red flowers in late winter to early spring

- Plant several containers with a selection of spring bulbs, concentrating your choice on the earliest species, such as *Galanthus nivalis* (snowdrop), crocuses and early *Narcissus* cvs., sinking them into the beds as temporary displays; lift them as soon as they have finished flowering and store them out of the way, ready to re-pot for next year

- Put extra containers on the patio with evergreen and early flowering shrubs – skimmias, hebes, *Erica* (heath) and *Euonymus* – to give foreground interest

- Plant *Primula* cvs. (polyanthus) in autumn for late winter and spring flowering and leave them in place, planting your new crops of salads and vegetables around them until they're well advanced; the polyanthus will enjoy the partial shade and can then be lifted, divided and put into small containers ready to plant again next autumn

- Include winter cabbages, cauliflowers and curly kale in your crop rotation to give structure and greenery all winter

- Plant ornamental cabbages, which do not actually grow in the winter so you must put out strong plants in early autumn; lift and discard them in spring as you need the space for other plants

- Grow a few plants of ornamental sweetcorn with different colours of kernel and leave some on the plants to dry to give you a winter ornament; you might need to support the dead main stalk with a cane

Mediterranean

The warm climate and typical geology of many Mediterranean regions have resulted in an instantly recognizable style of garden. To re-create such a garden in a different type of climate requires an understanding of the features that make it so distinctive – the warm, natural materials, the bright plants and careful use of water – and the informal way in which they are put together.

What makes this a good Mediterranean-style garden?

✓ Lots of warm, bright Mediterranean colours – white walls, terracotta and blue tiles and cream-coloured stone
✓ A simple, functional design in which the plants, materials and ornaments provide the real interest
✓ Plants with spiky foliage and bright, bold flowers
✓ A cooling water feature for hot sunny days
✓ Shady areas for shelter during the heat of the day

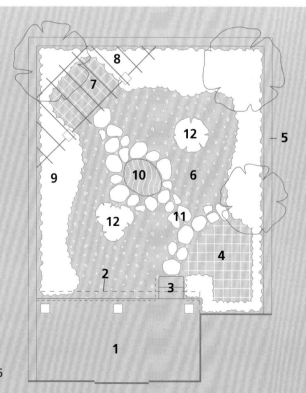

Garden elements key

1 Raised shade terrace and loggia
2 Railing
3 Step up to shade terrace
4 Tiled sun terrace
5 White-painted and pantiled garden wall
6 Limestone chippings
7 Tiled shade area
8 Wooden overhead shade structure

Mix and match

If you like this garden, but would prefer a different feature, see pages 250–251 for possible variations.

Key features

Wall pots

Make bright displays of annuals, such as scarlet pelargoniums, in pots mounted on white or pale-coloured walls, to add a Mediterranean feel to a garden. Use the sunniest walls where the annuals will thrive best. If your walls are natural stone or brick, think about giving them a pale colourwash to lighten them up.

Shade trees

In a hot, dry climate natural shade trees are predominantly evergreen to give year-round protection from the sun. Use varieties that respond well to pruning where space is limited. In a more temperate climate shade is better achieved with deciduous trees, which will be leafless in winter when the sun is low and weak, and the need for shade is gone.

Tender plants in containers

Add to the Mediterranean appearance of your garden by planting exotic but frost-prone varieties of plants in terracotta containers. Treat them as annuals and bring them into a protected area as soon as temperatures start to drop. As they are in containers, you can change your planting scheme each year for variety, and also move them around whenever you feel like a change.

Ornamental gravel area

For a modest outlay and little effort you can create a striking feature using simple, readily available materials to form a platform or plinth on which you can place an ornamental feature, such as a statue or container.

A simple combination of gravel and stone paving makes an ideal setting for a feature container.

You will need

Ornamental edging stones, such as
  barley twist, scalloped or plain
Fine soil
Sand and cement (optional)
Round gravel
Mulching fabric
A statue, sculpture or other feature

Step by step

1 Mark out a square, 1–1.2m (3–4ft)
wide and across, with one edge
against your lawn and the rest of it
sitting inside the border.

2 Dig a narrow trench around the
square and place the edging stones
in it, checking for levels as you go.
Use fine soil to adjust them for height
and level. For a more permanent
arrangement, bed them in with
cement/sand mortar.

3 Backfill any remaining space with
fine soil and firm it down.

4 Level the soil within the square and
cover with the fabric.

5 Place the chosen feature in the
centre and cover the rest of the fabric
with gravel.

How to minimize water loss

Some containers, particularly unglazed terracotta, are porous and in hot
weather lose a lot of moisture through the sides as well as through the
leaves of the plant. This means that the plant dries out faster than is
desirable and could be at risk unless you are able to water it frequently.

• Paint the inside of the container with bitumastic paint or a proprietary
  pond sealant to make it waterproof

• Line the containers with polythene before filling with growing medium
  – don't forget to make a drainage hole in the bottom

• Mix moisture-retaining gel (sold as dry crystals) with your growing
  medium, following the manufacturer's directions about quantity
  because too much gel can make the compost wet and soggy, resulting
  in badly rooted and unstable plants

• Position the container so that it is shaded from the heat of the sun by
  another plant or container or stand it at the side of a raised bed so
  that the plant itself remains in the sun

Stone chippings or gravel make an attractive mulch for all types of container
planting, including this narcissus.

Planting

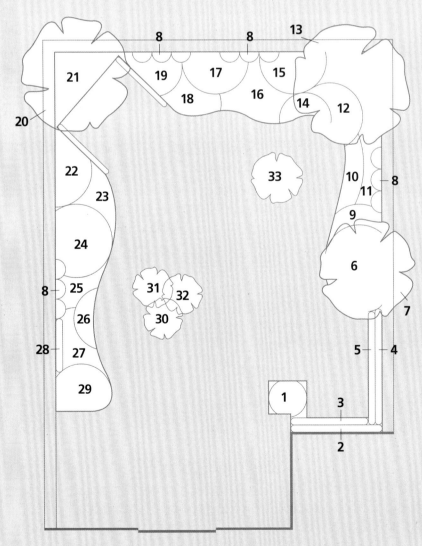

The best plants for this garden

Although the planting is designed to give the appearance of a Mediterranean setting, the plants are also suitable for more temperate climates. Herbs are used as much for their aromatic qualities as for their appearance, while other plants, such as hibiscus and *Campsis*, have rather exotic, brightly coloured flowers. Plants that are not fully hardy have been used to add to the effect and these are grown in containers so that they can be moved into a sheltered spot in the winter if necessary.

Planting key

1 *Yucca flaccida* 'Golden Sword'
2 *Eccremocarpus scaber* (on wall)
3 *Lavandula stoechas* (at base of wall)
4 *Solanum laxum* (on wall)
5 *Crocosmia* 'Firebird' (at base of wall)
6 *Myrtus communis*
7 *Thymus vulgaris*
8 *Pelargonium* red cv. (in pots on wall)

9 *Cichorium intybus*

10 *Helianthemum* 'Henfield Brilliant'

11 *Gladiolus communis* subsp. *byzantinus*

12 *Helleborus argutifolius*

13 *Arbutus unedo*

14 *Origanum laevigatum*

15 *Foeniculum vulgare* 'Giant Bronze'

16 *Salvia officinalis* 'Tricolor'

17 *Hibiscus syriacus* 'Hamabo'

18 *Agapanthus campanulatus*

19 *Verbascum* Cotswold Group 'Pink Domino'

20 *Laurus nobilis*

21 *Vitis* 'Brant' (on shade structure)

22 *Acanthus spinosus*

23 *Dahlia* 'Bishop of Llandaff'

24 *Cordyline australis* 'Torbay Dazzler'

25 *Asphodeline lutea*

26 *Osteospermum ecklonis*

27 *Iris pallida* 'Variegata'

28 *Campsis radicans* f. *flava* (on wall)

29 *Cistus ladanifer*

30 *Brugmansia* cv. (in pot)

31 *Agave americana* 'Variegata' (in pot)

32 *Aloysia triphylla* (in pot)

33 *Citrus limon* (in pot)

Alternative planting for a Mediterranean climate

1 *Abutilon vitifolium*

2 *Eryngium* x *tripartitum*

3 *Bougainvillea spectabilis*

4 *Pelargonium* red cv.

5 *Lavandula stoechas*

6 *Citrus sinensis*

7 *Arundo donax* var. *versicolor*

8 *Lantana camara* white cv.

9 *Araucaria heterophylla*

10 *Cistus albidus*

11 *Punica granatum*

12 *Teucrium creticum*

13 *Dictamnus albus*

14 *Verbascum longifolium*

15 *Olea europaea*

16 *Linum narbonense*

17 *Agapanthus* Headbourne hybrids

18 *Polygonatum* x *hybridum*

19 *Trachycarpus fortunei*

20 *Lantana camara* rose pink cv.

21 *Plumbago auriculata*

22 *Tecoma capensis*

23 *Nerium oleander*

24 x *Citrofortunella microcarpa* (calamondin orange)

25 *Aloe vera*

26 *Myrtus communis* subsp. *tarentina*

27 *Cordyline australis* 'Albertii'

28 *Acanthus mollis* Latifolius Group

A Mediterranean corner

Plants naturally at home in a Mediterranean climate – *Citrus* spp., *Bougainvillea*, *Nerium oleander*, *Hibiscus rosa-sinensis*, verbena, palms and *Olea europaea* (olive) – will need protection in a cooler climate, so grow them in pots and move them to a sheltered position in winter. Some hardier plants that will create a similar effect include:

- Woody herbs and other plants with aromatic foliage, such as lavender and thyme
- Perennials and shrubs that like hot, dry conditions, such as *Acanthus*, *Agapanthus*, *Teucrium*, *Ballota* and *Helianthemum* (rock rose, sun rose)
- Plants with bold, bright flowers, such as achilleas, crocosmias, pelargoniums (annual cvs.), *Tropaeolum* (annual nasturtium) and *Malva*
- Plants with bold, spiky foliage, such as yuccas, irises, cordylines, phormiums, junipers and cypresses

Best shrubs for a Mediterranean look

- *Cistus* x *hybridus* (rock rose, sun rose)
- *Cytisus battandieri* (pineapple broom)
- *Fremontodendron californicum* (flannel bush)
- *Genista aetnensis* (Mount Etna broom)
- *Hibiscus syriacus*
- *Lavandula* cvs.
- *Lavatera olbia*
- *Rosmarinus officinalis*
- *Teucrium fruticans* (shrubby germander)
- *Yucca gloriosa* (Spanish dagger)

In the jungle

In a large garden you can create different spaces by using mixed borders to both screen and frame views. In a small garden, space for subdividing planting is limited unless you adopt a tiered approach, with lots of tall planting underplanted with smaller plants that thrive in the shady conditions below. The result is a jungle-like effect, particularly if you can select plants with bold, dramatic foliage or exotic flowers.

What makes this a good jungle garden?

✓ Although it occupies a small plot, the garden is divided into three distinct spaces by generous, tall planting
✓ Tall shrubs and trees create a canopy underplanted with smaller species
✓ Different areas of light and shade mimic the feel of a jungle or forest
✓ The enclosing white weatherboarding accentuates the shady pockets and picks out the foliage of individual plants
✓ Natural materials used in the hard landscaping are in sympathy with the planting

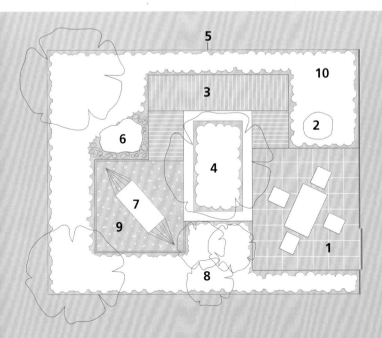

Garden elements key

1 Flagstone patio
2 Large feature rock
3 Raised timber deck walkway
4 Sleeper-edged raised bed
5 White weather-boarded boundary fence

6 Water feature

7 Free-standing hammock

8 Bamboo

9 Timber-edged gravel area

10 'Jungle' planting

Mix and match

If you like this garden, but would prefer a different feature, see pages 250–251 for possible variations.

Key features

Sleeper edging

Heavy timbers, such as old railway sleepers, are a really cheap and easy way to make a low raised bed. You can also use other heavy wooden beams provided they are durable. Sometimes, though, they can exude sticky resin or bitumen, so if you wanted to sit on the edge of your sleeper bed, nail or screw some new, clean and smooth boards on top to act as a coping and stain them with a suitable preservative to tone it down.

Weatherboard fence

When you're using plants with strong, bold foliage shapes, make the background against which they're seen white or very light. Any variations in light and shade among the plants will stand out much more obviously than if the wall or fence behind was very dark. By contrast, if your planting is very bright, for example a yellow themed border, you could paint your fence a very dark colour to contrast.

Hammock

Traditionally you needed two good strong trees at the optimum distance apart before you could put up a hammock. Nowadays, you can buy free-standing hammocks that can be placed wherever you like – in the shade on a very hot day, or maybe somewhere to catch the last gentle warmth of late afternoon sun.

Space dividers

Dividing a garden, even a small one, into two or more distinct spaces adds greatly to its character and charm. What you use to divide the space and how you use it can vary according to your own needs and how you want the garden to look.

This fence creates a perforated screen that softens the boundary of the garden.

Formal, solid dividers

These dividers usually take the form of a fence or wall, which makes an obvious barrier or boundary. Unless you intend to make a deliberate feature of them, they will require some form of softening with wall shrubs or climbers. The advantage is that you have an instant effect and can purposely use them to create shade on the side away from the sun.

Open or perforated screens

These are most likely to be built from some sort of trellis-work. Lightweight trellis or wrought iron will only give a hint of a divider, while much heavier wooden designs can look quite dense. Screens like these are useful if you don't want a completely solid effect, and they can be supplemented with climbers for extra softening yet still allow some light and limited views through.

Hedges

Hedges do not provide an instant barrier as walls, fences or trellis do, but they are softer in colour and texture. You can make them formal, by using clipped yew, or informal, by using flowering shrubs such as roses. Size can also vary. To block and separate a space completely a 1.8m (6ft) conifer hedge would be useful, but if you want to suggest a division of space, you could plant a low hedge of *Hebe albicans* or lavender.

Planting

The least formal way to divide space is with a mixed border of trees, shrubs, grasses and perennials. To create a solid screen you could have a backbone of tall shrubs with one or two trees interplanted, with some perennials in front for colour. For a more open 'screen', you could mix the plants in size to allow brief or restricted views through to the other side.

This stunning array of foliage provides a dense, 'jungle-like' screen that hides the rest of the garden from view.

Planting

The best plants for this garden

The planting has been selected to create a rather exotic, luxuriant feel to the garden, and the different species have been chosen with this in mind. Most are reasonably hardy, however, and the relatively mild microclimate encountered in towns and cities, resulting from the hard, heat-retaining surfaces, will help the plants grow to their full potential.

Planting key

1 *Romneya coulteri*
2 *Ligularia* 'The Rocket'
3 *Phyllostachys aureosulcata* f. *spectabilis*
4 *Photinia serratifolia*
5 *Sorbaria arborea*
6 *Astilboides tabularis*
7 *Embothrium coccineum* Lanceolatum Group
8 *Fatsia japonica* 'Variegata'
9 *Osmunda regalis*
10 *Hydrangea serrata* 'Grayswood'
11 *Idesia polycarpa*
12 *Sasa veitchii*
13 *Paeonia delavayi* var. *ludlowii*
14 *Fargesia nitida*
15 *Inula racemosa*
16 *Trachycarpus fortunei*
17 *Abutilon vitifolium*
18 *Melianthus major*
19 *Phormium* 'Sundowner'
20 *Hakonechloa macra* 'Aureola'
21 *Clerodendrum bungei*

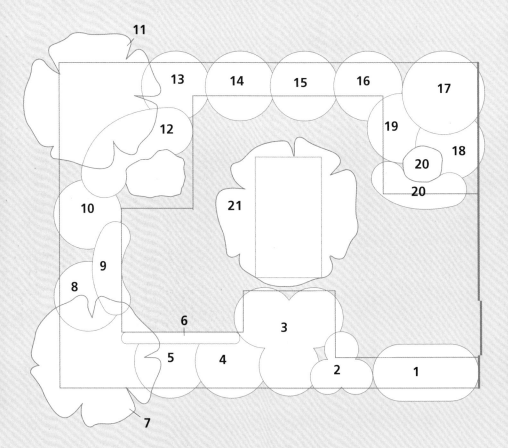

Creating a planting screen

Natural screens consisting of planting can be divided into two types: solid and 'open'. Solid screens that eventually make solid visual barriers can be used to screen an ugly outbuilding or maybe to create an area of privacy. 'Open' screens can be used to soften views without blocking them or just to give a suggestion of division or definition to a space.

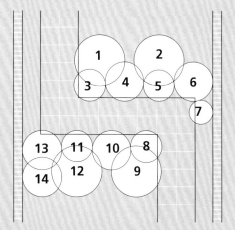

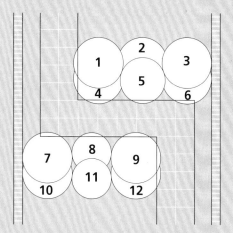

A solid planting screen

1 *Ligustrum ovalifolium* 'Argentum'
2 *Viburnum* x *bodnantense* 'Dawn'
3 *Spiraea japonica* 'Goldflame'
4 *Photinia* x *fraseri* 'Birmingham '
5 *Berberis thunbergii* f. *atropurpurea* 'Rose Glow'
6 *Mahonia japonica*
7 *Hebe* 'Great Orme'
8 *Potentilla fruticosa* 'Bewerley Surprise'
9 *Buddleja lindleyana*
10 *Ribes sanguineum* 'King Edward'
11 *Mahonia aquifolium*
12 *Pyracantha* 'Mohave'
13 *Kerria japonica* 'Pleniflora'
14 *Fargesia nitida* 'Nymphenburg'

An 'open' planting screen

1 *Buddleja* 'Pink Delight'
2 *Skimmia japonica* 'Rubella'
3 *Forsythia* x *intermedia* 'Arnold Giant'
4 *Viburnum davidii*
5 *Aronia arbutifolia* 'Erecta'
6 *Caryopteris* x *clandonensis* 'Worcester Gold'
7 *Leycestria formosa*
8 *Potentilla fruticosa* 'Tilford Cream'
9 *Osmanthus* x *burkwoodii*
10 *Prunus laurocerasus* 'Otto Luyken'
11 *Miscanthus sinensis* 'Gracillimus'
12 *Lavandula* x *intermedia* 'Grappenhall'

Contemporary urbanscape

In towns and cities the challenge can be to create the feeling of an open, airy space in a garden that is surrounded by walls and fences and overlooked by neighbouring houses. This design scheme provides an up-to-date solution to the problem, creating private sitting areas and a modern selection of easy-to-grow plants.

What makes this a good contemporary urbanscape?

✓ Generous paved areas, crisply edged and detailed
✓ A garden divided into three separate and distinct areas
✓ Contemporary layout, ornaments and garden furniture
✓ A private and enclosed hot tub
✓ Boundary walls softened by planting
✓ Extremely low maintenance

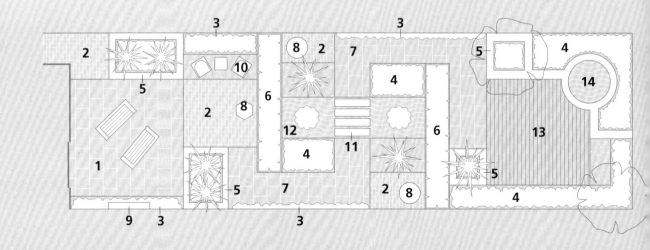

Garden elements key

1 Patio
2 Brick paving
3 Wall planting
4 Beds and borders
5 Raised bed with built-in seat
6 Bamboo screen
7 Concrete flag paving
8 Modern sculptures
9 Modern wall sculpture
10 Fibreglass/GRP chairs and table
11 Stepping stone bridge
12 Formal 'canal' water feature
13 Decking
14 Hot tub

Mix and match

If you like this garden, but would prefer a different feature, see pages 250–251 for possible variations.

Key features

Hot tub and deck

The tub is sited in a sheltered, private part of the garden, so that you can relax at leisure. Decking next to hot tubs and other water activities is comfortable on the feet and pleasant to lie around on, but make sure it can dry out well and doesn't become slippery; where possible, site decking in a sunny position. Alternatively, use smooth (but non-slip) concrete paving flags or hard bricks, which will absorb the heat of the sun during the day and gently release it later on.

Raised beds

Building one or more raised beds is an excellent way of introducing changes of level in a flat garden. Make one or more of the walls wide enough and high enough to act as a seat, and use brick, stone or concrete to sit on. If you don't want to use cushions, fix smooth wooden slats to the top to match the hot tub.

Sculptures

Use sculptures and other ornaments to add the finishing touches to your garden. A contemporary design will need modern features, made of concrete, stainless steel or even plastic or of natural materials, such as stone and wood, sculpted and polished into abstract, organic forms.

The garden by night

Gardens need not be daytime-only places. With a little bit of investment and imagination you can fit out your garden with lights and completely transform it.

Low-voltage systems could be installed, especially if there are children, but they require individual transformers, which need to be concealed, or ones that are built into the lighting unit, which can add to the cost. Mains voltage systems are less suitable where there are children but are generally more versatile, especially in large gardens.

The most effective garden lights are those that illuminate the object or space being viewed, not the viewer.

Subtle, indirect garden lighting is often more effective than overhead, direct lighting.

Avoid large, powerful floodlights, which are bright and can swamp a large area with light and make everything appear flat and featureless. Use several less powerful units spread out to create several smaller, downward-pointing, overlapping pools of light.

Uplighting

Fix wider-angled lights into the ground underneath pointing up into the canopy of trees to reveal them in a completely different way from the daytime.

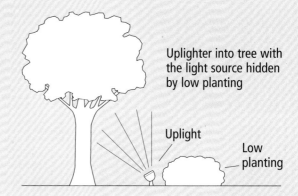

Uplighter into tree with the light source hidden by low planting

Uplight

Low planting

Backlighting

A backlighter is ideal for putting behind plants, casting shadows and showing stems and foliage in silhouette against a pale background, such as a white-painted wall or golden evergreen.

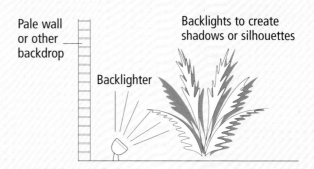

Pale wall or other backdrop

Backlights to create shadows or silhouettes

Backlighter

Spotlighting

Use spotlights to pick out individual features — a wall sculpture, a particular plant or an ornament — using side lighting to emphasize the relief shapes.

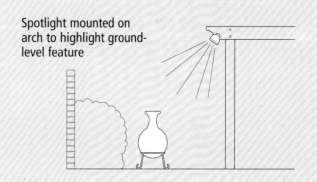

Spotlight mounted on arch to highlight ground-level feature

Downlighting

Low, hooded lights on short spikes or poles can be used to cast light down on a path or steps for safety and to create a gentle mood.

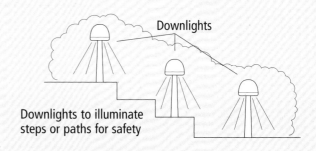

Downlights

Downlights to illuminate steps or paths for safety

Planting

The best plants for this garden

The garden contains plenty of evergreen species for year-round effect and low maintenance. The emphasis is on foliage and shape, and there are several spiky-leaved and upright species. Narrow screens of living bamboo take the place of walls and fences to divide up the garden.

Planting key

1 *Carpinus betulus* 'Fastigiata'
2 *Taxus cuspidata* 'Straight Hedge'
3 *Vinca minor* 'Argenteovariegata' (underplanted against yew hedge)
4 *Juniperus* x *pfitzeriana* 'Gold Coast'
5 *Fargesia murieliae* 'Simba'
6 *Phormium tenax* Purpureum Group
7 *Stipa gigantea*
8 *Juncus* 'Silver Spears'
9 *Festuca glauca* 'Azurit'

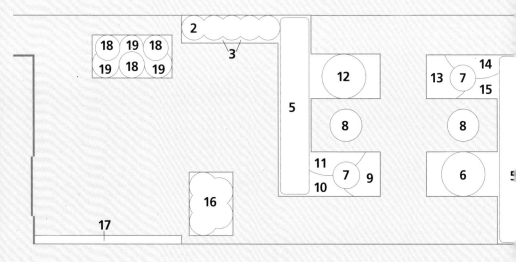

10 *Acorus gramineus* 'Ogon'
11 *Molinia caerulea* subsp. *caerulea* 'Variegata'
12 *Phormium tenax* 'Variegatum'
13 *Luzula sylvatica* 'Marginata'
14 *Carex oshimensis* 'Evergold'
15 *Nassella trichotoma*
16 *Yucca flaccida* 'Golden Sword'
17 *Iris graminea*
18 *Juniperus chinensis* 'Aurea'
19 *Rubus* 'Betty Ashburner'
20 *Cotoneaster congestus*
21 *Laurus nobilis* 'Aureus'
22 *Cornus alba* 'Kesselringii'
23 *Carpinus betulus* 'Fastigiata'

Some species of bamboo make excellent screens or hedges if you are looking for an alternative to the neat formality of tightly clipped *Taxus baccata* (yew) and the informality of a shrubby hedge of roses.

Living bamboo screens

There are bamboos to suit almost all extremes of sun and shade. Sun for at least part of the day is best for most species, but they will grow in full sun as long as the soil is moisture retentive. Your choice will depend on the ultimate height you require. Remember that you cannot take the top off bamboo as you can with a hedge of a plant such as beech, hawthorn or yew, so you must choose a variety that won't grow taller than your ideal height. Remember, too, that some bamboos spread rapidly, so only use these where you can restrict their run. Otherwise, choose varieties that grow by producing a slowly expanding central clump or crown.

Best bamboos for hedging

- *Fargesia dracocephala* (clump-forming) – 2.4m (8ft) or more tall
- *Fargesia murieliae* (clump-forming) – 3m (10ft) or more tall
- *Fargesia murieliae* 'Simba' (clump-forming) – 1.8m (6ft) or more tall
- *Fargesia nitida* (clump-forming) – 3m (10ft) or more tall
- *Hibanobambusa tranquillans* 'Shiroshima' (spreading) – 2.4m (8ft) or more tall
- *Phyllostachys aurea* (clump-forming) – 4m (13ft) or more tall
- *Phyllostachys nigra* (clump-forming) – 3.5m (11ft) or more tall
- *Pseudosasa japonica* (spreading) – 4m (13ft) or more tall
- *Semiarundinaria yashadake* var. *kimmei* (spreading) – 2.4m (8ft) or more tall
- *Yushania anceps* (clump-forming) – 4m (13ft) or more tall

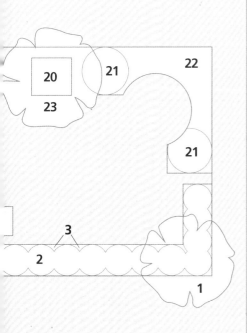

Follow the sun

Most people want a garden in which the main patio is in the sun for much if not all of the day, but in many gardens this is just not possible. The most challenging situations are those where the back of the house faces directly away from the midday sun and the space immediately behind it is in shade for much of the day. The easiest solution is to site the main patio or paved area in the sunniest part of the garden, even when this is far away from the house.

What makes this a good sunny garden?

✓ The large patio is in the right position to be in sun for most of the day and has plenty of space for furniture for entertaining

✓ There is a smaller paved area, which serves as an early morning or late afternoon sunspot or as a cool, shady place during the heat of the day

✓ The curved path linking the paved areas is practical and helps to disguise the long, narrow appearance of the garden

✓ The relatively simple planting provides background and structure and channels or interrupts views to break up the space visually

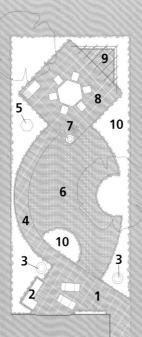

Garden elements key

1 Patio for morning and evening use

2 Built-in seating

3 Large urn

4 Path

5 Large obelisk

6 Lawn

7 Plants in containers

8 Main patio

9 Corner pergola and climbers

10 Planting

Mix and match
If you like this garden, but would
prefer a different feature, see pages
250–251 for possible variations.

Key features

Patio

Try to place your main patio or sitting area in a sunny part of the garden. It is a good idea, where there is space, to combine it with a simple shade structure for really hot days. If this sunny spot is not directly adjacent to your house, make sure that you provide a good, paved link between the two.

Ornamental grasses

Use ornamental grasses with shrubs and perennials in mixed borders or plant them on their own as individual specimens or as groups of the same variety. Dwarf grasses are good for edgings or for planting at the front of a bed. Taller varieties can be used as focal points and to give height and vertical emphasis where space is limited.

Obelisk

Obelisks make useful and decorative additions to a garden. They look good standing in some isolation, perhaps on stone paving or gravel. Alternatively, they can be dropped into planted borders to provide height and contrast, or be used as slender supports for slow-growing and delicate climbers.

Built-in seat

You can make a permanent built-in seat from paving materials that you've used elsewhere in the garden to provide a theme. The size of seat will depend on the dimension of the paving flags you use.

A carefully placed flagstone makes a neat seat at the edge of this timber raised bed.

You will need

Flagstones to match the patio to for the seat itself; minimum depth (front to back) 30cm (12in) but 45cm (18in) is ideal

Bricks (to match the path) to form the dwarf walls or 'legs' of the seat

Sand, cement for mortar

Cushions to put on the seat when it is in use

Step by step

As long as you have built your patio to a good standard, the seat can be built directly on top of it without extra foundations.

1 Mix mortar (in the proportion 1 part cement to 4 parts building sand) and lay bricks on top of each other to form short, low walls to support the flagstones. The finished height should allow for the thickness of the flagstone, but five bricks, 37.5cm (14¾in), is about right. Make sure the vertical joints in the walls are staggered for maximum strength – you'll need to cut some bricks in half for this, so make sure you wear goggles and a dust mask.

2 Put a bed of mortar on top of each support and lay a flagstone on top, checking that it is level.

3 Make or buy cushions to put on the seat. You can take them indoors when the seat is not being used.

Building the garden

The hard landscaping is relatively easy to build, apart from the curved path, which is an important feature of the design and requires extra care. The pergola and seating will require some woodworking skills but are not difficult.

- Lay the main patio and work back from it, then the curved path and finally the paved area by the house. This will give you clean access and provide usable space

- Erect the corner pergola and plant the trees for some vertical structure, and continue with the larger shrubs to provide the basic framework for your planting scheme

- Build the seat by the house and complete the beds with the smaller shrubs, perennials and grasses

- Lay the lawn (using turf if you want to use it as soon as possible or, alternatively, seed it for a more economical but longer-term solution)

Maintaining the garden

The choice of plants and materials makes maintenance straightforward and undemanding.

- Wooden features should be re-stained every three to four years, but this isn't necessary if the wood was pressure-treated to start with.

- Clean paving with a proprietary cleaner in the spring

- Trim evergreen shrubs in late winter and again in midsummer if it is necessary

- Prune spring-flowering shrubs after flowering and prune summer-flowering shrubs in late winter or early spring

- Tidy up perennials and grasses after the first frosts in autumn or leave them until early spring

Planting

The best plants for this garden

Many of the plants in this design are suitable for sunny situations – particularly at the far end of the garden. Others are chosen for the cooler, shadier locations at the base of walls. All of the plants are very easy to care for with no special requirements. There is a good mix of varieties to provide long periods of interest and taller varieties are used to break up the narrowness of the garden.

Planting key

1 *Zantedeschia aethiopica* 'Crowborough'
2 *Rhododendron yakushimanum*
3 *Symphytum* 'Goldsmith'
4 *Filipendula ulmaria* 'Variegata'
5 *Taxus cuspidata* 'Straight Hedge'
6 *Hosta* 'Gingko Craig'
7 *Lysimachia punctata*
8 *Perovskia atriplicifolia* 'Filigran'
9 *Viburnum plicatum* f. *tomentosum* 'Mariesii'

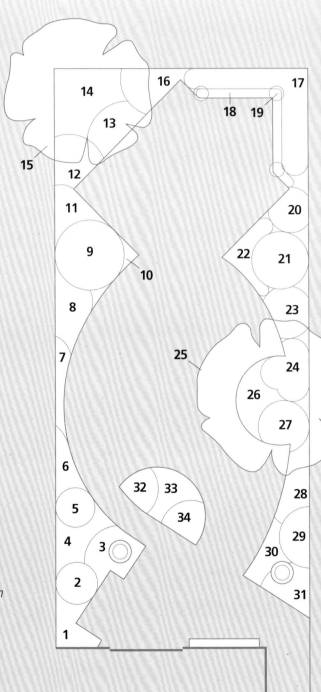

10 *Schizostylis coccinea* 'Major'
11 *Phygelius aequalis* 'Yellow Trumpet'
12 *Hebe* 'Great Orme'
13 x *Halimiocistus* 'Ingwersenii'
14 *Viburnum tinus* 'Variegatum'
15 *Prunus* 'Ukon'
16 *Spiraea japonica* 'Shirobana'
17 *Prunus lusitanica*
18 *Santolina chamaecyparissus*
19 *Wisteria sinensis* 'Rosea' (on pergola)
20 *Ceanothus* x *delileanus* 'Gloire de Versailles'
21 *Buddleja* 'Pink Delight'
22 *Lavandula* x *intermedia* 'Grappenhall'
23 *Elaeagnus* x *ebbingei* 'Gilt Edge'
24 *Skimmia laureola*
25 *Betula ermanii* (multistemmed)
26 *Euphorbia amygdaloides* var. robbiae
27 *Potentilla fruticosa* 'Maanelys'
28 *Darmera peltata*
29 *Chaenomeles* x *superba* 'Knap Hill Scarlet'
30 *Hypericum* x *moserianum* 'Tricolor'
31 *Astilbe* x *arendsii* 'Snowdrift'
32 *Hakonechloa macra* 'Alboaurea'
33 *Stipa calamagrostis*
34 *Molinia caerulea* 'Variegata'

Ornamental grasses

Ornamental grasses can range in size from tiny specimens no more than 15cm (6in) tall to giants of 3–4m (10–13ft) or more, especially bamboos, which are botanically a form of grass. The distinctive leaf shapes and habit make them an excellent choice for mixing with shrubs and perennials to provide contrast and foils. However, as a group in their own right they can look equally dramatic, particularly if each one is given sufficient room to develop to its full height and spread.

Island bed

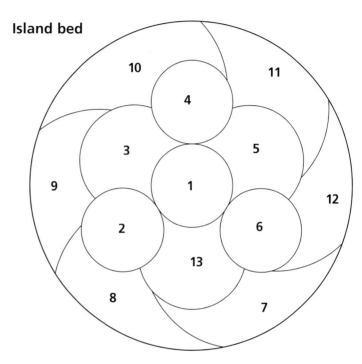

One-sided border

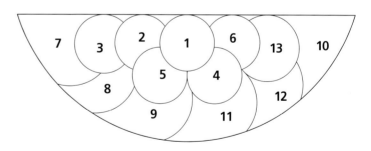

1 *Miscanthus sinensis* 'Silberfeder'
2 *Stipa gigantea*
3 *Carex comans* 'Frosted Curls'
4 *Calamagrostis* x *acutiflora* 'Karl Foerster'
5 *Stipa arundinacea*
6 *Panicum virgatum* 'Rubrum'
7 *Molinia caerulea* subsp. caerulea 'Variegata'
8 *Festuca glauca* 'Elijah Blue'
9 *Hakonechloa macra* 'Aureola'
10 *Luzula sylvatica* 'Aurea'
11 *Uncinia rubra*
12 *Carex morrowii* 'Fisher's Form'
13 *Carex buchananii*

Waterways

In many gardens the water feature is a secondary element in the design. This scheme, however, is designed around ponds and a stream, and these features are the main focus of the plan. The serpentine curves of the stream are mirrored by the gently sloping path, while a series of level platforms – patio, sun deck and brickweave sitting area – offer places to relax in the garden and to observe it from several vantage points.

What makes this a good water garden?

✓ The water features are an integral part of the design rather than being afterthoughts in an existing layout

✓ The planting is sympathetic to the hard landscaping required to construct the ponds and paths

✓ Sitting areas allow the design to be viewed from different places within the garden

✓ Although the design is intricate, the upkeep is not onerous

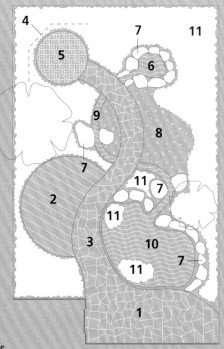

Garden elements key

1 Crazy paving patio
2 Sun deck
3 Crazy paving path
4 Reed fencing screen

5 Brickweave sitting area
6 Upper pool
7 Rocks

8 Gravel bed
9 Stream
10 Large, lower pond
11 Planting

Mix and match
If you like this garden, but would prefer a different feature, see pages 250–251 for possible variations.

Key features

Reed fencing

Fencing panels made from natural materials, such as reed, willow and hazel, can be used in lots of garden situations for a quick and sympathetic screen. Use reed fencing as a feature in its own right or as a background to your planting. It weathers and lasts better in a sunny, open position, especially if mounted on a simple timber framework.

Sun deck

Most decking is best positioned where it will be in the sun for a good part of the day, especially in temperate climates. For an informal effect, cut the deck edges with a jigsaw to produce curves. Or, for square and rectangular decks, lay the boards at 45° to the edges for an interesting herringbone look. To avoid rot and damp, always make sure that your deck boards are supported clear of the ground to allow air to circulate beneath them.

Stream

You don't need a garden with a serious slope in order to create a stream. A fall of only a few centimetres (inches) will be enough to allow water to flow downhill. In small gardens, make your stream meander from side to side for a layered waterscape. Try and introduce gentle cascades for added sound and movement and position them, if possible, where the moving water will catch and reflect sunlight.

Creating cascades

Cascades allow water to drop from a higher level to a lower one. The basic principle involves squeezing water between two larger rocks, forcing it to go over the edge of a flat rock at a higher level so that it falls into the next pool or stream section below. Cascades often fail because the rock or stone over which the water falls is

You only need a small change in level to create a very effective cascade in your garden.

unsuitable, creating a dribble or a series of vigorous drips that causes the water to run back under the lip of the cascade and then down the face of the rock that supports it. This may be because:

• The pump is not powerful enough and there is insufficient flow of water

• The edge of the cascade is too thick or is rounded

The ideal cascade profile resembles a chisel point (easily achieved by grinding the edge with a small grinder), or you can use a thin piece of slate, which will not need shaping. Make sure the cascade overhangs by at least 2.5–3.5cm (1–1½in).

If your water feature is formal or in a modern style you can use a thin sheet of zinc or aluminium, bent up slightly at the sides to channel the water over the lip.

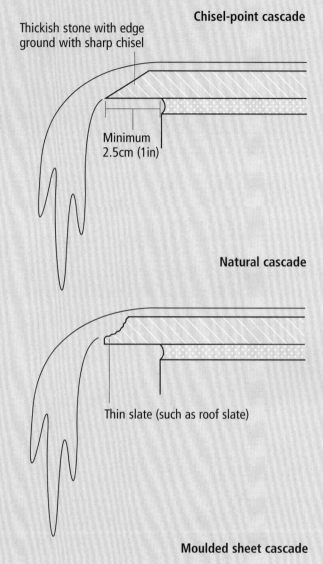

Chisel-point cascade

Thickish stone with edge ground with sharp chisel

Minimum 2.5cm (1in)

Natural cascade

Thin slate (such as roof slate)

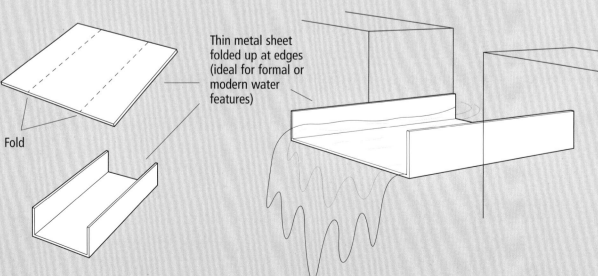

Moulded sheet cascade

Thin metal sheet folded up at edges (ideal for formal or modern water features)

Fold

Planting

The best plants for this garden

The style of planting is loose and informal to complement the ruggedness of the rocks and the curves of the other built features. There are no vivid flower colours so that the planting does not detract from the main feature of the garden – the waterway. Nevertheless, the plant associations are carefully chosen to enhance and complement the water.

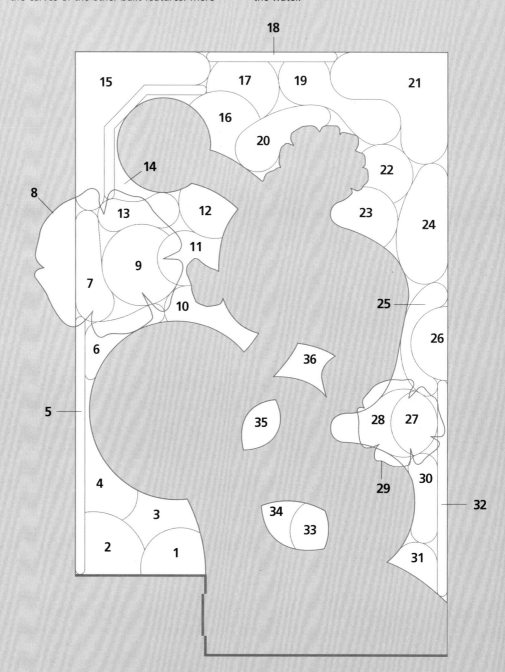

Planting key

1 *Abelia* x *grandiflora*
2 *Miscanthus sinensis* 'Kleine Fontane'
3 *Iris unguicularis*
4 *Rudbeckia fulgida* var. *deamii*
5 *Clematis flammula* (on fence)
6 *Aster amellus* 'Rosa Erfüllung'
7 *Ligularia dentata* 'Othello'
8 *Salix magnifica* (male form)
9 *Tiarella cordifolia*
10 *Carex morrowii* 'Evergold'
11 *Dicentra eximia*
12 *Stipa calamagrostis*
13 *Anchusa azurea* 'Loddon Royalist'
14 *Anemone sylvestris*
15 *Kerria japonica* 'Pleniflora'
16 *Helleborus niger*
17 *Meconopsis betonicifolia*
18 *Hedera canariensis* 'Gloire de
   Marengo' (on fence)
19 *Rhododendron* 'Persil' (azalea)
20 *Erica* x *darleyensis* 'Darley Dale'
21 *Pseudosasa japonica*
22 *Spiraea betulifolia* var. *ameliana*
23 *Pinus mugo* 'Winter Gold'
24 *Rhododendron* 'Elizabeth'
25 *Convallaria majalis*
26 *Acer griseum*
27 *Hosta* 'Big Daddy'
28 *Primula florindae*
29 *Sorbus koehneana*
30 *Astilbe* 'Deutschland'
31 *Digitalis ferruginea*
32 *Akebia quinata* (on fence)
33 *Iris pseudacorus* 'Variegata'
   (marginal in pond)
34 *Sagittaria sagittifolia* (marginal
   in pond)
35 *Caltha palustris* var. *alba*
   (marginal in pond)
36 *Juniperus communis* 'Repanda'

Aquatic planting

There are two types of aquatic plant that you can use primarily for ornamental purposes: marginals and floating-leaved plants. For most marginals – that is to say plants growing right at the edge of a pond – it is only necessary to provide between 15cm (6in) and 20cm (8in) depth of water. Some miniature water lilies can grow in as little as 45–60cm (18–24in) of water which is ideal for tiny ponds, but in larger ponds 75–90cm (30–36in) will enable you to grow a wider range successfully and this is a more favourable minimum depth if you're going to keep one or two fish.

Planting for a large pool

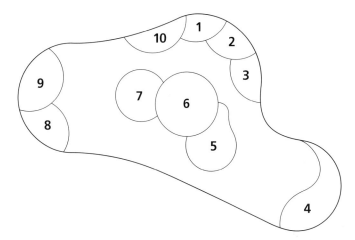

1 *Juncus patens* 'Carman's Gray'
2 *Glyceria maxima* var. *variegata*
3 *Pontederia cordata*
4 *Iris pseudacorus* 'Variegata'
5 *Aponogeton distachyos*
6 *Nymphaea* 'Marliacea Rosea'
7 *Orontium aquaticum*
8 *Lobelia* 'Queen Victoria'
9 *Caltha palustris* 'Flore Pleno'
10 *Sagittaria sagittifolia*

Planting for a small pool

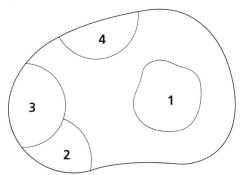

1 *Nymphaea tetragona*
2 *Juncus decipiens* 'Curly-wurly'
3 *Iris ensata*
4 *Acorus gramineus*

Romantic

Herbaceous borders mixed with roses, flowering shrubs and old-fashioned climbers are reminiscent of traditional cottage gardens. When they are combined with weathered bricks, natural stone paving and other period features, the overall effect is nostalgically romantic. Delicate colours and scent add to the effect and create a peaceful and harmonious garden.

What makes this a good romantic garden?

✓ An informal, rather meandering structure of stone paving, reflecting the fabric and age of the house

✓ A traditional herbaceous border combined with larger flowering shrubs to provide permanent framework and a selection of old-fashioned roses

✓ The traditional period features – arch, obelisks and arbour in ornamental 'gothic' style, old stone sculptures and sundial, a Victorian bench seat enclosed by a classic box hedge

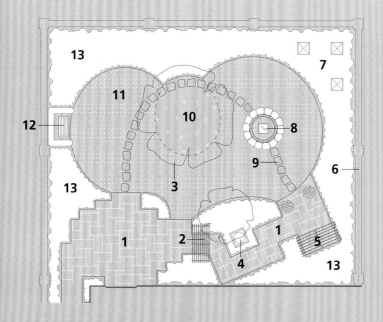

Garden elements key

1 Flagstone paving
2 Gothic rose arch
3 Old fruit tree
4 Statue or sculpture
5 Gothic arbour

6 Stone or brick boundary wall
7 Gothic obelisks
8 Stone and tile plinth and sundial

9 Stepping stones through lawn

10 Rough grass and spring bulbs

11 Lawn

12 Seat enclosed by low hedge

13 Border planting

Mix and match

If you like this garden, but would prefer a different feature, see pages 250–251 for possible variations.

Key features

Obelisks

Obelisks vary considerably in size, design and material, so you are likely to find one to suit your own garden design. Use them as features in their own right, either individually or in small groups, or combine them with climbers, perhaps permanent varieties like pillar roses and large-flowered clematis, or annuals such as sweet peas for an added scent bonus.

Old fruit tree

When redesigning an established garden, don't automatically cut down and remove all the existing trees and shrubs. Look to see if any can be incorporated in your new design – old apple and pear trees are fabulous in flower, and you could underplant them with spring bulbs to naturalize, perhaps mixed in with some old fashioned shade-loving perennials like astilbe or primulas.

Flag paving

A garden with many different features can sometimes look very busy or fragmented. Link them all together with a single paving material such as natural flagstones or old brick – these will harmonize and blend in with all other materials.

Circular tile edging

Terracotta tiles set on edge make an attractive and appropriate edging detail for paths and other paved areas. A project like this requires a certain amount of time and patience, but it is not too difficult if you prepare the ground properly.

You can economize on tiles by using halves or broken ones as long as one complete edge is undamaged. Because the broken edge may be uneven, you'll probably need to use a thicker bed of mortar to compensate.

You can create a totally different paving effect by using tiles on edge rather than flat.

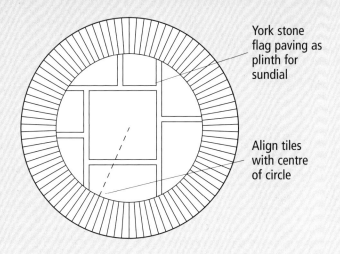

York stone flag paving as plinth for sundial

Align tiles with centre of circle

You will need

Terracotta tiles (or other tiles of your choice); make sure they are frost-proof and that the edges will give you the effect you want because this is the part that will be visible

Hardcore (crushed brick, concrete or stone)

Sand and cement for mortar

A straight length of softwood batten at least as long as the radius of the circle

Wooden peg, nail and string line

Step by step

1 Hammer the wooden peg into the ground to the desired height for your finished circle. Tap the nail into the top of the peg, leaving about 1.5cm (¾in) proud. Make a loop in the string, pass it over the nail and mark or knot the other end of the string at the radius of your circle plus about 5cm (2in).

2 Scribe a circle on the ground, using the knot or mark on the string. Dig a trench just wider than the length of the tiles and deep enough to accommodate the depth of the tile plus a bed of mortar 2.5–5cm (1–2in) deep and 8–10cm (3–4in) of compacted hardcore.

3 Place hardcore in the trench and compact it thoroughly. Blind the surface with sand to fill in any holes or cracks.

4 Lay a bed of soft mortar (1 part cement to 4 parts sand) 2.5–5cm (1–2in) thick on the hardcore and insert the tiles on edge, making sure they are level and that the tapered gap between adjacent tiles is not wider at its widest point than the thickness of the tile itself. Make sure your tiles are level and at the correct distance from the centre by using a spirit level taped to a batten with one end of the batten loosely nailed to the centre peg.

5 Brush an almost dry mixture of 1 part cement to 3 parts sand into the gaps and tamp down with the edge of a trowel. Add more mix to bring it level. Gently water it in with a fine rose on the watering can.

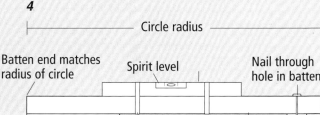

2

Circle

Fixed peg

Sharp peg

String

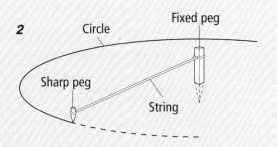

4

Circle radius

Batten end matches radius of circle

Spirit level

Nail through hole in batten

Tile

Tape to secure level

Batten

Peg at finished level

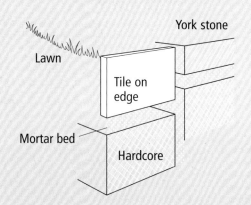

York stone

Lawn

Tile on edge

Mortar bed

Hardcore

Planting

The best plants for this garden

The planting is based on a traditional herbaceous border interspersed with familiar flowering shrubs and old-fashioned roses. Flower colours are deliberately restricted to yellow, white, blue and pink, which adds to the romantic atmosphere. There are no intense reds and oranges to catch the eye. Many of the individual plants listed are improved forms of older species and cultivars.

Planting key

1 *Rosa* x *francofurtana* 'Empress Josephine'
2 *Hemerocallis* 'Cream Drop'
3 *Delphinium* Blue Bird Group
4 *Hydrangea macrophylla* 'Mariesii Perfecta'
5 *Geranium pratense* 'Mrs Kendall Clarke'
6 *Digitalis purpurea* Excelsior Group
7 *Aquilegia* 'White Star'
8 *Potentilla fruticosa* 'Abbotswood'
9 *Delphinium* Astolat Group
10 *Alchemilla mollis*
11 *Astrantia major*
12 *Buddleja* 'Lochinch'
13 *Heuchera pulchella*
14 *Digitalis purpurea* Excelsior Group
15 *Rosa* 'Bourbon Queen'
16 *Campanula persicifolia*
17 *Aster amellus* 'Brilliant'
18 *Potentilla fruticosa* 'Primrose Beauty'
19 *Buxus sempervirens* (hedge)
20 *Delphinium* Black Knight Group

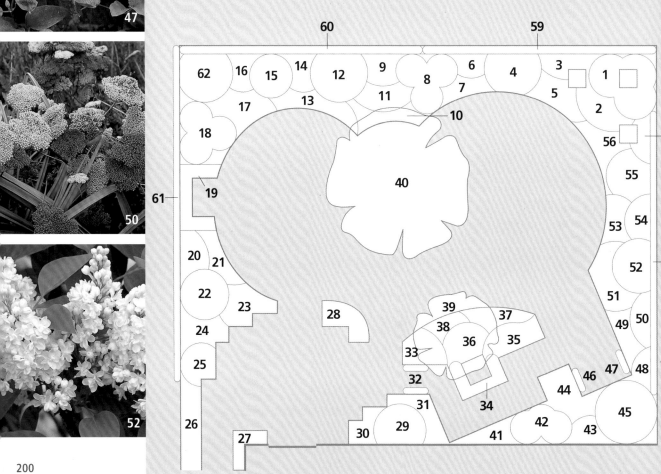

Romantic island bed

In a large garden it's a good idea to break up long vistas or create hidden areas by using island beds. This example is designed with plants in a romantic style, taking advantage of changing levels of sun and shade.

21 *Geranium* x *oxonianum* 'Claridge Druce'
22 *Viburnum plicatum* f. *tomentosum* 'Pink Beauty'
23 *Anthemis tinctoria* 'E.C. Buxton'
24 *Anemone* x *hybrida* 'Lady Gilmour'
25 *Rosa* 'Madame Hardy'
26 *Chaenomeles speciosa* 'Geisha Girl'
27 *Paeonia lactiflora* 'Sarah Bernhardt'
28 *Lavandula angustifolia*
29 *Camellia* x *williamsii* 'Mary Christian'
30 *Achillea* 'Taygetea'
31 *Iris* 'Blue Rhythm' (tall bearded)
32 *Rosa* 'Iceberg' (on rose arch)
33 *Iris* 'White City' (tall bearded)
34 *Artemisia* 'Powis Castle'
35 *Asphodeline lutea*
36 *Geranium phaeum*
37 *Dianthus* 'Doris'
38 *Papaver orientale* 'Kleine Tänzerin'
39 *Magnolia stellata* 'Waterlily'
40 Apple 'Bramley's Seedling'
41 *Verbascum* 'Helen Johnson'

42 *Rosa* 'Blanche de Vibert'
43 *Alcea rosea* salmon pink cv.
44 *Anchusa azurea* 'Loddon Royalist'
45 *Ceanothus* x *veitchianus*
46 *Lonicera caprifolium* (on arch)
47 *Clematis* 'Mrs Cholmondeley' (on arch)
48 *Alcea rosea* rose pink cv.
49 *Leucanthemum* x *superbum* 'Snowcap'
50 *Achillea filipendulina* 'Gold Plate'
51 *Rosa* 'Cécile Brünner'
52 *Syringa vulgaris* 'Madame Lemoine'
53 *Aster amellus* 'King George'
54 *Verbascum* Cotswold Group 'Gainsborough'
55 *Potentilla fruticosa* 'Tilford Cream'
56 *Clematis* x *eriostemon* 'Hendersonii'
57 *Alcea rosea* yellow cv.
58 *Clematis tangutica*
59 *Lonicera periclymenum* 'Graham Thomas'
60 *Clematis flammula*
61 *Solanum laxum*
62 *Philadelphus virginale*

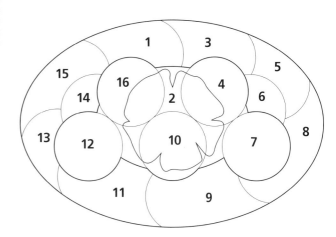

1 *Astilbe* x *arendsii* 'Venus'
2 *Malus* x *purpurea* 'Lemoinei'
3 *Hosta* 'Royal Standard'
4 *Cornus mas* 'Variegata'
5 *Crocosmia* x *crocosmiiflora* 'Emily McKenzie'
6 *Perovskia atriplicifolia*
7 *Rosa* 'Buff Beauty'
8 *Geranium clarkei* 'Kashmir White'
9 *Scabiosa caucasica* 'Clive Greaves'
10 *Spiraea* 'Arguta'
11 *Hemerocallis* 'Golden Chimes'
12 *Rosa glauca*
13 *Iris* 'Rajah' (tall bearded)
14 *Campanula persicifolia* 'Telham Beauty'
15 *Geranium phaeum*
16 *Hydrangea serrata* 'Bluebird'

An unsheltered garden

In more exposed gardens, strong gusts can cause plants to suffer stress, and trees and shrubs may even be deformed if they are continually exposed to a strong prevailing wind. Sheltering the whole garden with a windbreak of trees and large shrubs is practicable only in large gardens. In smaller gardens it is usually easier to use small groups of plants and structures to create sheltered microclimates in selected parts of the garden.

What makes this a good garden in an exposed position?

✓ A well-planted perimeter border with a few trees and some larger shrubs helps to break up and deflect the wind

✓ Simple structures – trellis and summerhouse – provide some immediate shelter and extend the garden's use

✓ The larger plants are robust and will thrive in the prevailing conditions

✓ The localized shelter provided by the larger plants makes it easier to grow smaller plants that would otherwise not do well

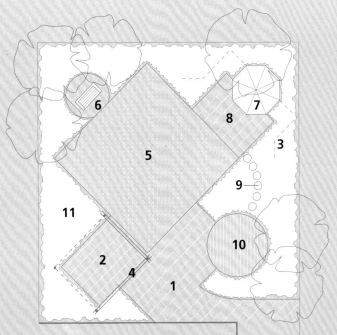

Garden elements key

1 Main patio for calm days

2 Sheltered patio

3 Trellis screen

4 Overhead beams with climbers and wind chimes

5 Lawn

6 Bench in copse, wind
chimes in trees

7 Summerhouse
8 Summerhouse patio

9 Stepping stone path
10 Raised sun deck
11 Planting

Mix and match
If you like this garden, but would
prefer a different feature, see pages
250–251 for possible variations.

Key features

Summerhouse

Makes a very strong focal point – provide a small patio in front and make it into an alternative sitting area, perhaps in a part of the garden that catches the late afternoon sun. Choose a style and materials to harmonize with the rest of the garden. Plan the garden to provide an electricity supply to the summerhouse for lights so you can use it in the evenings as well.

Raised sun deck

Wooden decking makes a contrast with stone paving and raising it by about 15cm (6in) provides another element of interest. Position your deck areas where they'll get the maximum amount of sun so that the surface of the wood doesn't harbour unsightly algae or mosses. Stain them in colours to match or complement other wooden features – pergola, trellis, arches etc.

Planting

Tall, hardy shrubs and trees can be used to break up prevailing winds and make your garden more sheltered. Identify those areas in the garden where shelter planting is needed and make your beds here generous with the taller plants at the back and medium to small plants in the front where it's more protected. Try to include some large evergreens to give year-round protection.

Choosing a summerhouse

There are so many different summerhouses available – from tiny ones in kit form that you can put up in an afternoon to massive, multi-roomed structures that you can almost live in – that the choice can be bewildering. Narrow down your choice by following a few guidelines.

A dark-coloured summerhouse framed by planting is less intrusive that a bright-coloured summerhouse in isolation.

Style

Match the summerhouse to your garden style or theme. A rustic model would suit a country cottage garden, but one built in a modern style with modern materials would be best for a city garden.

Colour

Be guided by your garden design but remember that a summerhouse painted in a dark shade will be less intrusive than a pale or brightly coloured one.

Shape and size

If your summerhouse is primarily a visual feature and the inside will be used only occasionally, choose a shape that fits in with your overall design. However, if you plan to sit in and use the summerhouse on a regular basis, make sure it will comfortably accommodate your garden furniture. Remember that a square structure will provide more floor space than an octagonal or hexagonal one of the same diameter.

Location

Decide if you want the summerhouse to be a bold, obvious feature – that is, it will stand in some isolation as a focal point – or if you would rather have something less obvious, perhaps hidden slightly behind some shrubs or tucked into a border.

Access

Unless you are going to use the summerhouse on very rare occasions, you'll need to get to it along a hard-wearing path. Unless your garden has a strictly formal layout, don't take this path in a direct line from your house to the summerhouse. Instead, introduce some gentle changes of direction, perhaps linking with or passing by other features *en route*.

Use the wind to make a garden more interesting

- Wind chimes – but don't overdo it; one or two sets will be enough and think of your neighbours

- Mobiles of shiny plastic, tough glass or polished metal will reflect light but make sure they're suitable for outdoor use and are strong

- Individual hanging ornaments – glass spheres, chrome-plated stars and moons, for example – will brighten a dark corner

- Bamboos and tall grasses will sway in the wind and make gentle rustling noises

- Shrubs with leaves that have contrasting tops and undersides, such as *Elaeagnus*, look good when moving in strong winds

Wind chimes are a simple way to take advantage of breezy conditions in your garden.

Planting

28

39

41

50

The best plants for this garden

The main framework planting of trees and shrubs is made up of plants that will thrive in an exposed situation. In front, smaller shrubs and perennials are planted to take advantage of this first line of defence; these then create small sheltered spots for planting less robust plants.

Planting key

1 *Iris sibirica* 'Perry's Blue'
2 *Lavatera* x *clementii* 'Barnsley'
3 *Aquilegia* McKana Group
4 *Spiraea thunbergii*
5 *Berberis julianae*
6 *Indigofera heterantha*
7 *Clematis orientalis* (on trellis/overheads)
8 *Heuchera* 'Persian Carpet'
9 *Geranium* x *cantabrigense* 'Biokovo'

10 *Syringa vulgaris* 'Charles Joly'
11 *Rubus thibetanus*
12 *Hypericum* x *inodorum* 'Elstead'
13 *Genista lydia*
14 *Phlox paniculata* 'Mount Fuji'
15 *Sambucus racemosa* 'Plumosa Aurea'
16 *Ligustrum lucidum*
17 *Prunus padus*
18 *Osmanthus delavayi*
19 *Lamium maculatum* 'Roseum'

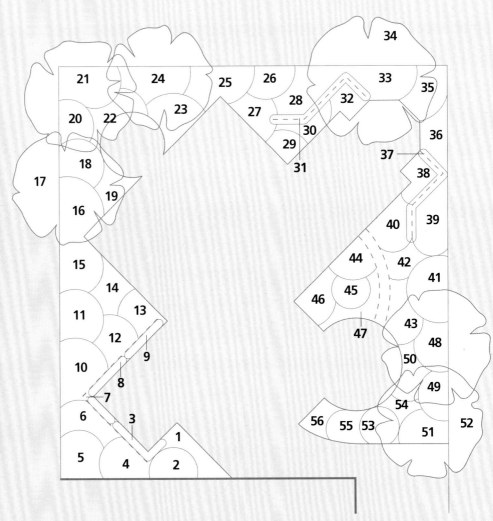

20 *Ilex aquifolium* 'Aurea Marginata'
21 *Amelanchier lamarckii*
22 *Geranium* x *monacense*
23 *Digitalis purpurea* Excelsior Group
24 *Viburnum sargentii* 'Onondaga'
25 *Buddleja globosa*
26 *Ilex aquifolium* 'Flavescens'
27 *Potentilla fruticosa* 'Abbotswood'
28 *Philadelphus* 'Virginal'
29 *Euphorbia dulcis* 'Chameleon'
30 *Anemone* x *hybrida* 'Richard Ahrens'
31 *Akebia quinata* (on trellis)
32 *Syringa pubescens* subsp. *microphylla* 'Superba'
33 *Corylus maxima* 'Purpurea'
34 *Acer cappadocicum* 'Aureum'
35 *Elaeagnus* x *ebbingei*
36 *Viburnum betulifolium*
37 *Jasminum nudiflorum* 'Aureum' (on trellis)
38 *Caryopteris* x *clandonensis* 'Kew Blue'
39 *Tamarix tetrandra*
40 *Tradescantia* Andersoniana Group 'Isis'
41 *Spartium junceum*
42 *Miscanthus sinensis* 'Undine'
43 *Acanthus mollis*
44 *Teucrium chamaedrys*
45 *Yucca filamentosa*
46 *Lavandula angustifolia* 'Twickel Purple'
47 *Hemerocallis* 'Hyperion'
48 *Pyracantha* 'Golden Charmer'
49 *Holodiscus discolor*
50 *Geranium psilostemon*
51 *Viburnum tinus* 'Purpureum'
52 *Salix alba* subsp. *vitellina* 'Britzensis' (pollarded)
53 *Weigela florida* 'Albovariegata'
54 *Euphorbia palustris*
55 *Crocosmia* 'Spitfire'
56 *Asphodeline lutea*

Plants for shelter

Understanding how plants break up air flows and make calm, sheltered areas will enable you to position trees and shrubs for maximum effect in breaking up the wind. The larger a windbreak – in terms of width as well as height – the greater the area it will protect immediately behind it, and as you move further away from it the effect gradually diminishes.

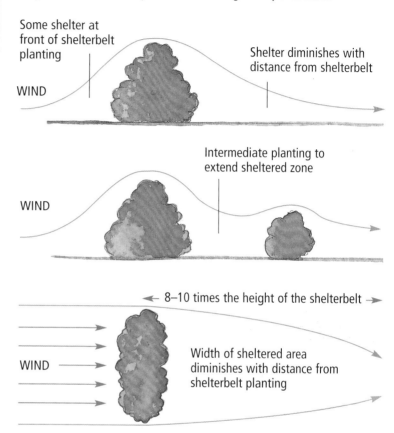

Some shelter at front of shelterbelt planting

Shelter diminishes with distance from shelterbelt

WIND

Intermediate planting to extend sheltered zone

WIND

8–10 times the height of the shelterbelt

WIND

Width of sheltered area diminishes with distance from shelterbelt planting

Best trees for a windbreak

Many trees and shrubs will survive in a windy, exposed position, but they will not necessarily thrive. For trees to act as a windbreak they must grow well and put on plenty of growth to protect lesser plants and create shelter.

- *Acer campestre* (field maple)
- *Betula* spp. (birch)
- *Crataegus monogyna* and cvs. (common hawthorn, quickthorn)
- *Fraxinus excelsior* and cvs. (common ash)
- *Larix decidua* (larch)
- *Pinus nigra* (European black pine), *P. sylvestris* (Scots pine)
- *Quercus robur* and cvs. (English oak)
- *Salix alba* and cvs. (white willow)
- *Sorbus aria*, *S. intermedia*, *S. aucuparia* (whitebeam and mountain ash)
- *Tilia cordata* (small-leaved lime)

In the shade

Sometimes, in small, mostly urban gardens, only a small proportion of the area is in the sun, while the remainder receives either none at all or perhaps a small amount in early morning and early evening in summer when the sun is at its zenith. If you are to make the most of this type of garden the paved area or patio must be located in the sunniest corner, which means that the rest of the garden is likely to be in varying degrees of shade.

What makes this a good shaded garden?

✓ The patio is in the best place to receive maximum sun
✓ The simple, bold design makes a striking framework for the planting
✓ Mirrors reflect light back into the garden
✓ The hard landscape materials are in warm, light colours
✓ The simple pool works with the mirrors to reflect the brightness of the sky and surrounding planting
✓ The plants are selected not only for their ability to thrive in shady places but also to give lots of interest to brighten the border

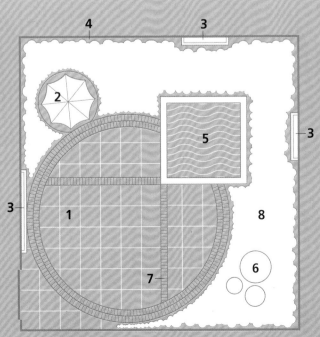

Garden elements key

1 Patio of exposed aggregate concrete flags

2 White-painted wrought iron gazebo

3 Wall-mounted mirrors

4 White-painted walls

5 Reflection pool

6 Large earthenware pots

7 Warm orange brick
edging

8 Planting

Mix and match
If you like this garden, but would
prefer a different feature, see pages
250–251 for possible variations.

Key features

Wall-mounted mirrors

Use mirrors in any small garden to create a feeling of extra light and space. Fix them securely to solid walls or frames in a position where they won't be at risk from footballs or bikes! You'll need to clean them on a regular basis for them to be most effective.

Planting

There are lots of attractive plants that will thrive in varying degrees of shade. Those that tolerate heavy shade can be used in the darker corners of a garden, while those that require perhaps a small amount of sun can be planted in more open positions, on the edges of patios and paths for example.

Reflection pool

A shallow pool filled to the brim with water can be used as a horizontal mirror to reflect the sky or an attractive feature behind the pool. Make use of it at night as well by lighting a tree or ornament to be reflected on the water's surface, or put lights directly in the pool itself. To achieve maximum reflections for any given size of pool, it is best to have the water level as near to ground level as possible.

How to make a reflection pool

A pool can act like a mirror and reflect both light and individual objects or plants within a garden, thereby doubling the effect. Because the water's surface acts as the mirror, the depth of the pool is relatively unimportant, which makes it a potentially easy feature to build.

The water in a garden pool can make a striking – and safe – mirror.

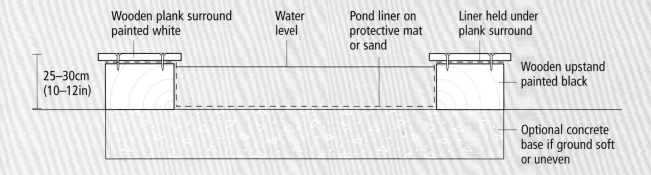

Wooden plank surround painted white

Water level

Pond liner on protective mat or sand

Liner held under plank surround

25–30cm (10–12in)

Wooden upstand painted black

Optional concrete base if ground soft or uneven

You will need

Sand, gravel and cement to make a simple concrete base (unless the ground where the pool is going is hard enough already)

Heavy pieces of wood to form the upstand of the pool, about 20 x 30cm (8 x 12in), length to suit; alternatively, use concrete blocks

Softwood planks, 1.5–2cm (about ¾in) thick, to form the top of the surround; the overall width to match that of the upstand plus a small overhang each side of about 2.5cm (1in)

Flexible pond liner and protective matting or soft sand

White paint and black paint or stain

Screws and fixings to attach wooden surround to upstand

Step by step

1 Level the area for the pool. If the ground is soft or unstable, dig out 7.5–10cm (3–4in) and spread concrete to form a solid level base.

2 Build the upstand. Lay the heavy timbers in a square or rectangle around the edge of the base and make sure they are level. Use spots of mortar to adjust the level if necessary. Alternatively, lay a level course of concrete blocks.

3 When the upstand is complete, place the protective mat or a layer of soft sand, 2.5cm (1in) deep, in the bottom of the pool.

4 Place the liner in the pool. If there is a lot of spare liner, trim off some of the excess, but make sure you leave at least 25cm (10in) to trap under the wooden surround. This will make the fitting easier.

5 Fit the liner neatly into the corners by making triangular pleats. Use double-sided adhesive tape to hold it temporarily in place until the pool is filled with water.

6 Partly fill the pool to ensure that the pond liner is tight against the bottom corners.

7 Screw the wooden surround to the top of the upstand, trapping the edge of the pond liner under it as you go. You will need to make a small vertical slit in each corner of the liner from the edge down as far as the top of the upstand in the same way as the flaps of a cardboard box open and fold outwards.

8 Paint or stain the upstand black and paint the wooden top white. Fill the pool completely.

5

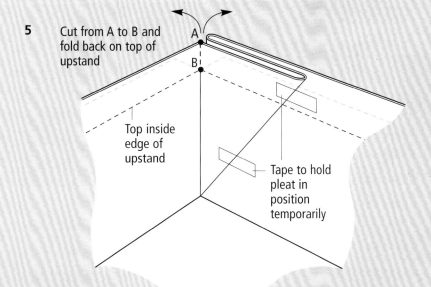

Cut from A to B and fold back on top of upstand

A

B

Top inside edge of upstand

Tape to hold pleat in position temporarily

Planting

The best plants for this garden

The plants have been chosen for their bright foliage and flowers or for their distinctive shape or form, which can be admired against the pale background and paving. Yellows, whites and purples predominate, and evergreens give structure to the garden when the perennials are dormant. They are carefully placed so that the most shade tolerant are in the sunless corners, while those that will benefit from a little sunlight will not be in complete shade all day.

Planting key

1 *Luzula sylvatica* 'Aurea'
2 *Heuchera* 'Rachel'
3 *Scrophularia auriculata* 'Variegata'
4 *Ribes sanguineum* 'Brocklebankii'
5 *Ilex aquifolium* 'Silver Queen'
6 *Taxus baccata* 'Semperaurea'
7 *Primula* (polyanthus) mauve/purple cvs.

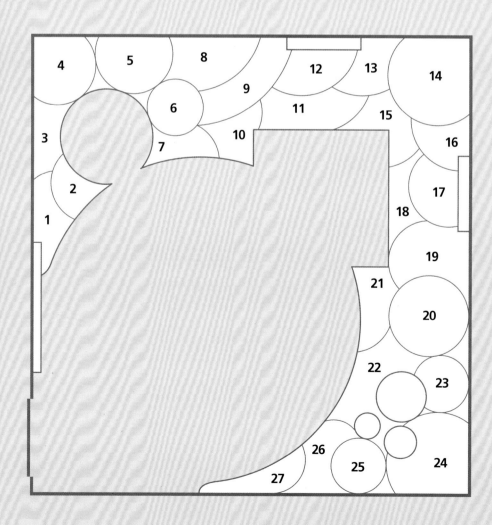

There are many plants, such as *Lamium*, that will grow well in a shady position and provide groundcover.

A shady evergreen corner

For ultimate low-maintenance planting a group of evergreens will take some beating once they are established. They will cover the ground and consequently prevent weeds from growing. These plants are suited to shady conditions and will thrive there.

Best evergreen plants for a shady garden

- *Epimedium* spp.

- *Vinca minor* spp.

- *Skimmia japonica*

- *Polystichum polyblepharum*

- *Viburnum davidii*

- *Prunus laurocerasus* 'Otto Luyken'

- *Iris foetidissima*

- *Mahonia aquifolium* 'Apollo'

- *Euonymus fortunei* varieties

- *Helleborus argutifolius*

Cottage creative

Part of the appeal of a traditional cottage garden is the rather rustic, rough-edged feel to the paths, arches and other features. However, the demands of modern life make this kind of approach impracticable, and although they are 'cottagey' or rustic in appearance, the features for a 'modern' cottage garden must be built to last.

What makes this a good modern cottage garden?

✓ There is plenty of space and features so that it can be used as a family garden, making it more practical than a traditional cottage garden
✓ The materials for the features – patio, arches, fencing – have been selected for durability as well as appearance
✓ Reliable plants re-create the feel of a traditional cottage garden
✓ The enclosed kitchen garden is screened from view.
✓ The low-maintenance design suits a busy, modern lifestyle

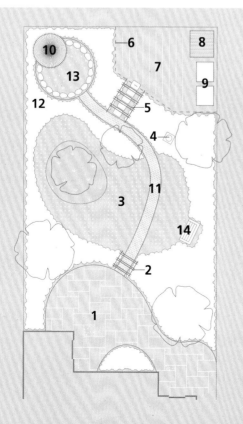

Garden elements key

1 Patio	5 Pergola
2 Arch	6 Willow hurdle fence
3 Lawn	7 Kitchen garden
4 Birdbath	8 Garden store

9 Compost bins
10 Rustic gazebo
11 Brick path
12 Planting

13 Gravel and stone
   sitting area
14 Bench

Mix and match
If you like this garden, but would prefer a different feature, see pages 250–251 for possible variations.

Key features

Birdbath

Finish off your garden with individual features such as obelisks, statues and birdbaths. Don't just drop them into the garden randomly; position them with thought so that they can be seen from different viewpoints. Even in the depths of winter, birdbaths are valuable to birds.

Rustic gazebo

Gazebos are pleasant places to sit and take in the atmosphere of your garden. Either make them a strong focal point that can be seen from the house, or tuck them away – perhaps hidden by planting – to form a secret, quiet area. Choose a style and materials that will complement the rest of your garden features, and maybe have a small patio adjacent for a table and chairs.

Serpentine path

Bricks are an excellent material for paths and paving, and because of their small size, compared with paving flags, are more suitable for irregular shapes and curves. Check with your supplier to make sure that any bricks you use are frost-proof. For a formal effect, use very hard engineering bricks and point the joints between them with cement:sand mortar. To get a softer, more informal appearance use textured bricks laid in herringbone fashion and just brush sand into the joints.

Willow hurdle fencing

Fence panels made from natural willow, reed or bamboo fit in well with cottage-garden planting and designs. If they are not installed with some care, however, they can become unsightly and quickly deteriorate. When they are fixed to a proper frame of posts and rails, they will not only last for many years but will also continue to look good.

Willow hurdle fencing makes a natural and sympathetic boundary to a traditional cottage garden.

You will need

Willow hurdle fence panels (or similar)

10 x 10cm (4 x 4in) section (or round) pressure-treated softwood posts, 45cm (18in) longer than the overall height of the fence

Pressure-treated softwood rails 3.8 x 7.5cm (1½ x 3in)

Galvanized nails

Galvanized wire

Stain (optional)

Sand, gravel and cement for concrete (optional)

Step by step

1 Dig post holes, about 25 x 25cm (10 x 10in) and 45cm (18in) deep, and concrete in the posts. Alternatively, on firm ground, use pointed stakes and drive them in with a proper post-driver.

2 Nail the rails horizontally to the face of the posts to allow about 5cm (2in) overhang of the fence panel at both top and bottom. For higher fence panels – those over about 1.8m (6ft) – put in an intermediate rail between top and bottom.

3 Stain the posts and rails if required.

4 Attach the fence panels to the rails by nailing through the thicker upright supports of the panel and by tying in the thinner stems of willow with twists of galvanized wire. Pre-drilling the nail holes will avoid splitting the upright supports.

Rustic arches and pergolas

Originally, cottage gardeners used virtually any fairly straight pieces of wood to build their garden structures. They often relied on young conifer thinnings from forests and woodlands. These would soon become unstable or fall prey to rot, and the bark, which was usually left on, would become host to all sorts of garden pests and diseases.

Modern techniques and materials make it easy to build a rustic structure, with none of the inherent pitfalls of their predecessors.

Untreated timbers will not last long in a outdoor situation, so use treated wood for your garden features.

Planting

The best plants for this garden

A mixture of trees, shrubs, perennials and climbers has been used to re-create the effect of traditional borders. The plants have been selected for their reliability and good health and because they require minimal maintenance. No special growing conditions are needed, apart from ensuring that the soil is well drained, and all the plants will benefit from regular mulching.

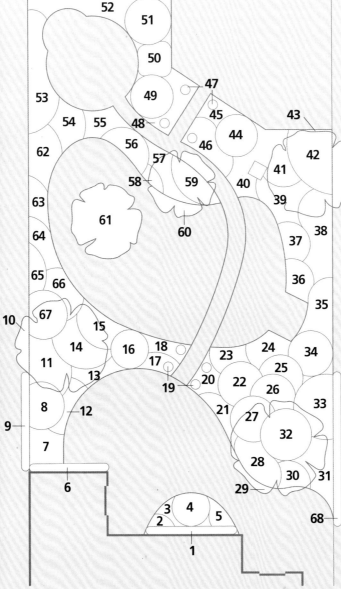

Planting key

1 *Rosa* 'Della Balfour' (on wall)
2 *Nerine bowdenii* 'Pink Triumph'
3 *Ballota* 'All Hallows Green'
4 *Lavandula* 'Helmsdale'
5 *Dianthus* 'Devon Dove'
6 *Jasminum officinale* f. *affine*
7 *Geranium himalayense* 'Gravetye'
8 *Rosa* 'Pink Grootendorst'
9 *Clematis henryi*
10 *Prunus sargentii*
11 *Campanula persicifolia* 'Bennett's Blue'
12 *Alchemilla alpina*
13 *Leucanthemum* x *superbum* 'Snowcap'
14 *Phlox paniculata* 'Prince of Orange'
15 *Aster novi-belgii* 'Lady in Blue'
16 *Rosa* 'Geranium'
17 *Eryngium variifolium*
18 *Achillea* 'Anthea'
19 *Wisteria* 'Caroline'
20 *Aquilegia* 'Red Star'
21 *Artemisia* 'Powis Castle'
22 *Rosa* 'Buff Beauty'
23 *Dicentra* 'Adrian Bloom'
24 *Salvia* x *sylvestris* 'Blauhügel'
25 *Crocosmia* 'Lucifer'
26 *Aconitum* 'Bressingham Spire'
27 *Phlox paniculata* 'Eva Cullum'

28 *Viola riviniana* Purpurea Group
29 *Crataegus laevigata* 'Paul's Scarlet'
30 *Tradescantia* Andersoniana Group 'Purple Dome'
31 *Geranium sylvaticum*
32 *Anemone* x *hybrida* 'Whirlwind'
33 *Filipendula rubra* 'Venusta'
34 *Hydrangea macrophylla* 'Mariesii Perfecta'
35 *Iris sibirica* 'Dreaming Yellow'
36 *Astilbe* x *arendsii* 'Elizabeth Bloom'
37 *Helleborus argutifolius*
38 *Hosta* 'Blue Moon'
39 *Geranium psilostemon* 'Bressingham Flair'
40 *Aquilegia* 'Blue Star'
41 *Acanthus mollis* Latifolius Group
42 *Persicaria amplexicaulis* 'Atrosanguinea'
43 *Acer davidii*
44 *Rosa glauca*
45 *Astrantia major* 'Sunningdale Variegated'
46 *Geum rivale* 'Leonard's Variety'
47 *Rosa* 'Clarence House' (on pergola)
48 *Ajuga reptans* 'Pink Surprise'

49 *Weigela middendorffiana*
50 *Anemone* x *hybrida* 'Richard Ahrens'
51 *Kerria japonica*
52 *Delphinium* Black Knight Group
53 *Miscanthus sinensis* 'Silberfeder'
54 *Rudbeckia fulgida* var. *sullivantii* 'Goldsturm'
55 *Aster amellus* 'King George'
56 *Bergenia* 'Wintermärchen'
57 *Campanula persicifolia* var. *alba*
58 *Pulmonaria longifolia*
59 *Doronicum* 'Miss Mason'
60 *Laburnum* x *watereri* 'Vossii'
61 Apple 'Bramley's Seedling'
62 *Agapanthus* 'Blue Giant'
63 *Geranium clarkei* 'Kashmir White'
64 *Echinacea purpurea* 'Rubinstern'
65 *Thalictrum flavum* subsp. *glaucum*
66 *Hemerocallis* 'Little Wine Cup'
67 *Philadelphus coronarius* 'Variegatus'
68 *Lonicera periclymenum* 'Graham Thomas' (on fence)

Alpine 'pavement'

On large paved areas you can plant some alpines and dwarf perennials here and there between paving flags or in small pockets and still leave reasonably generous amounts of space for garden furniture and general relaxation without putting the plants at risk. Where this is not possible you could create a small section of paving away from the main patio that won't be used, although the plants can be admired.

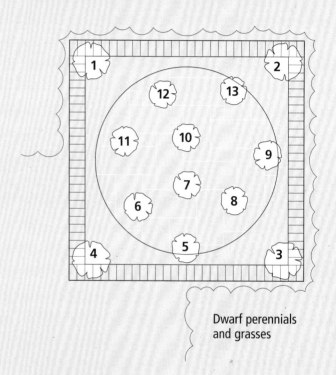

Dwarf perennials and grasses

1 *Iberis sempervirens*
2 *Helianthemum* 'Sudbury Gem'
3 *Thymus richardii* subsp. *nitidus*
4 *Artemisia schmidtiana* 'Nana'
5 *Campanula carpatica* 'Chewton Joy'
6 *Aubrieta* 'Doctor Mules'
7 *Arabis procurrens* 'Variegata'
8 *Phlox subulata* 'Temiskaming'
9 *Veronica prostrata*
10 *Sedum spathulifolium* 'Cape Blanco'
11 *Linum flavum* 'Compactum'
12 *Diascia barberae* 'Ruby Field'
13 *Crepis incana*

Geometric garden

A geometric garden differs from a formal garden in the relationship between the shapes and the style of planting. Symmetry is not an essential element of the design; instead, the plan is an abstract combination of shapes or has a single theme based on the repetition of a single shape. In this design, the plants are a complete contrast with the underlying structure, appearing soft and informal against the crisp outlines and edges of the paving and walls.

What makes this a successful geometric garden?

✓ The combination of geometric shapes – squares and circles – in the garden design
✓ The repetition of the geometric themes in greater detail in the concentric circles of the brick path, the square patterns within the brickweave patio and the sharp-edged rectangular stone edgings
✓ The deliberately informal planting, which incorporates a range of colours and textures and a degree of informality that are in marked contrast to the well-defined hard landscaping

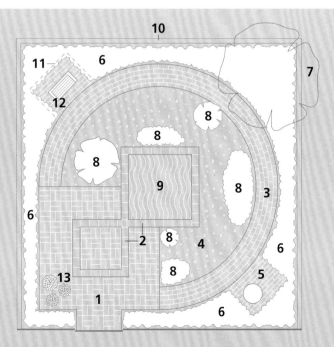

Garden elements key

1 Red brick patio
2 Stone edging
3 Brick path
4 Gravel bed
5 Barbecue area
6 Border planting
7 Tree
8 Specimen planting in gravel bed
9 Pond
10 Brick boundary wall

11 Trellis arbour and
    climbers

12 Sitting area and
    seating

13 Container planting

Mix and match

If you like this garden, but would
prefer a different feature, see pages
250–251 for possible variations.

Key features

Pond

This is a central feature of the design, forming the focal point around which the other garden features are grouped. For more movement and sound you could introduce a small fountain, but make sure that it's not so high that the spray can be caught by strong winds and land away from the pond! Alternatively, keep the pond as a still water body to act as a mirror and reflect light and colour.

Specimen planting

Spacing individual plants well apart in a central bed is an excellent way to appreciate their full attractions of shape, colour and flower. Plant single specimen shrubs or trees but, for a better effect, plant perennials (especially smaller ones) in groups of three, five or even seven. Keep weeds at bay by covering the ground with a weed-suppressing mulch mat covered with coarse bark or shingle.

Barbecue area

In large gardens where there's plenty of room you can construct a built-in barbecue as part of the design. Here, an area of paving is dedicated for a mobile barbecue so that the chef can stand in any position upwind. Keep your barbecue area away from the main space for sitting and relaxation, but make sure it is easily accessible to the seating area and also to the kitchen for extra supplies.

A square pond

Constructing a square pond with vertical sides is in many ways more difficult than building a more informal one with shallow margins and gently curved edges covered with a flexible pond liner.

You need to build what is, in effect, a below-ground box that is strong enough to withstand outward pressure from the water within the pond and inward pressure from the soil behind the vertical walls. The bottom of the box must be strong enough to

Several plants other than grass can be used to give the impression of a lawn, and, once established, they require far less maintenance.

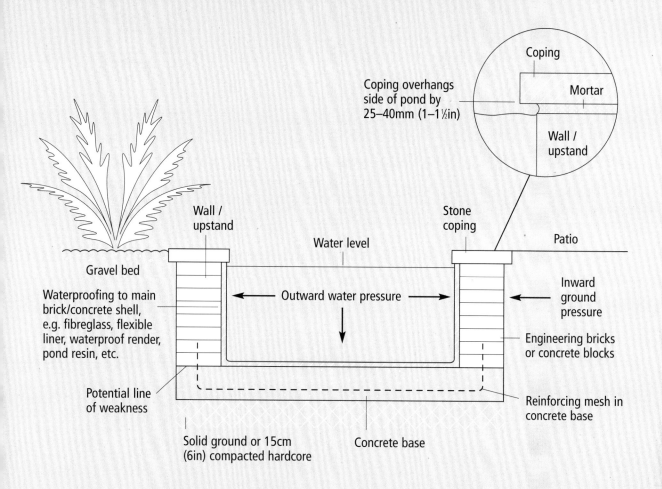

Coping

Mortar

Coping overhangs
side of pond by
25–40mm (1–1½in)

Wall /
upstand

Wall /
upstand

Stone
coping

Patio

Water level

Gravel bed

Waterproofing to main
brick/concrete shell,
e.g. fibreglass, flexible
liner, waterproof render,
pond resin, etc.

Outward water pressure

Inward
ground
pressure

Engineering bricks
or concrete blocks

Potential line
of weakness

Reinforcing mesh in
concrete base

Solid ground or 15cm
(6in) compacted hardcore

Concrete base

bear the weight above it without
moving or settling and be joined to
the vertical walls so that no cracks
(and potential leaks) develop.

You will need

Hardcore, such as crushed brick or
  concrete
Sharp sand, 1.9cm (¾in) gravel and
  cement for the concrete base
Steel reinforcing bars
Steel reinforcing mesh
Engineering bricks or dense hollow
  concrete blocks to build the
  upstands
Flexible pond liner
Stone or concrete paving flags to
  make the pond edging

Step by step

1 Excavate a hole for your pond,
making sure that you have made
allowances for the thickness of the
upstands and the base.

2 Put hardcore in the bottom of the
hole and compact it well to give a
finished depth of at least 15cm (6in).

3 Make concrete (cement:sand:gravel
in the ratio 1:2:4) and pour it onto
the hardcore. Spread a layer 7.5cm
(3in) thick. Place the reinforcing mesh
on top of this while it is still wet and
immediately add another 7.5cm (3in)
layer of concrete on top.

4 Push reinforcing bars
(30–40cm/12–16in long), vertically
into the concrete around the edge to

coincide with the centre line of the
upstands. These will help tie the
upstand to the base.

5 Build the four upstand walls using
bricks or hollow concrete blocks
mortared together with cement:sand
mortar in the ratio 1:4. Make sure the
reinforcing bars are surrounded with
mortar to key them into the walls.

6 Once the walls and base are strong
enough, fit the pond liner using
pleats at the corner to ensure a tight
fit (see page 211).

7 Fold the top edge of the pond liner
over the upstand and trap it using
the flagstone edgings on a bed of
mortar (cement:sand mortar in the
ratio of 1:4).

Planting

The best plants for this garden

The planting is informal, and the plants have been chosen to give a mixture of colours and textures, ranging from tall bamboos to neat, low mounds of hebes. All the plants will tolerate a range of growing conditions and are fairly undemanding. In the central area the specimen plants are displayed to highlight their form, texture and colour.

Planting key

1 *Berberis thunbergii* f. *atropurpurea* 'Atropurpurea Nana'
2 *Choisya* 'Aztec Pearl'
3 *Abeliophyllum distichum* 'Roseum'
4 *Anthemis tinctoria* 'E.C. Buxton'
5 *Cotoneaster horizontalis*
6 *Iris* 'Pogo' (dwarf bearded)
7 *Rosa sericea* subsp. *omeiensis* f. *pteracantha*
8 *Liatris spicata*
9 *Chaenomeles* x *superba* 'Crimson and Gold'
10 *Schizostylis coccinea* 'Major'
11 *Pyracantha* 'Orange Glow'
12 *Vitis vinifera* 'Purpurea' (on trellis)
13 *Viburnum opulus* 'Roseum'
14 *Ilex aquifolium* 'J.C. van Tol'
15 *Iris* 'Braithwaite' (tall bearded)
16 *Philadelphus* 'Silberregen'
17 *Forsythia suspensa* f. *atrocaulis*

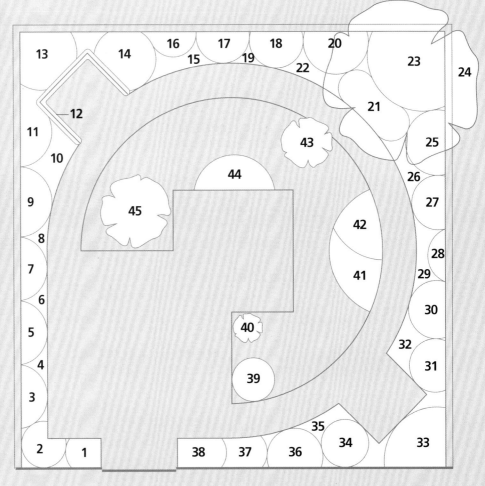

18 *Viburnum opulus*
  'Compactum'
19 *Phlox carolina* 'Bill Baker'
20 *Hydrangea serrata* 'Diadem'
21 *Daphne odora*
  'Aureamarginata'
22 *Melissa officinalis* 'Aurea'
23 *Rhododendron* 'Pink Pearl'
24 *Malus* 'Royalty'
25 *Weigela* 'Looymansii Aurea'
26 *Brunnera macrophylla*
27 *Mahonia japonica*
28 *Hydrangea anomala* subsp.
  petiolaris
29 *Persicaria bistorta*
  'Superba'
30 *Berberis darwinii*
31 *Fargesia nitida*
  'Nymphenburg'
32 *Lamium maculatum* 'White
  Nancy'
33 *Prunus lusitanica*
34 *Berberis* x *ottawensis* f.
  purpurea 'Superba'
35 *Geranium* 'Johnson's Blue'
36 *Hydrangea paniculata*
  'Kyushu'
37 *Hebe* 'Marjorie'
38 *Brachyglottis* Dunedin
  Group 'Sunshine'
39 *Cornus sanguinea*
  'Midwinter Fire'
40 *Zantedeschia aethiopica*
  'Crowborough'
41 *Iris sibirica* 'Tropic Night'
42 *Hosta* 'Frances Williams'
43 *Pinus mugo* 'Ophir'
44 *Rodgersia pinnata*
45 *Acer palmatum* var.
  dissectum Dissectum
  Atropurpureum Group

Specimen plants

Individual plants or groups of the same species can often be seen to best advantage when they are planted as spot features, perhaps surrounded by gravel or bark to set off their characteristics. Sometimes, however, a well-spaced group of several different types can produce an even more effective display, especially when they have been chosen for colour, shape and texture.

In this context, 'specimen' means a plant that can be grown in isolation, perhaps with one or two others, rather than a large 'instant' plant. Some plants are best appreciated when grown away from other plants – they may, for example, need lots of room to develop their characteristic shape.

Choose specimens that will relate to the available space. A tree that will, after ten years, be large and spreading needs room to develop. A narrower plant, such as a single fastigiate tree, will look out of proportion in a wide, open space. In such an area a group of three or even five of the same cultivar will have a more dramatic effect.

You can site a specimen plant wherever there is room. Don't, however, place them randomly because they need to be seen as focal points. Plant them where they can be seen from a window or sitting area, or perhaps position one just around the corner of a path so that it will surprise you as you turn the corner.

Hot and sunny specimen planting

1 *Berberis* x *media* 'Red Jewel'
2 *Yucca gloriosa*
3 *Halimium ocymoides*
4 *Ceratostigma willmottianum*
5 *Pittosporum tenuifolium* 'Irene Paterson'

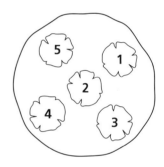

Damp and shady specimen planting

1 *Ligularia* 'The Rocket'
2 *Astilboides tabularis*
3 *Hosta* 'Frances Williams'
4 *Hydrangea aspera*

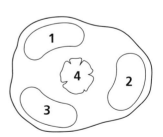

Foliage specimen planting

1 *Hydrangea quercifolia*
2 *Brachyglottis* Dunedin Group 'Sunshine'
3 *Pinus mugo* 'Winter Gold'
4 *Phormium tenax* Purpureum Group

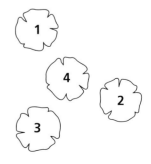

The secret garden

Houses are often overlooked by adjacent buildings, especially in urban areas. Putting up high fences and walls or planting a tall hedge doesn't always solve the problem, particularly if the neighbouring houses are two storeys high. Often, it's not necessary to block off a view in (or out) of your garden but merely to camouflage or soften it so that it becomes less obvious.

What makes this a good secret garden?

✓ There are three zones, two where some privacy is essential (patio and stone circle) and one where it is not so important (lawn)

✓ Trees with light foliage break up the outline of neighbouring buildings without casting excessive shade

✓ Tall, upright-growing shrubs provide some lower level screening and soften and break up the line of boundary fences or walls

✓ The trellis and pergola around and over the patio give extra privacy without making it excessively dark and shady

✓ The live bamboo/trellis screen creates a private, intimate sitting area

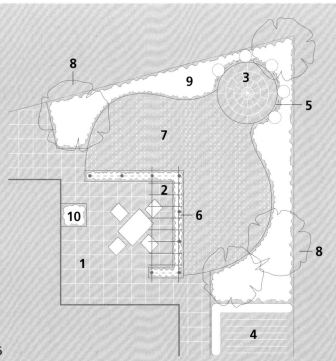

Garden elements key

1 Patio
2 Pergola/overheads
3 Ornamental stone circle feature

4 Vegetable garden
5 Bamboo and trellis screen
6 Climber on trellis

7 Lawn

8 Light foliage trees to break up the outline of neighbouring buildings

9 Planting

10 Evergreen shrubs for quick seclusion

Mix and match

If you like this garden, but would prefer a different feature, see pages 250–251 for possible variations.

Key features

Deciduous trees

As well as providing height and structure to any garden, trees are useful for masking or disguising unsightly views and objects. When you use them in this way, select light-foliaged varieties that will not cast too much shade into your own garden. If you have a very sunny garden you might want to try some more densely foliaged deciduous trees, such as maples, which will provide welcome shade in summer but allow light through in winter.

Bamboo/trellis screen

A mixture of natural and artificial screening is an excellent way to provide some privacy – trellis gives an instant effect, while the bamboos soften the hard edges and as they grow will increase the amount of screening. You can use all sorts of combinations of plants and materials for different effects by varying the height, colour and texture of the various elements.

Lawn

A well-kept lawn can really lift an otherwise average garden. Keep it immaculate by cutting with a well-sharpened mower and by feeding and weeding regularly as well as watering in extended dry periods. Make sure that your patio or terrace is linked, at least in part, to your lawn to give you extra space for relaxation in the summer.

How to make a trellis-and-bamboo screen

The combination of living plants and trellis panels makes an unusual but effective screen.

A carefully chosen bamboo can make a quick and effective evergreen screen.

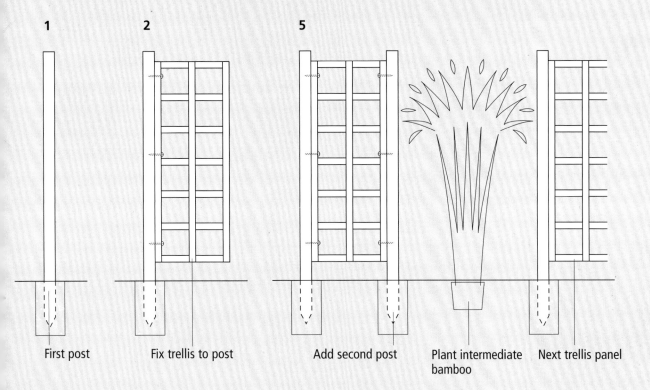

1 First post

2 Fix trellis to post

5 Add second post — Plant intermediate bamboo — Next trellis panel

You will need

Trellis panels, ideally 1.8m (6ft) high and 40–60cm (16–24in) wide; select panels with relatively small gaps to give extra privacy

Posts (2 for each panel), the length to suit trellis plus about 45cm (18in) to fix in the ground; use narrower posts than you would for large trellis or fence panels, about 5–6cm (2–2½in) square or diameter (if using machined round section posts), which will be more in proportion with the narrow panels

Bamboos — one per gap

Sand, gravel, cement for concreting in the posts if the ground is soft or loose

Step by step

1 Drive the first post into the ground to the desired height or dig a hole and concrete it in if the ground is soft.

2 Drill two or three pilot holes through one long edge of a trellis panel and screw it to the first post.

3 Drive in the second post tight against the free edge of the trellis panel and fix this edge as in step 2.

4 Repeat with successive panels, leaving gaps of 60cm (24in) between successive panels.

5 Plant the bamboos in the centre of the gaps between the panels and water in thoroughly.

Planting

The best plants for this garden

The scheme includes deciduous trees with light or delicate foliage that are quite twiggy in winter and still provide an element of screening and softening. Large shrubs with an upright habit of growth give plenty of height without taking up too much horizontal space. Bamboos and tall grasses are ideal for breaking up plain fence lines and making screens where space is limited. Finally, fast-growing deciduous climbers are good for summer screening.

Planting key

1 *Robinia pseudoacacia* 'Frisia'
2 *Hydrangea aspera* Villosa Group
3 *Helleborus orientalis*
4 *Tradescantia* Andersoniana Group 'Pauline'
5 *Cornus sericea* 'Flaviramea'
6 *Berberis thunbergii* f. *atropurpurea* 'Helmond Pillar'
7 *Ilex aquifolium* 'Pyramidalis'

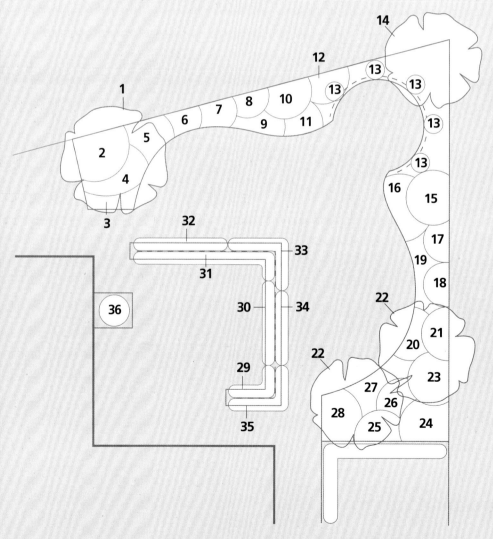

A well-placed large shrub is sometimes all that is needed to provide privacy for a small corner-bench or seat.

Creating a small secluded spot

Sometimes you might want to screen only a small, specific area, such as immediately outside your back door so that you can sit in privacy and have a cup of tea. All it would take to create this space would be some plants that were tall enough to hide you when you were sitting down – maybe no more than 1.2m (4ft) or so high and wide. It would be a mistake to look through your gardening books and select a plant you liked that ultimately reached a height of about 1.2m (4ft), because it might take ten years to get there! The ideal plant needs to have a much greater potential for growth so that it reaches the height you want much sooner but also needs to be tolerant of regular trimming or pruning so that it doesn't outgrow its position. In addition, if it were evergreen you would have a year-round private spot.

Trimmable evergreens for (relatively) quick seclusion

* *Berberis darwinii*

* *Ceanothus* spp.

* *Choisya ternata* cvs. (Mexican orange blossom)

* *Cotoneaster lacteus*

* *Elaeagnus* x *ebbingei* cvs.

* *Escallonia* cvs.

* *Photinia* x *fraseri* 'Red Robin'

* *Prunus lusitanica* (Portugal laurel)

* *Pyracantha* cvs. (firethorn)

* *Viburnum tinus* (laurustinus)

A small family garden

If you have one or two young children you will want a garden that provides a range of attractions for all the family, even if the limited size of your garden means that you have to compromise on some less important features. As the children grow, you will want the flexibility to add or replace features, such as a pond, that you could not include when your children were young.

What makes this a good family garden?

✓ The good sized patio is easily supervised when the children are outside
✓ The generously sized play area covered with bark chippings is ideal for active children who would quickly wear out a small lawn, which would be muddy in winter
✓ A separate barbecue area can also be used for a 'quiet' spot to relax in
✓ There is plenty of storage space
✓ The safe planting is easy to maintain but good to look at
✓ There is no potentially dangerous water feature
✓ There is a small area for kitchen gardening

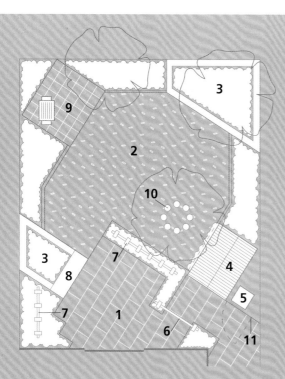

Garden elements key

1 Patio
2 Bark play area
3 Raised bed
4 Garden store
5 Bin and utility area
6 Arch
7 Screen
8 Built-in seat and storage
9 Barbecue area
10 Log steps
11 Trellis and gate

Mix and match

If you like this garden, but would prefer a different feature, see pages 250–251 for possible variations.

Key features

Play area

In a small garden it is sometimes sensible to dispense with a lawn altogether because it won't stand up to wear and tear. Use bark chippings or wood chips instead, spread on top of a proprietary, weed-suppressing mulching fabric to give a neat, maintenance-free surface all year round. Later on, as the family grows, there'll probably be less pressure on this part of the garden and you could then seed or turf it to make a 'proper' lawn.

Raised bed with seat

This combined feature is a simple way to introduce a change of level in a flat garden. Using old railway sleepers makes it even simpler to build, and you can fill it with good-quality topsoil and compost so that you can grow salads and vegetables. The built-in seat gives extra sitting room and you can incorporate front-opening cupboards or a hinged lid to provide extra storage space.

Patio

A good-sized patio is essential – especially if you need extra outdoor space in wet weather or want to entertain outdoors in summer. Putting a patio at an angle to the boundaries and house makes the most of the available space, and the post-and-rope screen makes an effective 'division' between the patio and the play area but still allows you to keep an eye on the children.

Post-and-rope screen

Separating different areas of a garden will add interest and character, but you may not always want to use a solid barrier, such as a fence or wall or even a screen of plants. An 'open' screen can be effective. A simple arrangement of posts, linked with lengths of heavy, natural fibre rope, is ideal for a family garden because it doesn't completely block views. A bonus is that it is easy and economical to make.

Heavy rope and rustic posts make a simple yet striking support for climbers such as this clematis.

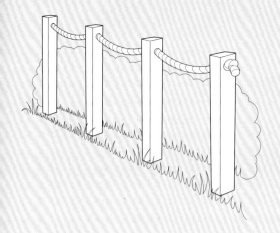

You will need

Pressure-treated softwood posts, 15 x 5cm (6 x 2in) and about 2.4m (8ft) long (or less for a lower 'screen')

Thick, natural fibre rope, such as hemp, at least 2.5cm (1in) thick

Sand, gravel and cement for concreting in the posts (optional)

Woodstain to match or complement the fence and raised beds (optional)

Step by step

1 Drill a single hole (using an auger bit) through each post, about 7.5cm (3in) from the top. The holes must be large enough to take the rope.

2 Stain all the posts and leave them to dry.

3 Dig a hole for each post, about 40cm (16in) deep by 20–25cm (8–10in) across, and at the chosen distance apart – say 45cm (18in).

4 Secure the posts in the holes, placing the long edges parallel to each other, tamping the topsoil firmly around them. If the ground is soft or loose mix concrete (in the proportions 1 part cement, 2 parts sand and 4 parts gravel) and set the posts in this in the holes. Check that the posts are vertical and leave the concrete to set.

5 Knot one end of the rope and feed the unknotted end through successive post holes. Tie a knot in the other end and cut off any excess rope.

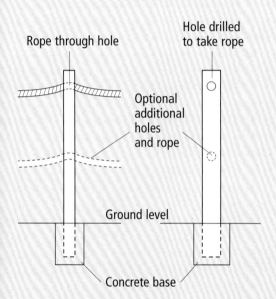

Rope through hole

Hole drilled to take rope

Optional additional holes and rope

Ground level

Concrete base

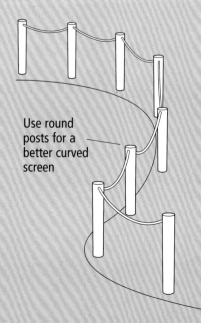

Use round posts for a better curved screen

Alternative post-and-rope screens

- Choose different sizes of post, even round ones, and vary the height for different purposes – you might want a low divider to separate two different areas of planting in contrasting styles

- Drill more holes in the post, say 30cm (12in) apart, and fit extra ropes to give a loose trellis appearance

- Vary the heights of the posts to create a serpentine effect

- Plant the posts with annual or delicate climbers, fixing wires to the posts to make it easier for the climbers to grip

- Place the posts in a curved line or to follow the edge of a border

- Use posts in pairs across a path to make a rope archway or narrow pergola with or without lightweight climbers

Planting

7

13

16

24

The best plants for this garden

Small ornamental and fruit trees give height and structure, while easy-care shrubs, perennials and climbers are safe where there are small children and robust enough to put up with the inevitable damage. Salad crops and easy vegetables are grown in raised beds to give a fresh supply of carrots, cabbage and herbs.

Planting key

1 *Clematis alpina* (on post and rope)
2 *Perovskia atriplicifolia* 'Blue Spire'
3 *Tradescantia* Andersoniana Group 'Innocence'
4 *Bergenia cordifolia* 'Purpurea'

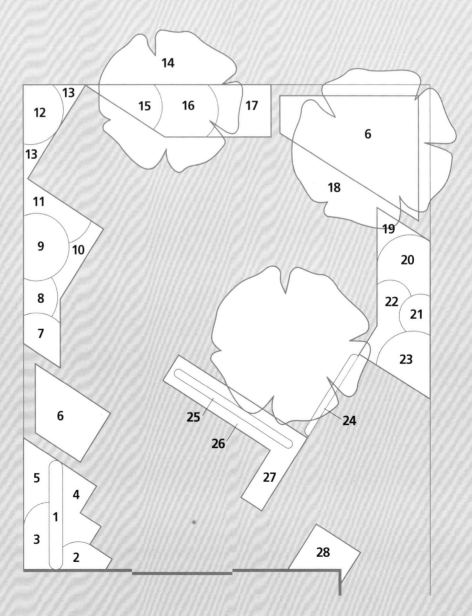

5 *Anemone* x *hybrida* 'Richard Ahrens'
6 Salad and vegetables
7 *Spiraea japonica* 'Goldflame'
8 *Miscanthus sinensis* 'Variegatus'
9 *Weigela* 'Florida Variegata'
10 *Geranium ibericum*
11 *Hemerocallis* 'Sammy Russell'
12 *Viburnum farreri*
13 *Geum* 'Borisii'
14 *Sorbus aria* 'Lutescens'
15 *Aster novi-belgii* 'Little Pink Beauty'
16 *Prunus laurocerasus* 'Otto Luyken'
17 *Abelia* x *grandiflora*
18 'Family' apple tree
19 *Iris sibirica* 'White Swirl'
20 *Cornus alba* 'Spaethii'
21 *Miscanthus sinensis* 'Gracillimus'
22 *Solidago* 'Cloth of Gold'
23 *Ceanothus* 'Burkwoodii'
24 *Jasminum nudiflorum* (on store)
25 *Lathyrus odoratus* (on post and rope)
26 *Euonymus fortunei* 'Emerald 'n' Gold' (low hedge)
27 *Potentilla fruticosa* 'Princess'
28 *Choisya ternata* 'Sundance'

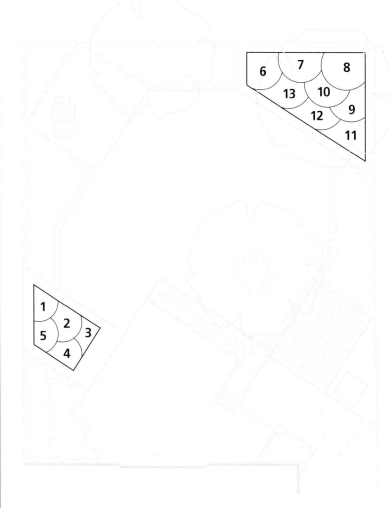

Edible to ornamental

If you don't want or need to grow your own salad crops and vegetables, fill the raised beds with ornamental plants to add extra colour and interest.

Ornamental plants for raised bed

1 *Miscanthus sinensis* 'Morning Light'
2 *Skimmia japonica* var. *reevesiana*
3 *Helianthemum* 'The Bride'
4 *Persicaria vaccinifolia*
5 *Aster* x *frikartii* Mönch'
6 *Weigela florida* 'Foliis Purpureis'
7 *Osmanthus delavayi*
8 *Aucuba japonica* 'Picturata'
9 *Rudbeckia fulgida* var. *sullivantii* 'Goldsturm'
10 *Hydrangea arborescens* 'Annabelle'
11 *Vinca minor* 'Argenteovariegata'
12 *Geranium* x *riversleaianum* 'Russell Prichard'
13 *Cotoneaster congestus*

The concrete garden

Concrete has had a bad press and is frequently regarded as the poor relation of materials such as brick, wood and natural stone. Nevertheless, if it is detailed and used with imagination and confidence, concrete in its 'natural' form or finish can provide the backbone of an exceptionally attractive garden.

What makes this a good concrete garden?

✓ An imaginative layout for a small plot makes full use of all the available space

✓ The unusual use of pre-cast concrete pipes, channel sections and other products as garden features rather than their originally intended mundane purpose as drains or kerb stones

✓ The different surface textures, ranging from smooth to hammered to exposed aggregate, add extra interest

✓ The simple use of concrete units to create changes in level

✓ The balance between the concrete surfaces and the planting, which softens the hard lines and edges and shows off the various textures to best effect

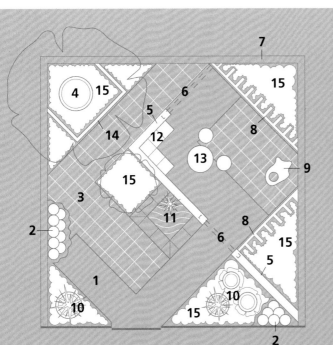

Garden elements key

1 *In situ* concrete with exposed aggregate finish

2 Pipe 'cascade' of trailing annuals

3 Concrete flag paving with 'hammered' or 'tooled' finish

4 Tree in concrete pipe container

5 Decorative concrete block wall

6 Climber on concrete lintel 'arch'

7 Boundary wall

8 Retaining wall made
from concrete U-shaped
channel sections

9 Concrete abstract
sculpture

10 Specimen shrub in pipe
container

11 Raised formal pool

12 Concrete 'bench' seat

13 Concrete stools and
table

14 Concrete planks on
edge for low raised bed

15 Planting

Mix and match

If you like this garden, but would
prefer a different feature, see pages
250–251 for possible variations.

Key features

Concrete pipes

Containers for plants needn't necessarily be traditional materials, such as terracotta or stone. Anything that is waterproof and weatherproof can be used as long as it's well drained. Concrete drain pipes are a perfect example and you can place them either individually, perhaps a very large pipe would hold a small tree or specimen shrub, or in groups, maybe planted with perennials or annual bedding.

Raised pool

Raised pools are a great idea where it's not possible to dig down for a more traditional construction. Make them about 45cm (18in) high with a wooden, stone or concrete coping, which will double up as seating.

Groundcover planting

Soften the hard edges of the paving with low groundcover planting. Where your paving is fairly bland and utilitarian, try and use ornamental plants with striking flowers or variegated foliage. However, if the paving is attractive and a feature in its own right, make your groundcover planting simpler, perhaps restricting it to plain foliage like ivy.

How to make a concrete stool or table

The instructions opposite are for the stools, but you can also make a small occasional table to the same design by using wider, longer sections of pipe to the approximate table size. Finish off with a table covering to match or complement the cushions. If you want more colour, paint the concrete with masonry paint.

A simple seat made from three concrete blocks is the perfect foil to this herbaceous border.

You will need

Sections of round or square concrete pipe, 30–40cm (12–16in) in diameter and 40–50cm (16–20in) long (high); you will need one section per stool

19–25mm (¾–1in) thick marine plywood

Castors (four for each stool)

Screws and fixing plugs

Cushions to fit

Step by step

1 Use a jigsaw to cut two pieces of plywood: one that exactly matches the bottom of the pipe and another for the top.

2 Drill four equidistant holes in both the bottom and top edges of the pipe with a masonry drill bit, plug them and screw a plywood circle (or square) to both ends of the pipe.

3 Screw four castors to the plywood at one end of the pipe; this will become the bottom of the stool.

4 Make or buy cushions to put on top of the stool.

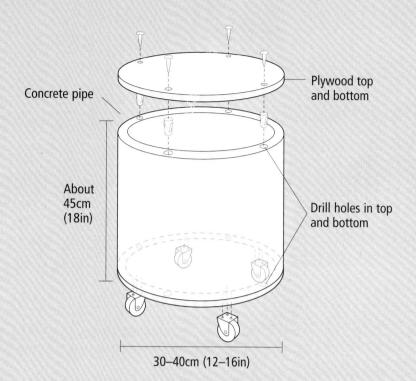

Concrete pipe

Plywood top and bottom

About 45cm (18in)

Drill holes in top and bottom

30–40cm (12–16in)

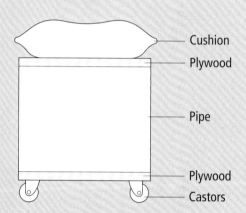

Cushion

Plywood

Pipe

Plywood

Castors

A quick bench seat

You can make a basic seat – or bench – with precast concrete 'U' channels, which are normally used for drainage. Simply turn them on their edge and make the tops comfortable with cushions.

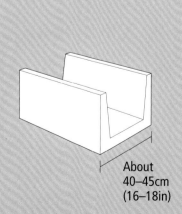

About 40–45cm (16–18in)

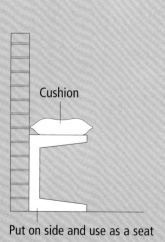

Cushion

Put on side and use as a seat

Planting

The best plants for this garden

Bold, simple planting complements the raw, basic feel of the concrete. There are distinctive foliage plants, such as hostas, acers and phormiums, and characterful individual trees and shrubs, including *Paulownia tomentosa* (foxglove tree), are underplanted with drifts of weed-suppressing perennials and grasses. The colours are mostly restrained, with an emphasis on foliage and form, but the occasional hotspot in the form of pelargoniums and rhododendrons lifts a corner or area.

Planting key

1 *Sophora tetraptera*
2 *Liriope muscari*
3 *Pelargonium* and *Lobelia* cvs. (in pipe feature)
4 *Acer shirasawanum* 'Aureum'
5 *Persicaria affinis* 'Superba'
6 *Hosta fortunei* var. *albopicta*
7 *Paulownia tomentosa* (in container)
8 x *Heucherella alba* 'Bridget Bloom'
9 *Hosta* 'Honeybells'
10 *Actinidia deliciosa* (on lintel)
11 *Ligustrum lucidum* 'Excelsum Superbum'
12 *Phormium* 'Bronze Baby'

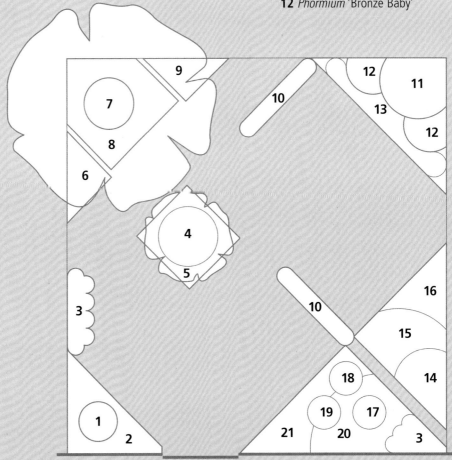

13 *Cotoneaster dammeri* 'Streib's Findling'
14 *Taxus baccata* 'Fastigiata'
15 *Hosta* 'Krossa Regal'
16 *Alopecurus pratensis* 'Aureus'
17 *Penstemon* 'Sour Grapes' (in container)
18 *Rhododendron* 'Chikor' (in container)
19 *Fuchsia* 'Snowcap' (in container)
20 *Heuchera micrantha* var. *diversifolia* 'Palace Purple'
21 *Hedera helix* 'Ivalace'

Alternative evergreen planting

1 *Piptanthus nepalensis*
2 *Ophiopogon planiscapus*
3 *Hedera helix* 'Little Diamond'
4 *Ilex* x *attenuata* 'Sunny Foster'
5 *Rubus* 'Betty Ashburner'
6 *Euphorbia* x *martini*
7 *Arbutus unedo* f. *rubra*
8 *Epimedium* x *cantabrigiense*
9 *Helleborus argutifolius*
10 *Lonicera japonica* 'Halliana'
11 *Mahonia lomariifolia*
12 *Phormium* 'Jester'
13 *Helianthemum* 'Rhodanthe Carneum'
14 *Juniperus scopulorum* 'Skyrocket'
15 *Bergenia* 'Bressingham Salmon'
16 *Carex oshimensis* 'Evergold'
17 *Phormium cookianum* subsp. *hookeri* 'Cream Delight'
18 *Tsuga canadensis* 'Jeddeloh'
19 *Hebe pinguifolia* 'Pagei'
20 *Erica* x *darleyensis* 'Silberschmelze'
21 *Vinca minor* 'La Grave'

Melianthus major is a superb shrubby perennial for foliage colour and shape.

Pruning

Many deciduous and evergreen trees and shrubs (though not all conifers) can be cut back hard during the dormant period without ill-effect. The benefit of this is that you can rejuvenate and reshape old plants that have perhaps been neglected for several years, with the added bonus that they will produce strong new growths with bigger, brighter leaves.

Best shrubs for green foliage interest

- *Alangium chinense*
- *Catalpa bignonioides* (Indian bean tree)
- *Chamaerops humilis* (dwarf fan palm)
- *Fatsia japonica*
- *Hydrangea quercifolia* (oak-leaved hydrangea)
- *Mahonia* spp.
- *Melianthus major* (honey bush)
- *Osmanthus armatus*
- *Paeonia delavayi* var. *ludlowii* (tree peony)
- *Phormium tenax* (New Zealand flax)

Traditional urbanscape

This design is for a rather long, narrow garden, which is typical in its proportions of many gardens found in towns and cities. The angular patio, diagonal paving and timber structures – trellis screen and pergola – combine with the planting to break up the space into several smaller areas and cleverly disguise its overall shape, making it more inviting and interesting.

What makes this a good urban garden?

✓ An unusual but relatively simple and achievable design
✓ Traditional planting for year-round interest and ease of maintenance
✓ All materials are readily available and inexpensive
✓ Can be built by anyone with reasonable DIY skills
✓ There are several individual areas to give a choice of privacy, sun and shade

Mix and match
If you like this garden, but would prefer a different feature, see pages 250–251 for possible variations.

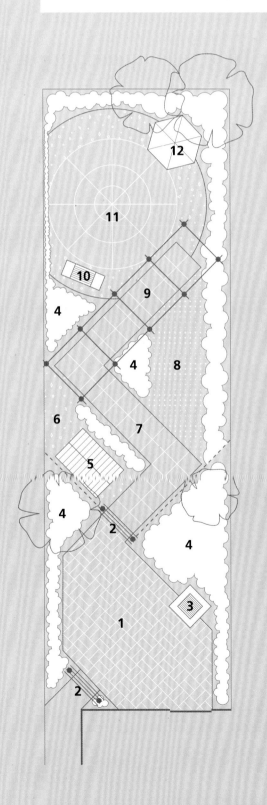

Garden elements key

1 Patio
2 Arch
3 Water feature
4 Planting
5 Garden store
6 Outside storage area
7 Stone-effect flag paving
8 Lawn
9 Pergola
10 Barbecue
11 Stone circle feature
12 Summerhouse

Key features

Secure water feature

Position small water features next to sitting areas or where they can be seen from inside the house. Make them safe for children by concealing a sump of water below ground and hiding the top with mesh, stones and boulders. Even the smallest garden will have space for one and benefit from the sound and movement.

Arch

On curving or irregular paths, build a series of arches to give a pergola effect without any complicated joins or angles to consider. You can make your arches very ornamental in design with a minimum of planting, or alternatively keep your costs down and build the simplest arch to act purely as a support for abundant climbing plants.

Garden store

Even the smallest garden will need a place where you can store gardening tools and other items, such as garden furniture, over the winter. If you've enough space, hide your store away and screen it with soft planting, hedges or trellis. Where you can't do this, make the store into a positive design feature with colour and decoration, perhaps putting real or imitation cedar shingles on the roof or adding fancy barge boards.

How to construct a simple arch

You can buy several styles of timber arch at garden centres, home improvement stores and woodworking specialists, but building your own gives you complete control over the size, quality and appearance, particularly when you want the arch to complement or match other features in your garden.

If you are going to plant rampant climbers, construct a simple arch as it will soon be hidden.

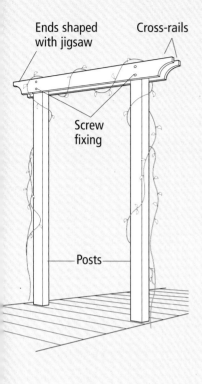

Ends shaped with jigsaw

Cross-rails

Screw fixing

Posts

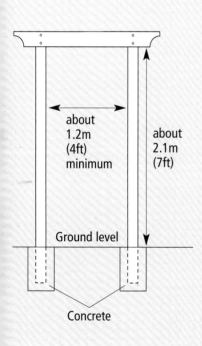

about 1.2m (4ft) minimum

about 2.1m (7ft)

Ground level

Concrete

You will need

2 pressure-treated softwood posts (7.5 x 7.5cm/3 x 3in); length to suit the height of arch plus 45cm (18in) extra for fixing in ground

2 softwood rails (3.8 x 12.5cm/ 1½ x 5in); length to suit width of arch plus 20cm (8in) overhang each side

Sand, gravel and cement to make concrete or 2 proprietary metal spike post fixings (to drive into ground)

Screws

Woodstain

Step by step

1 Dig a post hole measuring about 25 x 25cm (10 x 10in) and about 50cm (20in) deep.

2 Mix concrete (in the proportions 1 part cement, 2 parts sand and 4 parts gravel) and set the posts in this in the holes.

3 Make sure the tops of the posts are level and that they are vertical.

4 Cut the rails to the required length. Shape the ends with a jigsaw, if you desire.

5 Stain the posts and rails before you assemble the arch.

6 Screw rails to either side of the posts, making sure the overhangs are equal.

Securing a post

Making sure that posts for fences, arches and pergolas that are set in concrete stay perfectly upright until the concrete has 'gone off' can be a problem, especially if it is windy or if they could be accidentally knocked by children or pets. To avoid this, take a length of fairly thin softwood batten, about 2.5 x 3.8cm (1 x 1½in), and when the post is more or less in the right position, drive the batten into the ground at an angle of about 45°, so that it is flush against the post face. Check with a spirit level that the post is vertical and then tap in a thin nail through the batten, just far enough to 'bite' into the post. Repeat this with another batten on the adjoining face. The post will not move.

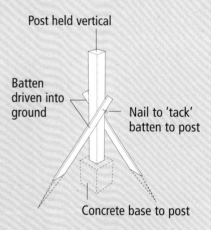

Post held vertical

Batten driven into ground

Nail to 'tack' batten to post

Concrete base to post

Alternatively, put a nail in each face of the post about halfway up and use lengths of strong cord fixed either to pegs in the ground or to other fixed objects in the manner of tent 'guy ropes'.

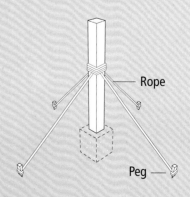

Rope

Peg

Planting

The best plants for this garden

A traditional mixture of trees, shrubs, perennials and grasses will give varying and continued interest throughout the seasons and suit the different degrees of sun and shade. None of the plants is too demanding, and all are readily available from hardy plant nurseries and good garden centres.

Planting key

1 *Aucuba japonica* 'Variegata'
2 *Rosa* 'Pink Grootendorst'
3 *Viburnum tinus* 'Eve Price'
4 *Hydrangea* 'Preziosa'
5 *Amelanchier lamarckii*
6 *Carpinus betulus* 'Fastigiata'
7 *Corylus maxima* 'Purpurea'
8 *Pseudosasa japonica*
9 *Elaeagnus* x *ebbingei*
10 *Philadelphus coronarius* 'Aureus'
11 *Hydrangea paniculata* 'Tardiva'
12 *Escallonia* 'Peach Blossom'
13 *Leycesteria formosa*
14 *Weigela florida* 'Foliis Purpureis'
15 *Miscanthus sinensis* 'Variegatus'
16 *Spiraea* x *vanhouttei*
17 *Buddleja* 'Lochinch'
18 *Malus* 'John Downie'
19 *Photinia* x *fraseri* 'Red Robin'
20 *Hibiscus syriacus* 'Oiseau Bleu'
21 *Berberis darwinii*
22 *Hemerocallis* 'Stafford'
23 *Pennisetum alopecuroides* 'Hameln'
24 *Euonymus fortunei* 'Emerald Gaiety'
25 *Nepeta* x *faassenii*
26 *Juniperus* x *pfitzeriana* 'Gold Coast'
27 *Liriope muscari*
28 *Campsis* x *tagliabuana* 'Madame Galen'
29 *Rosa* 'Zéphirine Drouhin'
30 *Cotoneaster horizontalis*
31 *Elaeagnus pungens* 'Dicksonii'
32 *Helleborus niger*
33 *Hydrangea macrophylla* 'Madame Emile Moullière'
34 *Chimonanthus praecox*
35 *Abelia* x *grandiflora*
36 *Hemerocallis* 'Burning Daylight'
37 *Deutzia* x *kalmiiflora*
38 *Aster novi-belgii* 'Lady in Blue'
39 *Cornus alba* 'Elegantissima'
40 *Pittosporum tenuifolium*
41 *Betula utilis* var. *jacquemontii*
42 *Spiraea nipponica* 'Snowmound'
43 *Pyracantha* 'Orange Glow'
44 *Physocarpus opulifolius* 'Dart's Gold'

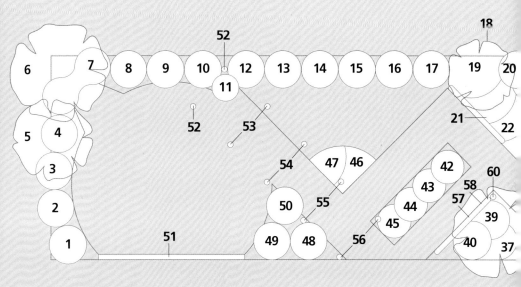

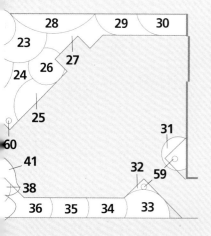

Choosing trees for small gardens

Trees are the ultimate plants in terms not only of their potential age but also their stature. Even one tree planted in a garden can make a huge difference to its appearance. You must choose trees for small gardens carefully, bearing in mind that not only will the crown of the tree become larger with time but the below-ground section – the roots – will do the same.

A bad choice of tree may lead to problems for both you and possibly your neighbours. Where space is very limited, plant large shrubs, which can be trained as small trees.

The silver willow-leaved pear (*Pyrus salicifolia pendula*) makes a perfect tree for a small garden.

Look for the following when choosing a tree:

• Slow-growing forms

• Species and cultivars that have only a modest ultimate height

• Trees with light, delicate foliage

• Trees with a narrow, upright habit of growth

Trees to avoid

• Fast-growing species, such as *Salix* (willow) and *Populus* (poplar)

• 'Forest' species, such as *Quercus* (oak) and *Fagus* (beech)

• Species with vigorous, dense root systems, such as *Fraxinus* (ash), *Salix* (willow) and *Populus* (poplar)

• Species that produce dense canopies of large, shade-creating leaves, such as *Acer pseudoplatanus* (sycamore) and *Aesculus* spp.

• Forms with wide-spreading crowns, such as *Arbutus* x *andrachnoides* (strawberry tree)

Best trees for small gardens

• *Acer palmatum*

• *Acer palmatum* 'Bloodgood'

• *Amelanchier lamarckii*

• *Crataegus laevigata* 'Paul's Scarlet'

• *Gleditsia triacanthos* 'Sunburst'

• *Magnolia* x *soulangeana*

• *Malus* (crab apples)

• *Photinia villosa*

• *Prunus* x *subhirtella* 'Autumnalis'

• *Sorbus aucuparia* and cvs.

Mix and match

Boundaries and dividers

Decking

Decoration and ornaments

Edging

Gravel and rocks

Lawns

Paths

Index

Acknowledgements

Eric Crichton/Design: Stephen Roberts, Isobel Kendrick, RHS Tatton Park Flower Show 1999 198 right **Garden Picture Library**/Mark Bolton 182 centre left top/Eric Crichton 186 right/Suzie Gibbons 133/John Glover 128 bottom left/Juliet Greene; Design: Jacquie Gordon, RHS Chelsea Flower Show 1999 222 right/Neil Holmes 134 top left/Clive Nichols 61/JS Sira 81, 104 centre left top, 146 bottom left/Janet Sorrell 105, 169/Friedrich Strauss 135/Ron Sutherland 145/Juliette Wade 104 centre left bottom **John Glover** 20 top left, 39, 44 top left, 50 centre left top, 78 bottom left, 116 bottom left, 128 centre left bottom, 164 top left, 170 bottom left, 176 top left, 176 bottom left, 182 centre top/Design: Bradley/Carey 115 bottom/Design: McNeil/Leeves 114 right /Design: Steve Woodham 115 top **Jerry Harpur** 32 centre left bottom, 98 bottom left, 147, 182 centre left bottom/Design: Mr. Ashdown, Alresford 246 right/Design: Jeff Bale 120 right/Design: Michael Balston 231/Barzi & Cabares, Buenos Aires, Argentine 30 right/Patricia Larson Boston 139 top/Design: Raymond Hudson/Free Island Pines 72 right/Design: Luciano Giubbilei, Kensington, London 180 right/Design: Naila Green, Dawlish 108 bottom right/Design: Bernard Hickie, Dublin 175/Tom Hobbs, Vancouver 171/Bruan Hubbard, Del Mar 32 bottom left/Design: Bruce Kelly 213/Kate Kend 48 right/Design: Hoichi Kurisu 183/Lambeth Palace 240 right/Design: Gunilla Pickard 45/Design: Erik De Maeijer and Jane Hudson for Cancer Research UK, RHS Chelsea Flower Show 2003 96 bottom right **Marcus Harpur** 50 centre left bottom, 62 top left, 116 top left, 218 centre left bottom, 236 centre left top/Creagh, Co. Cork, Ireland 170 centre left bottom/Harvey's Garden Plants 212 centre left bottom/RHS Wisley 176 centre left bottom/; Design: Shooting Star Trust, RHS Hampton Court 2003 99/Cherry Williams, Bungay, Suffolk 242 top left **Andrew Lawson** 20 centre left top, 20 centre left bottom, 32 centre left top, 62 bottom left, 62 centre left top, 62 centre left bottom, 92 top left, 92 centre left top, 132 right, 134 centre left top, 164 bottom left, 204 right, 210 bottom right, 212 top left, 218 bottom left, 228 right, 236 top left/Design: Jinny Blom 234 right/Design: Katy Collity 205/Design: Wendy Lauderdale 42 bottom right/Design: Anthony Noel 103/Design: Dan Pearson 117/Design: Dipika Price 24/Design: Sara Woolley 54 bottom right **S & O Mathews** 50 centre left bottom, 63, 92 bottom left, 116 centre left top, 146 centre left bottom, 165, 168 right, 176 centre left top, 230 centre left bottom **Octopus Publishing Group Limited**/38 bottom left, 98 centre left bottom, 104 top left, 146 top left, 152 top left/Mark Bolton 12 bottom right, 19, 67 centre/ Design: Elizabeth Apedaile, RHS Hampton Court Flower Show 2001 151/Design: Nigel Boardman & Stephen Gelly, RHS Hampton Court Flower Show 2001 192 right/Design: Christopher Costin, RHS Hampton Court Flower Show 2001 2/Design: Christopher Costin, RHS Hampton Court Flower Show 2001 223 top/Design: Paul Dyer, RHS Hampton Court Flower Show 2001 3/Design: Sarah Eberle, RHS Hampton Court Flower Show 2001 91 top/Design: Sheila Fishwick, RHS Chelsea Flower Show 2001 144 right/Design: Naila Green, Pecorama, Devon 216 bottom right/Design: Stephen C. Markham Collection, RHS Chelsea Flower Show 2001 150 right/Design: Prof. Masao Fukuhara, Masahiro Yoshida, Jun Takada & Team RHS Chelsea Flower Show 2001 126 bottom right/Design: Tom Stuart-Smith, RHS Chelsea Flower Show 2001 7/Design: Carole Vincent, RHS Chelsea Flower Show 2001 90 right/Michael Boys 14 centre left bottom, 32 top left, 44 centre left bottom, 56 top left, 56 centre left top, 74 centre left top, 74 centre left bottom, 146 centre left top, 152 bottom left, 158 centre left bottom, 170 top left, 192 centre left top, 212 bottom left, 230 top left, 243/Jerry Harpur 44 centre left top, 50 top left, 56 bottom left, 56 centre left top, 68 centre left bottom, 80 top left, 80 centre left top, 80 centre left bottom, 98 top left, 128 top left, 128 centre left top, 158 top left, 158 bottom left, 158 centre left top, 164 centre left top, 194 centre left bottom, 224 top left, 230 centre left top, 236 bottom left, 242 centre left top, 248 centre left top/Marcus Harpur 68 centre left top, 122 centre left top/Neil Holmes 152 centre left top/Andrew Lawson 14 top left, 14 bottom left, 18 bottom right, 26 top left, 26 bottom left, 26 centre left top, 44 bottom left, 68 top left, 80 bottom left, 92 centre left bottom, 110 top left, 110 centre left top, 110 centre left bottom, 122 top left, 122 bottom left, 122 centre left bottom, 134 centre left bottom, 140 top left, 140 centre left top, 140 centre left bottom, 188 bottom left, 188 centre left bottom, 194 top left, 200 bottom left, 200 centre left top, 206 top left, 206 bottom left, 206 centre left top, 206 centre left bottom, 224 bottom left, 224 centre left bottom, 230 bottom left, 242 centre left bottom, 248 bottom left/Howard Rice 55, 86 centre left top, 110 bottom left, 134 bottom left, 170 centre left top, 200 top left, 224 centre left top, 236 centre left bottom, 249/David Sarton 141, 162 bottom right/Design: Mark Ashmead, RHS Hampton Court Flower Show 2002 1/Design: Diana Beddoes, RHS Hampton Court Flower Show 2003 36 bottom right/Design: Cherry Burton, RHS Hampton Court Flower Show 2002 223 bottom/Design: Janette Lazell, Design in Green, RHS Hampton Court Flower Show 2003 66 centre right/Design: Sarah Lloyd, RHS Hampton Court Flower Show 2003 218 top left/Design: Erik de Maeijer & Jane Hudson 174 bottom right/Design: May & Watts Garden Design, RHS Hampton Court Flower Show 2002 9/Design: Mark Walker & Sarah Wigglesworth, RHS Chelsea Flower Show 2002 156 right/Design: Geoffrey Whiten, Goldfish Bank Ltd. RHS Chelsea Flower Show 2003 91 bottom/Design: Geoffrey Whiten, RHS Chelsea Flower Show 2001 8/Mark Winwood 139 bottom, 217, 218 centre left top/Steve Wooster 37/George Wright 14 centre left top, 26 centre left bottom, 38 top left, 74 top left, 86 top left, 86 centre left bottom, 116 centre left bottom, 140 bottom left, 164 centre left bottom, 182 bottom left, 188 top left, 188 centre left top, 194 bottom left, 248 centre left bottom/Mel Yates 67 top left/James Young 20 bottom left, 38 centre left top, 38 centre left bottom, 68 bottom left, 74 bottom left, 86 bottom left, 98 centre left top, 104 bottom left, 152 centre left bottom, 200 centre left bottom, 212 centre left top, 242 bottom left, 248 top left.

Executive Editor: **Sarah Ford**
Managing Editor: **Clare Churly**
Editor: **Katy Denny and Lydia Darbyshire**
Executive Art Editor: **Rozelle Bentheim**
Design: **'ome**design
Diagrams: **David Beswick**
Illustrations: **Mark Burgess, Kevin Dean, Nicola Gregory, Jenny Hawksley and Gill Tomblin**
Picture Researchers: **Christine Junemann and Jennifer Veall**
Production Manager: **Louise Hall and Martin Croshaw**